RADIO FREQUENCY IDENTIFICATION

Edited by **Paulo Cesar Crepaldi**
and **Tales Cleber Pimenta**

Radio Frequency Identification
http://dx.doi.org/10.5772/62606
Edited by Paulo Cesar Crepaldi and Tales Cleber Pimenta

Contributors
M.V. Bueno-Delgado, Francesc Burrull, Pablo Pavón-Mariño, Tiago M. Fernández-Caramés, Paula Fraga-Lamas, Manuel Suárez-Albela, Yang Zhao, Zijian Xing, Paulo Cesar Crepaldi, Piotr Jankowski-Mihułowicz

Published by InTech
Janeza Trdine 9, 51000 Rijeka, Croatia

Publishing Process Manager Edi Lipovic
Technical Editor SPi Global
Cover InTech Design team

First published November, 2017
Printed in Croatia
Legal deposit, Croatia: National and University Library in Zagreb

Additional hard copies can be obtained from orders@intechopen.com

Radio Frequency Identification, Edited by Paulo Cesar Crepaldi and Tales Cleber Pimenta
p. cm.
Print ISBN 978-953-51-3629-3
Online ISBN 978-953-51-3630-9

For EU product safety concerns:
IN TECH d.o.o., Prolaz Marije Krucifikse Kozulić 3, 51000 Rijeka, Croatia,
info@intechopen.com or visit our website at intechopen.com.

Meet the editors

Prof. Paulo Cesar Crepaldi holds a degree in Electrical Engineering (Emphasis in Electronics) from the Universidade Federal de Itajubá—formerly UNIFEI—(1994) and an MSc degree in Electrical Engineering (Automation and Industrial Electrical Systems) from the Universidade Federal de Itajubá in 2010. He is currently an associate professor at UNIFEI, working at the Institute of Systems Engineering and Information Technology (IESTI) and the Microelectronics Group (GMicro). He has experience in electrical engineering, with emphasis on analog and/or digital CMOS circuits for low-voltage/low-power applications, biomedical applications, signal conditioning, sensors/transducers, and applications involving field programmable gate array (FPGA) and (FPAA) devices.

Dr. Tales Cleber Pimenta obtained his BSc and MSc degrees in Electrical Engineering from the Universidade Federal de Itajubá in 1985 and 1988, respectively. He obtained his PhD degree from Ohio University in Electrical and Computer Engineering in 1992. He conducted his first sabbatical leave in 1997 at the Ohio State University in the area of low-voltage analog-integrated circuits, and the second one at the Virginia Polytechnic Institute and State University in 2005 in the area of ultrahigh-frequency integrated circuits, and the third one in circuits and systems for biomedical applications at the North Florida University in 2014. He is currently a professor at the Universidade Federal de Itajubá. He works on low-voltage/low-power integrated circuits, including IC for biomedical applications.

Contents

Preface

We have been witnessing a fascinating technological evolution in recent years. Products and processes from science fiction books and films are becoming a reality, and in some cases, they turned out to be indispensable.

Radio-frequency identification (RFID) is one of the modern names that is becoming increasingly popular, as a result of many years of researches and investigations. It is a promising technology to be used in virtually all areas of human activities.

Powerful hardware and software tools have contributed, and still do, to place the radio-frequency identification as a popular and widely used technology, from large corporations to individuals, and custom applications.

Although RFID offers many advantages over other technologies, it is essential to be aware of its limitations. Therefore, it will be possible to overcome the limitations and to increase its applications. As an example, cost, safety, security, transmissions formats, and international standards are important merit figures of continuous improvement.

In this book, we present important proposals that will certainly contribute to the evolution of RFID. Theoretical and practical aspects are presented and discussed by the authors, and thus we invite everyone for a pleasant reading.

The editors would like to express their deepest thanks to the InTech team for their constant support and everyone that somehow contributed to this publication.

Prof. Paulo Cesar Crepaldi
Universidade Federal de Itajubá,
Brasil

Prof. Tales Cleber Pimenta
Universidade Federal de Itajubá,
Brasil

Chapter 1

Introductory Chapter: RFID: A Successful History

Paulo Cesar Crepaldi and Tales Cleber Pimenta

Additional information is available at the end of the chapter

http://dx.doi.org/10.5772/intechopen.69602

Radio frequency identification (RFID) is a part of our daily life. This term is used to define any process that, by means of a radio communication, can exchange information between a stationary unit and a mobile unit or between mobile units [1].

In one end of the link, simpler devices, called tags, are used and, and at the other end, more complex devices such a multiprocessor unit can be found. Tags are generally small and inexpensive units that can be bulk acquired and are easily attached to the objects to be identified, and can be automatically operated.

Nevertheless, the roots of RFID date back to World War II. At that time, radar—which had been discovered in 1935 by Scottish physicist Sir Robert Alexander Watson-Watt—was used to alert of approaching aircrafts. Would they be our pilots returning home or would it be an enemy attack?

Germans, for instance, used an interesting maneuver in which their pilots rolled their planes as they return to base, so it would change the reflecting radio signal. This simple procedure alerted the ground radar crew of German planes returning and not allied aircrafts. It can be considered one of the first passive ways to identify an object by means of a radio frequency signal.

Still during the WWII, British researchers led by Watson-Watt developed a new system with a very clever idea. They put transmitter on all British planes, and when they received signals from radar stations on the ground, they began broadcasting a signal back that identified the aircraft as friendly. That is the basic concept of RFID operation: a signal is sent to a transponder, which wakes up and either reflects back a signal (this means a passive system) or broadcasts a signal (active system). This system was known as "identify friend or foe (IFF)."

Radar and RF communications had a great development in the 1950s and 1960s mainly with the contribution of researches in the USA and in Europe. Many scientific articles explain in detail how an energy in the RF range can be used in the detection and identification of objects and, more importantly, remotely.

In a remarkable article—Communications by Means of Reflected Power—dated from 1948, Harry Stokman wrote "Evidently, considerable research and development work has to be done before the remaining basic problems in reflected-power communication are solved, and before the field of useful applications is explored." This paper can be considered one of the first works exploring the RFID subject [2].

In the 1960s and 1970s, RFID systems were still embedded within a context of "secret technology." As an example, Los Alamos National Laboratory was asked by the Energy Department of United States of America to develop a system for tracking nuclear materials and control sensitive materials. Inventors, developers, academic institutions and government laboratories were intensively working on RFID.

Considered to be one of the first patents involving RFID, Mario W. Cardullo received the US patent for an active RFID tag with rewritable memory on January 23, 1973.

Technological developments in the 1980s and 1990s led to the manufacture of more sophisticated and comprehensive RFID systems in addition to reducing the costs involved. An important task has also begun: standardization for the interoperability of RFID equipment or systems. In the 1990s, the RFID systems reach a significant mark of millions of tags only in the USA, especially from the automotive sector.

In 1999, the Massachusetts Institute of Technology (MIT) created a research center (financed by Uniform Code Council, EAN International, Procter & Gamble and Gillette) specialized in automatic identification (including UHF RFID) named the Auto-ID center. Between 1999 and 2003, the Auto-ID center gained the support of more than 100 large end-user companies, plus the US Department of Defense and many key RFID vendors. It opened research laboratories in Australia, the United Kingdom, Switzerland, Japan and China and developed two air interface protocols.

The MIT Auto-ID center became the global Electronic Product Code, an organism in charge of promoting the EPC standard. Some of the biggest retailers in the world and the US Department of Defense have said they plan to use EPC technology. The Auto-ID center closed its doors in October 2003, and its research responsibilities were passed on to Auto-ID Labs.

In December 2004, EPC global emerged as a second-generation standard way for broad adoption. Many industries are moving to adopt this technology.

In 2010s, the decreased cost of equipment and tags, increased performance to a reliability of 99.9% and a stable international standard brought a major boost in the use of RFID systems. In March 2010, a Korean laboratory successfully created a printed chip using carbon nanotubes that resulted in a significant decrease in cost.

RFID technologies are used for hundreds, if not thousands, of applications and industrial sectors (aerospace, automotive, logistics, transport, health, life, etc.), and the International Standard Organization (ISO) took part in establishing technical and applicative standards that led to a high degree of interoperability or interchangeability.

Today, there are various RFID frequency bands from a few kilohertz to a microwave frequency band (2.4–2.5 GHz). One of the most recent is the UHF Generation 2, which operates at 860–969 MHz [3].

Summarizing, RFID is a fantastic technology that brings together a wide range of professionals and knowledge areas such as systems engineering, circuit technology, software development, integrated circuit design, network engineering, antenna theory, propagation theory, microware technology, materials technology, receiver and transmitter design, encryption theory and mechanical design [4].

And what about the future? Are there still challenges to overcome? Efforts to reduce costs, miniaturize tags, use of alternative energy sources and standardization are likely to be part of these challenges.

In this book, the reader can find very important contributions not only to understand the RFID systems but also to visualize interesting new search fields and approaches.

Author details

Paulo Cesar Crepaldi* and Tales Cleber Pimenta

*Address all correspondence to: crepaldi@unifei.edu.br

Microelectronics Group, Institute of Systems Engineering and Information Technologies, Federal University of Itajuba, Brazil

References

[1] Landt J. The history of RFID. IEEE Potentials. 2005;**24**(4):8-11. DOI: 10.1109/MP.2005.1549751

[2] Domdouzisa K, Kumarb B, Anumbaa C. Radio-Frequency Identification (RFID) applications: A brief introduction. Advanced Engineering Informatics. 2007;**21**(4):350-355

[3] James Chu. Applications of RFID technology. IEEE Microwave Magazine. 2015;**16**(6):64-65. DOI: 10.1109/MMM.2015.2419891

[4] Weinstein R. RFID: A technical overview and its application to the enterprise. IT Professional. 2005;**7**(3):27-33. DOI:10.1109/MITP.2005.69

Chapter 2

Near-Field Antenna of RFID System

Zijian Xing

Additional information is available at the end of the chapter

http://dx.doi.org/10.5772/intechopen.71427

Abstract

Radio frequency identification (RFID) technology is a very important part of the Internet of Things. The antenna used in RFID system reader is one of its most important equipment, has become a research hotspot. Compared to far-field applications, RFID antennas typically use high-gain circularly polarized antennas or antenna arrays to increase their read distance. Near-field RFID reader antenna requires strong magnetic field, wide band and low gain characteristics, while the resulting magnetic field should be evenly distributed to avoid leakage read phenomenon. The main contents of this chapter are as follows. The RFID reader near field antenna based on the principle of magnetic field coupling has developed rapidly in recent years. In this paper, a double-layer open-circuit antenna are proposed. The near-field antennas have wideband and strong magnetic field characteristics, and are compact and simple to process. The open-loop antenna of the double-layer terminal is located at the lower level and the upper layer is the radiation ring. The antenna size is smaller, and the feeder part and the radiation part of the isolation, a good deal to avoid interference between each other.

Keywords: RFID, near field, antenna, electrically large

1. Concept of near-field antenna

Radio frequency identification (RFID) technologies, which were developed during the World War II, provide wireless identification and tracking capability [1, 2]. The reader antenna is an important unit of RFID systems. Many new RFID antennas are developed for different applications [3–7]. Reader antennas can be classified into two types based on the working scope for different application purposes: near-field antenna and far-field antenna. Currently, ultra-high frequency (UHF) near-field RFID technology are fast developed in item-level identifications such as sensitive products tracking, biological products and medical products (blood, medicines, vaccines), biosensing applications and so on [8–12].

The basic consideration of UHF near-field RFID is to make it work in a short distance stable, just like what LF/HF near-field RFID does [8]. Inductive coupling systems are selected in most applications in near-field UHF RFID, because most of the reactive energy is stored in magnetic field. Inductive coupling is more stable than the capacitive coupling and hardly affected by liquid or metal [13].

In a near-field RFID system, the reader and the tag antennas are coupled mainly through magnetic field. If the tag antenna is electrically small, the magnetic field of reader antenna is perturbed by tag rarely, and coupling coefficient C could be shown by the equation [14, 15].

$$C \propto f^2 N_{\mathrm{tag}}^2 S_{\mathrm{tag}}^2 B^2 \alpha \tag{1}$$

where f is an operating frequency, N_{tag} is the number of turns of the tag coil, S is the cross-section area of the coil, B is the magnetic field density at the tag location and α is the antenna misalignment loss.

One of the challenges in UHF near-field RFID applications is to design a reader antenna with wide bandwidth and strong near magnetic field simultaneously. Strong near magnetic field is important for extending the reading range. Low gain could reduce interferences. Wide bandwidth antenna could be applied at 840–960 MHz, which covers both ETSI of Europe and FCC of North America. In some special application scenarios, smaller size antennas are required because of the limited system space.

Some near-field antennas have been reported to generate strong and even magnetic field. Many travelling wave antenna is proposed to extend the bandwidth [16]. A conventional travelling wave antenna called Mini-Guardrail from a famous company Impinj has wide bandwidth of more than 200 MHz at UHF band as well as low gain [17]. But because, loads of traveling wave antenna consume too much power, current and near magnetic field are not strong enough. The magnetic field should be lower than −13 dBA/m at any direction if the distance above antenna is larger than 2 cm. Conventional standing wave antenna could present a strong magnetic field, but its gain is too high and bandwidth is too narrow to cover a wide UHF RFID bandwidth. Typical standing wave antenna with strong magnetic field like eye shape is proposed by Li et al. [18], but −10 dB bandwidth is only 30 MHz which could only cover FCC band. Narrow bandwidth antenna is easily detuned by environmental changes.

2. Typical design of electrically large near-field RFID antenna

2.1. Structure and character of a near-field RFID antenna

The current distribution of the near-field antenna is in-phase. That is, the current on the loops has the same orientation. For example, a two-layer and open circuit shape near-field antenna made by PCB board is shown in **Figure 1**. The current character is explained by this example.

Figure 1(a) shows the structure of the antenna, which is composed of two PCB layers. The top layer is mainly composed of two quasi-half loops which are connected with two folded

http://dx.doi.org/10.5772/intechopen.71427

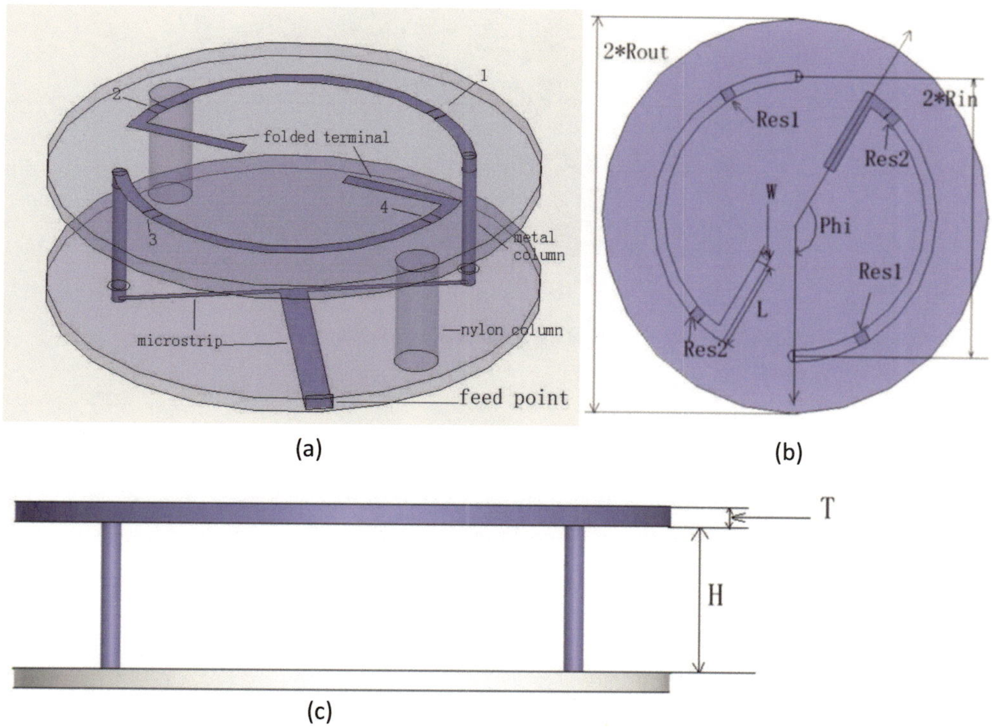

Figure 1. Model and structure of the proposed antenna: (a) 3D view, (b) top view and (c) side view.

straight terminals. The bottom layer is feed network with ground and lead are printed onto top and bottom surface, respectively. Fed at edge of bottom layer, 50 ohm microstrip line is connected with two 100-ohm lines, which are connected to two metal columns in another end. The other end of each column is connected to metal quasi-half loop strip. There are four loads on two quasi-half loops which are marked by 1, 2, 3 and 4 in **Figure 1(a)**. The two PCB boards are connected by two metal columns and fixed by two nylon columns.

Figure 1(b) shows the top view. Angle and radius of loop are marked by *Phi* and *Rin*, respectively. Length of folded terminal, width of metal strip and radius of PCB board are marked by *L*, *W* and *Rout*, respectively. The value of loads 1, 3 is Res1 and 2, 4 is Res2. **Figure 1(c)** shows the side view. The distance between two PCB layers and thickness of top PCB board are marked by *H* and *T*, respectively. Bottom layer has the same size and material as top layer.

2.2. Performance of the antenna

The proposed antenna can be printed onto any substrate and optimized at specific operating frequency by properly selecting the geometrical parameters. The antenna prototype is printed onto a FR4 substrate ($\varepsilon_r = 4.4$, $tan\delta = 0.02$, thickness $T = 2$ mm). The optimized antenna has parameters of $H = 15$ mm, $W = 2$ mm, $Rin = 25$ mm, $Rout = 34$ mm, $Res1 = 30$ ohm, $Res2 = 50$ ohm, $L = 8$ mm and $T = 2$ mm. As shown in **Figure 2(a)** and **(b)**, the antenna is fed by SMA port on the edge of the bottom layer. The new proposed antenna has many advantages such as strong magnetic field, low far-field gain, wide bandwidth, small size and so on.

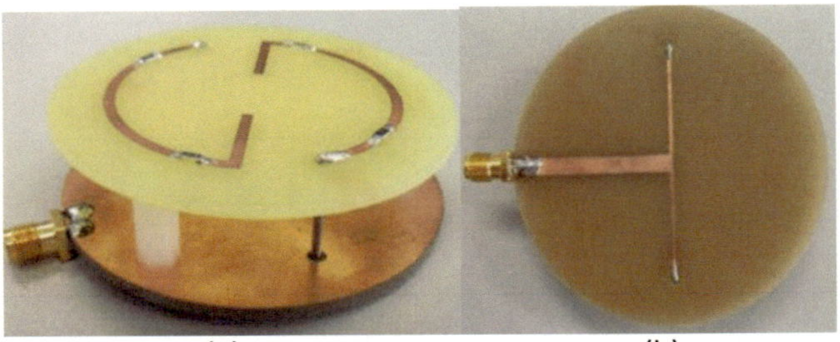

Figure 2. Photograph of the antenna: (a) 45° view of the antenna and (b) bottom view of the antenna.

2.2.1. *S11 performance*

The impedance matching measurement of the antennas was carried out using the Agilent N5230A vector network analyzer. **Figure 3** shows the simulated and measured return loss. The proposed antenna exhibits broadband impedance bandwidth, the frequency range for −15 dB return loss is from 826 to 950 MHz or 124 MHz bandwidth. The measured result agrees well with the simulation.

2.2.2. *Far-field gain and directivity*

The far-field gain and directivity are shown in **Figure 4**. It is clear that the gain is lower than −10 dB at any direction and about 15 dB lower than directivity.

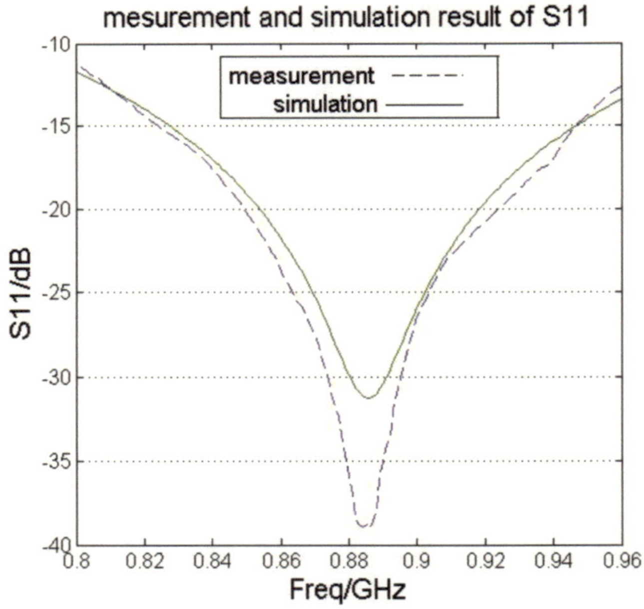

Figure 3. S11 of the actual antenna and simulation model.

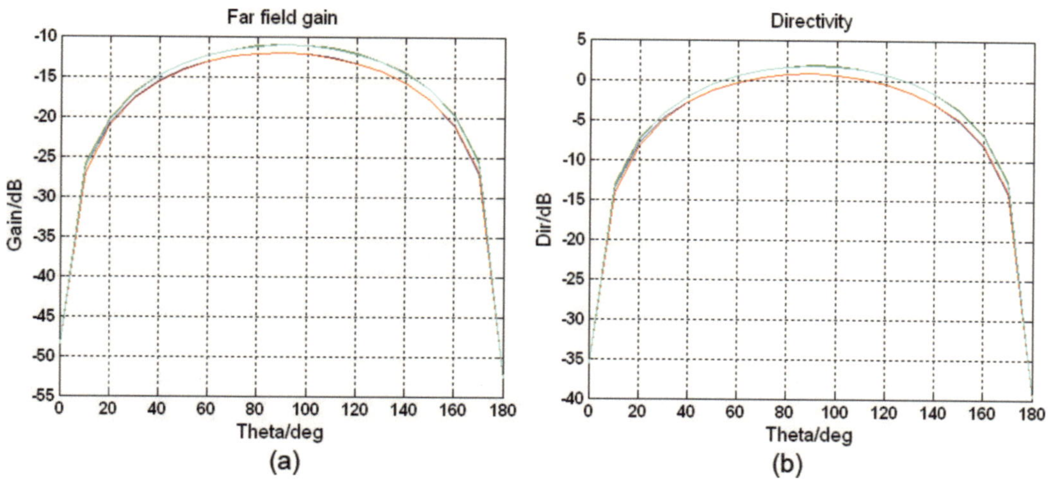

Figure 4. (a) Far-field gain versus theta at different Φ, which is 0, 90, 180 and 270°, and marked by four curves; (b) directivity versus theta at different Φ which is same as (a).

2.2.3. *Current distribution*

Figure 5 shows the current distribution of different phases. Different from conventional traveling wave antenna, current on the loop assumes standing wave distribution. One important factor of current is in-phase. Because magnetic field produced by the currents on the adjacent sides of the antenna cancel out each other and is thus very weak in the central portion of interrogation zone if the current distribution is out-phase. In **Figure 5**, current of this antenna is not out-phase because of small electrical length of the quasi-half loop. At the phases of 45, 90 and 135 degree, the currents are all strong. Actually, the magnetic field at these phases are also strong. The result could be verified by the comparison between **Figures 5** and **6**.

2.2.4. *Magnetic field distribution*

Figure 6 shows that magnetic field is concentrated and uniform around the center region of antenna at different phases (0°, 45°, 90°, 135°). Moreover, as a result of folded terminal, average current can be enhanced on the outer loop so that strong magnetic field intensity is obtained.

Figure 7(a) shows the magnetic field distribution at different z above the surface of antenna's top. The reason for choosing such a graduation scale is narrowly related with reading tag ability which will be discussed later. **Figure 7(b)** focuses on the magnetic field intensity attenuation versus z-axis.

Compared to other antenna, it could be found that the z-orientation magnetic field of the new antenna is much stronger. For example, referred by **Figure 7(b)**, the magnetic field of this antenna is significantly stronger than that of the proposed traveling wave antenna in [17] at same z. At $z = 2$ cm, two-layer and two quasi-half loops antenna has magnetic field intensity of −3 dBA/m, whereas the antenna from [17] has only −15 dBA/m. Taken **Figure 7(a)** as a reference, the magnetic field in center region of the antenna is also stronger than the another broadband

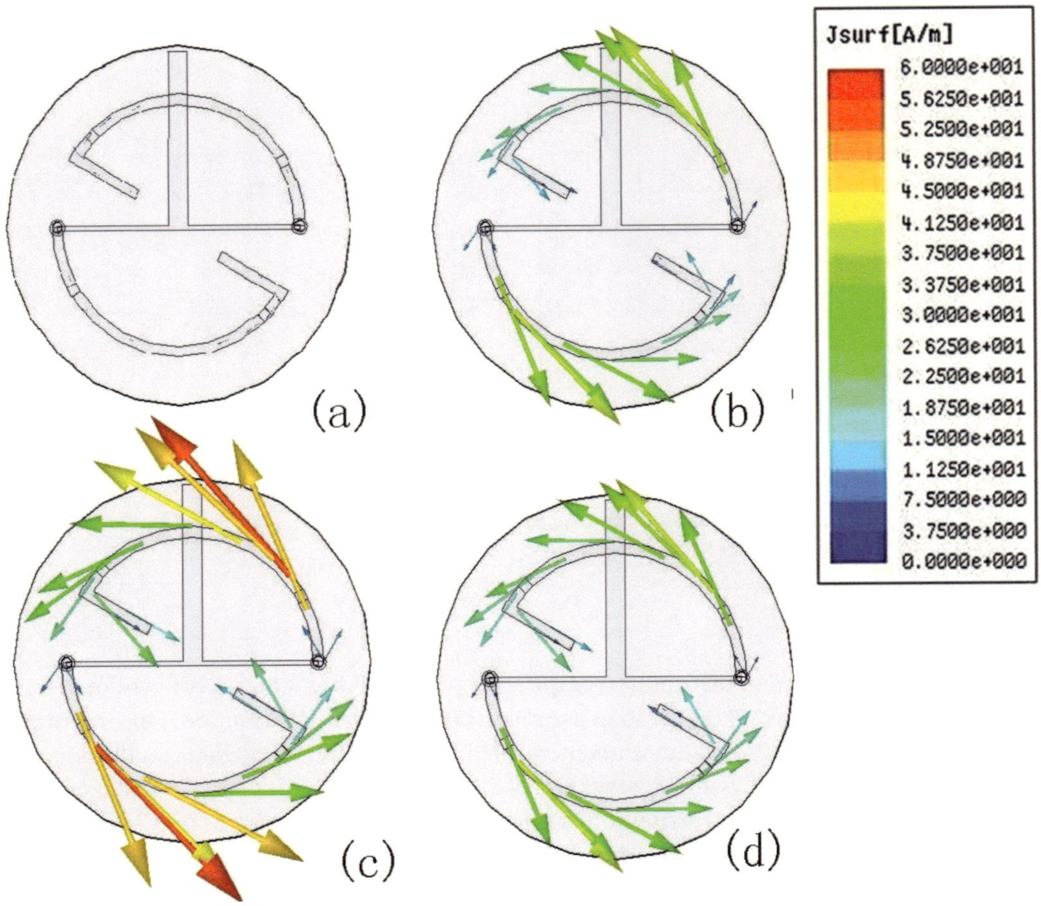

Figure 5. Current distribution on metal strip at different phases: (a) 0°, (b) 45°, (c) 90° and (d) 135°.

antenna which is proposed by Qing et al. [19]. It shows that magnetic field of the antenna from [19] is lower than −10 dBA/m at $z = 0.5$ mm, whereas two-layer and two quasi-half loops antenna is stronger than 0 dBA/m although at $z = 1$ cm.

2.3. Reading range

To further verify the performance of the proposed two-layer and two quasi-half loops antenna, the prototype was used as the reader antenna in a UHF near-field RFID system to detect UHF near-field tags. Test system is shown in **Figure 8(a)**, and the proposed antenna was connected to the reader operating at both 865–868 MHz of ETSI and 902–928 MHz of FCC with 30 dBm output to detect tag. Tag is positioned on a foam board, which has a size of 70 mm×70 mm, could be shown as **Figure 8(b)**. Grid is marked on the top of the foam board with the size of 1 cm×1 cm. The data of detected tag on each intersection were recorded.

This chapter adopts one annular tag which could be activated when magnetic field intensity is stronger than −13 dBA/m. The system choose ETSI band as the operating frequency because the operating mechanism of FCC is hopping frequency (HF).

http://dx.doi.org/10.5772/intechopen.71427

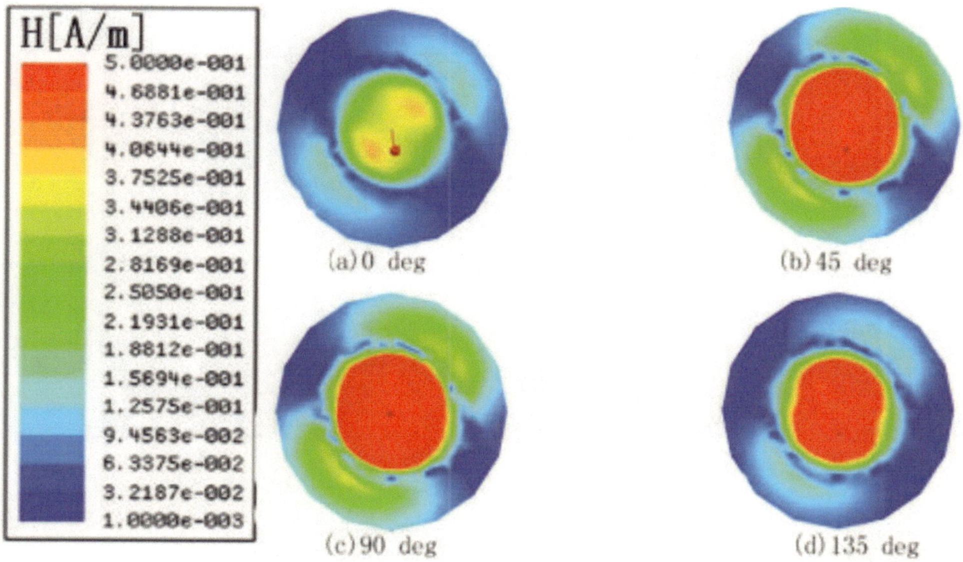

Figure 6. Different phases of *z*-orientation magnetic field distribution on the reference plane which is 1 cm above the top of antenna: (a) 0°; (b) 45°; (c) 90° and (d) 135°.

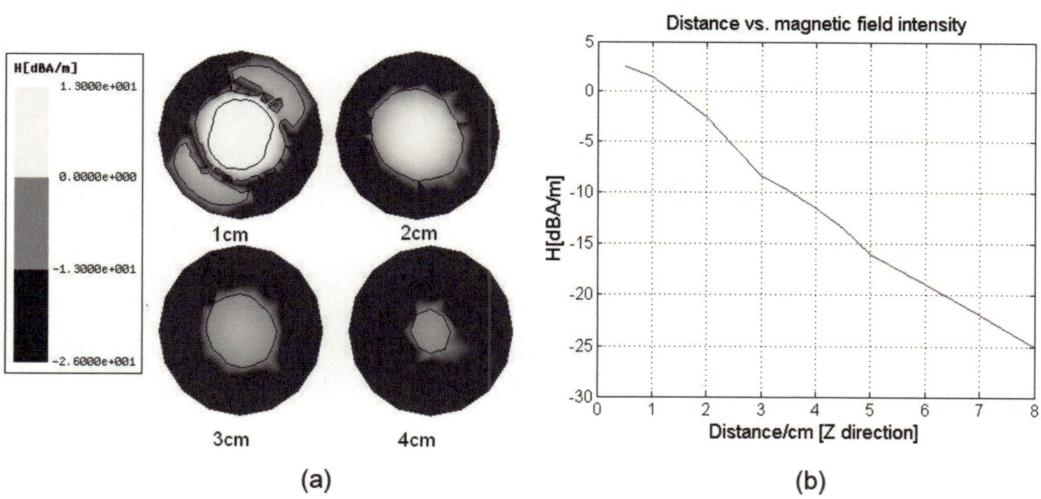

Figure 7. Simulated magnetic field distribution of the antenna operated at 868 MHz: (a) *z*-orientation magnetic field distribution at different *z*. Radius of reference plane is also 50 mm and (b) magnetic field intensity of the antennas along *z*-axis.

The measurement results of reading range are exhibited in **Figure 9**; it is clear that reading scope is reduced if distance increased. Compared between **Figures 9** and **7(a)**, it could be found that at each *z*, the reading range has a rough agreement with the magnetic field level line of −13 dBA/m. This is the reason for choosing such a graduation scale of z-orientation magnetic field in **Figure 7(a)**.

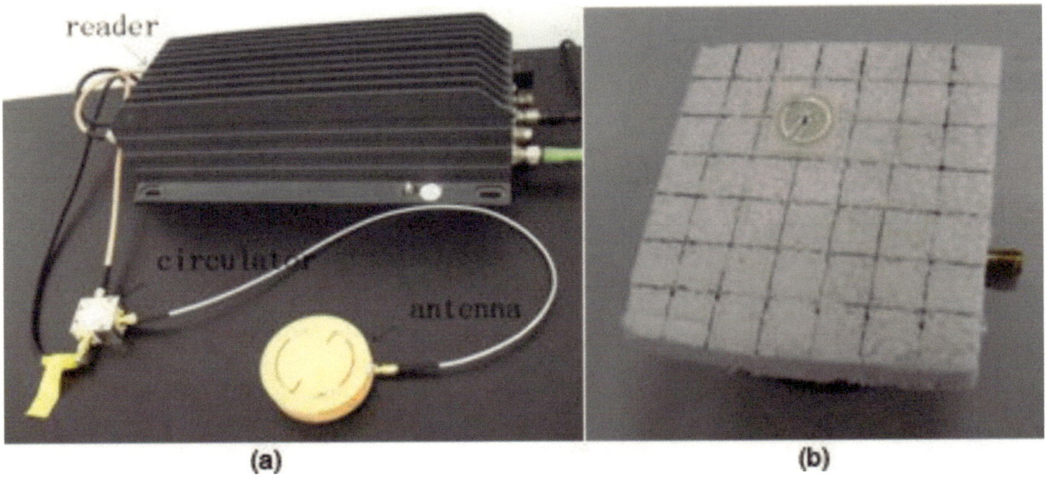

Figure 8. The configuration of reading range measurement. (a) Configuration of measurement scenarios: reader antenna, circulator and reader, which are connected with computer. (b) Foam board with tag is positioned above the antenna.

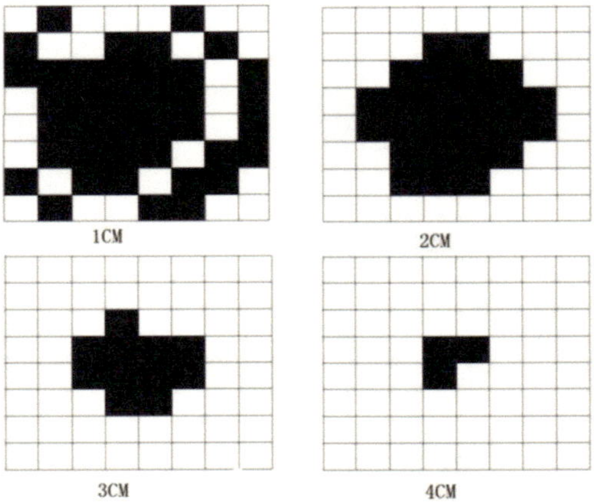

Figure 9. Reading scope of antenna at different distances, which are 1, 2, 3 and 4 cm. Black grid marked the intersection which could be read when tag is put on it, and white grid marked the opposite.

3. Optimization of near magnetic field

3.1. Parameter studies

The antenna's structure is a distorted symmetrical dipole. So, the length of metal loops and the input impedance could be estimated based on dipole theory. If resonant frequency is determined, the electric length of a metal column, quasi-half loop and folded terminal should match the resonant frequency.

$$L_{\text{loop}} = \frac{\text{phi}}{180} * \pi * R_{in} \tag{2}$$

where L_{loop} is the length of one quasi-half loop. It is needed to consider the quasi-half loop's mirror image function on the ground plane of microstrip during designing. Metal columns should be long enough because current mirror image is reversal and then it will cancel out a part of magnetic field. But if metal column is too long, magnetic field will be weak for the weak current on small quasi-half loop because of the unchangeable resonant frequency. Phase and magnitude of the current on both quasi-half loops are symmetrical so that magnetic field can be strengthened simultaneously by two quasi-half loops. Most of energy consumption of the antenna attributes to ohmic consumption on metal and loads, which could sharply reduce gain and broaden the bandwidth.

After extensive simulations, it is found that loads (*Res1* and *Res2*), the length of H and L_{loop} affect antenna performance significantly, whereas the other parameters show slight effects. The antenna with the parameters: R_{out}=34 mm, R_{in}=25 mm, *Phi*=160 degree, *L*=8 mm, *W*=2 mm, *Res1*=30 ohm, *Res2*=50 ohm, *H*=15 mm and *T*=2 mm was selected as a reference. All the simulation results of magnetic field distribution in this chapter are *z*-orientation. In this section, magnetic field is observed on the reference plane = 1 cm above the top of the antenna with radius of 50 mm. Set the upper surface of top layer as *z*=0, so that the distance between reference plane and antenna could be figured by the value of *z*. *z*-axis passes through the center of both top and bottom PCB boards.

3.1.1. Loads on quasi-half loops, Res1 and Res2

Figure 10(a) and **(b)** shows the magnetic field distribution of antennas at different values of *Res1* and *Res2*, respectively. It is observed that magnetic field distribution is sharply reduced with the increasing of *Res1* and *Res2* at the operating frequency. As shown in **Tables 1** and **2**, it could be found that the bandwidth and magnitude of S11 are also narrowly related with *Res1* and *Res2*.

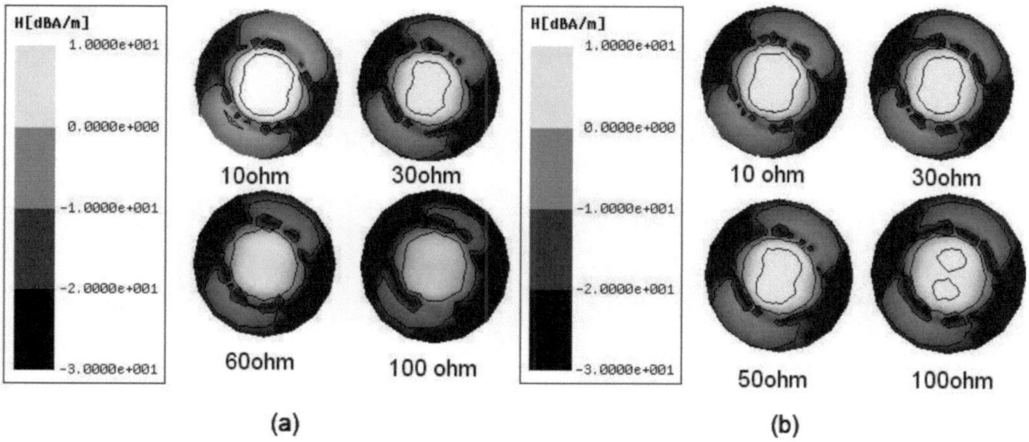

Figure 10. The relationship between loads and magnetic field at 868 MHz: (a) *Res1* versus magnetic field and (b) *Res2* versus magnetic field.

Res1	S11 at resonant frequency	–15 dB bandwidth	–10 dB bandwidth
10 ohm	–11.95 dB at 884 MHz	0 MHz	61 MHz (859–920 MHz)
30 ohm	–33.5 dB at 884 MHz	123 MHz (828–951 MHz)	190 MHz (808–998 MHz)
60 ohm	–13.81 dB at 884 MHz	0 MHz	179 MHz (818–986 MHz)
100 ohm	-8.35 dB at 893 MHz	0 MHz	0 MHz

Table 1. Relationship between the Res1, resonant frequency and bandwidth.

Res2	S11 at resonant frequency	–15 dB bandwidth	–10 dB bandwidth
10 ohm	–16.7 dB at 877 MHz	42 MHz (857–899 MHz)	124 MHz (817–941 MHz)
30 ohm	–21.7 dB at 879 MHz	72 MHz (844–916 MHz)	145 MHz (810–955 MHz)
50 ohm	–33.5 dB at 884 MHz	123 MHz (828–951 MHz)	190 MHz (808–998 MHz)
90 ohm	–25.4d B at 894 MHz	96 MHz (850–946 MHz)	184 MHz (811–996 MHz)

Table 2. Relationship between the Res2, resonant frequency and bandwidth.

Both magnetic field and return loss are more sensitive to *Res1* than *Res2*, because the current of *Res1* is much stronger than that of *Res2*. From **Tables 1** and **2**, it is found that *Res1* or *Res2* affects resonant frequency slightly and bandwidth and S11 at resonant frequency significantly.

3.1.2. *Effect of the space between two layers, H*

Figure 11(a) and **(b)** exhibits the magnetic field distribution of the antennas with varying heights of H at 868 and 915 MHz. The antennas are configured with identical length of R_{in}

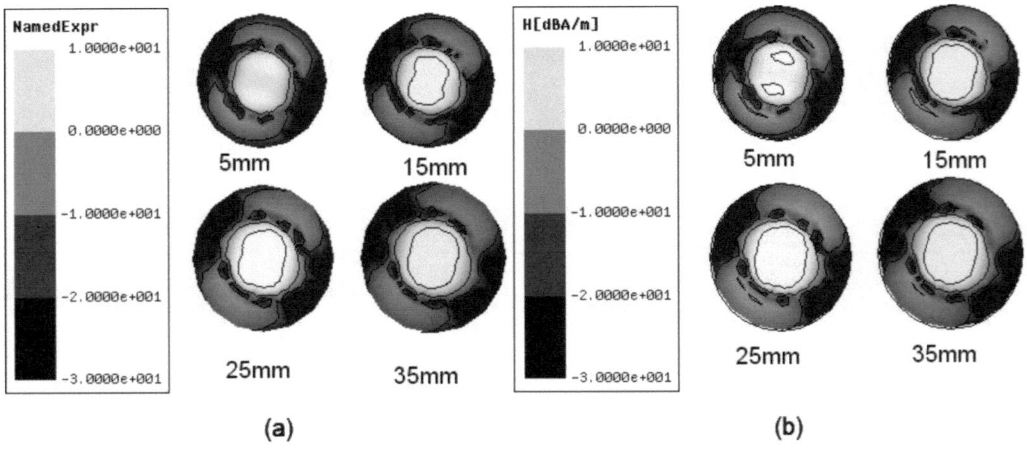

Figure 11. The relationship between the H and magnetic field at different frequencies: (a) 868 and (b) 915 MHz.

and L. It is observed that all the antennas have similar magnetic field except H=5 cm, when H changes from 5 to 35 mm. It could be inferred that the magnetic field is sharply cancelled out by current mirror image of the ground if H is too narrow. Current mirror image is too weak to influence the magnetic field when the length of H is longer than 15 mm.

3.1.3. *Radius of quasi-half loop* R_{in}

Radius of quasi-half loop is also an important influencing factor of magnetic field. In the experiments, other parameters are unchanged except R_{out} because radius of R_{out} is narrowly related with that of R_{in}. **Figure 12** shows how magnetic field changes with different R_{in}. It is clear that magnetic field should be weaker if the R_{in} is too small or large at 868 MHz. The total length of L_{loop} and L is far less than λ_4 (8.64 cm) and average current strength on the loop is naturally weak. But the reason for weak magnetic field at large R_{in} (40 mm) is the decentralization of magnetic field energy.

3.2. Structure improvement

Figure 13(a) shows the structure of the antenna. The top layer contains two quasi-half loops with two inductance-like terminals. The bottom layer is the feed network with the ground and lead. Fed at the edge, a 50 ohm microstrip line is connected to two 100 ohm microstrip lines which connect metal columns. The other end of each column is connected with a metal loop strip. On loops, there are four printed loads which are marked by 1, 2, 3 and 4 in **Figure 13(a)**. The two PCB boards are supported by two nylon columns.

Figure 13(b) shows the top view of antenna. The angle, width and radius of the quasi-half loop are marked by *Phi, W* and R_{in}, respectively. The radial and tangential length of the one circle of inductance structure is marked by L and *BW*, respectively. The number of the inductance loop is marked by N which is three in **Figure 13(b)**. Four resistors are printed on the top of antenna.

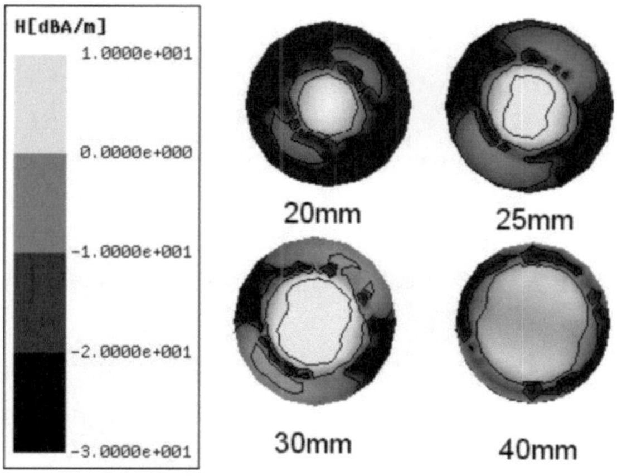

Figure 12. Magnetic field distribution of different R_{in} (868 MHz).

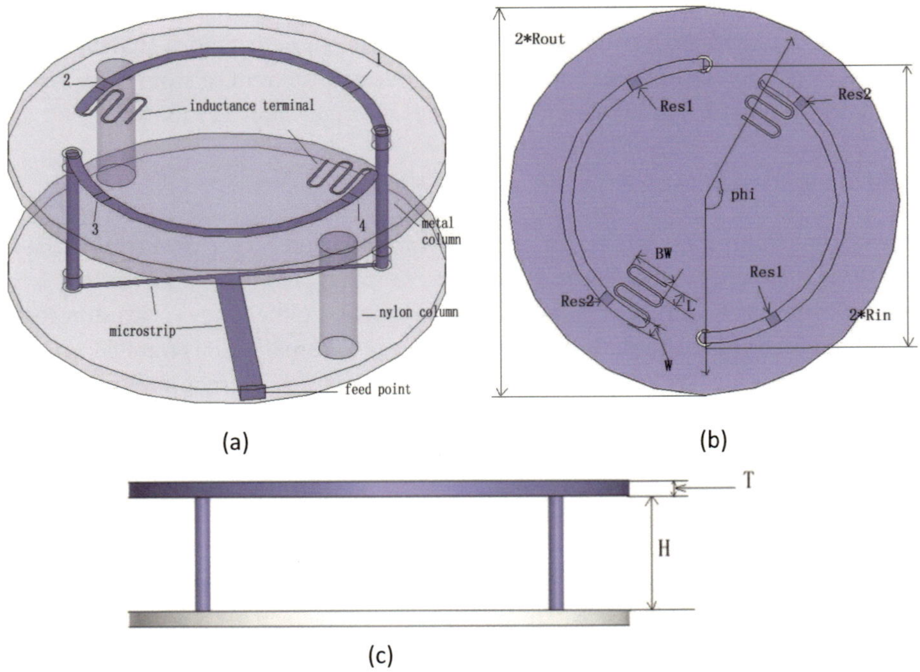

Figure 13. Model and structure of the proposed antenna: (a) 3D view, (b) top view and (c) side view.

4. Conclusion of near-field antenna of RFID system

It is challenging to design UHF near-field RFID antennas with strong magnetic fields and broad bandwidth. The UHF RFID antenna is demonstrated to be able to achieve a broad bandwidth and a low gain. The proposed antenna has also been proven to have strong magnetic fields with concentrated field distribution in the near-field region of antenna, which is very suitable for UHF near-field RFID reader applications.

Moreover, the investigation has shown that the UHF RFID antenna has produced the stronger magnetic field distribution. The most impact factor for near-field RFID antenna is magnetic field distribution. In recent years, near field radio frequency identification system has developed, many antennas are developed, but there are still have some problems. The combination of magnetic field construction and band widening technology is not perfect, especially the low-loss large-scale standing wave near-field antenna band widening technology is rarely reported.

The near-field theory is the research foundation of the near-field antenna. The breakthrough of the near-field electromagnetism theory and its innovation not only play an extremely important role in the development of the electromagnetism itself but also promotes the radio frequency identification directly and also a series of modern electronic technology development, so the analysis of the near-field problem is very basic in the electromagnetism, valuable and challenging research work.

Author details

Zijian Xing

Address all correspondence to: xingzijian2004@126.com

Northwestern Polytechnical University, China

References

[1] Wantc R. An introduction to RFID technology. IEEE Pervasive Computing. 2006;**5**(1):25-33

[2] Landt J. The history of RFID. IEEE Potentials. 2005;**24**(4):8-1

[3] Cole PH. A Study of Factors Affecting the Design of EPC Antennas & Readers for Supermarket Shelves. Auto-ID Center, north terrace, adelaide, Australia; 2002

[4] Liu ZM, Hillegass RR. A 3 patch near field antenna for conveyor bottom read in RFID sortation application. Antennas and Propagation Society International Symposium 2006, IEEE, July 2006, pp.1043-1046

[5] Ranasinghe DC, Ng ML, Leong KS, Jamali B, Cole PH. Small UHF RFID label antenna Design and Limitations. 2006 IEEE International workshop on Antenna Technology, March 6-8, 2006, pp. 200-204

[6] Nikitin PV, Rao KVS, Lazar S. An overview of near field UHF RFID, 2007 IEEE International Conference on RFID, Mar. 26-28, 2007, pp.166-174

[7] Zhang M, Chen Y, Jiao Y, Zhang F. Dual circularly polarized antenna of compact structure for RFID application. Journal of Electromagnetic Waves and Applications. 2006;**20**(14):1895-1902

[8] Harrop P. Near Field UHF vs. HF for Item Level Tagging [Online]. Available: http://www.eurotag.org/?Articles_and_Publications

[9] Desmons D. UHF Gen2 for item-level tagging, presented at the RFID World 2006. [Online]. Available: www.impinj.com/files/Impinj_ILT_RFID_World.pdf

[10] UHF Gen 2 for Item-Level Tagging Impinj RFID Technology Series Paper [Online]. Available: http://www.impinj.com/files/MR_GP_ED_00003_ILT.pdf

[11] Ajluni C. Item-level RFID takes off. RF Design Magazine. Sep. 2006

[12] Item-Level Visibility in the Pharmaceutical Supply Chain: A Comparison of HF and UHF RFID Technologies, Philips, TAGSYS, and Texas Instruments [Online]. Available: http://www.tagsysrfid.com/modules/tagsys/upload/news/TAGSYSTI-Philips White-Paper.pdf

[13] Wang S, Guan X, Wang D-W, Ma X, Su Y. Fast Calculation of Wide-Band Responses of Complex Radar Targets. Progress In Electromagnetics Research. 2007;**68**:185-196

[14] Qing X, Goh CK, Chen ZN. A broadband UHF near-field RFID antenna. IEEE Transactions on Antennas and Propagation. 2010;**58**(12)

[15] Ryu H-K, Woo J-M. Size reduction in UHF band RFID tag antenna based on circular loop antenna. 18th International Conference on Applied Electromagnetics and Communications, 2005;12-14

[16] Ling C. Antenna Project Handbook. Publishing House of Electronics Industry. Beijing, China; June 2002. p. 306-308

[17] Mini Guardrail Antenna Datasheet [online]. Available: http://www.bodetech.com/documents/MiniGuardrail_Antenna_Datasheet.pdf

[18] Li X, Liao J, Yuan Y, Yu D. Segmented coupling eye-shape UHF band near field antenna design. IEEE Microwave Asia Pacific Conf, Singapore, December 2009. pp. 2401-2404

[19] Qing X, Chen ZN, Goh CK. UHF near field RFID reader antenna with capacitive couplers. Electronics Letters. 2010;**46**(24)

Chapter 3

RFID Localization in Wireless Sensor Networks

Yang Zhao and Neal Patwari

Additional information is available at the end of the chapter

http://dx.doi.org/10.5772/65069

Abstract

Received signal strength (RSS)-based localization of people and assets through RFID has significant benefits for logistics, security and safety. However, the accuracy of RFID localization in wireless sensor networks suffers from unrealistic antenna gain pattern assumption, and the human body has a major effect on the gain pattern of the RFID badge that the person is wearing. In this book chapter, the gain pattern due to the effect of the human body is experimentally measured and modeled. A method is presented to estimate the model parameters from multiple RSS measurements. Two joint orientation and position estimators, four-dimensional (4D) maximum likelihood estimation (MLE) algorithm and alternating gain and position estimation (AGAPE) algorithm, are proposed to estimate the orientation and the position of the badge using RSS measurements from anchor nodes. A Bayesian lower bound on the mean squared error of the joint estimation is derived and compared with the Cramer-Rao bound with an isotropic gain pattern. Both theoretical and experimental results show that the accuracy of position estimates can be improved with orientation estimates included in the localization system.

Keywords: localization, radio propagation, wireless sensor network

1. Introduction

RFID localization of assets, robots and people has significant benefits for logistics, security and operations management. For example, GE Healthcare uses the AgileTrac platform [1] to track the physical location of each asset, via various real-time location system (RTLS) techniques. In RFID localization, many kinds of radio measurements can be used: time of arrival (TOA), time difference of arrival (TDOA), angle of arrival (AOA) and received signal strength (RSS) [2]. While RSS is low-cost and available in almost all standard wireless devices, most RSS-based localization methods make the assumption that the transmitters have isotropic gain patterns. However, even when the antenna of a transmitter badge is considered as isotropic, people or objects can affect the RFID badge's radiation, due to the fact that they are absorbing power, altering the antenna impedance and thus distorting the antenna gain pattern [3]. Previous studies have focused on characterizing the effects of a human body's location and orientation on RSS measurements [4–7]. In this book chapter, we present models and methods to handle, and in fact benefit from, the removal of the unrealistic isotropic gain pattern assumption.

Real-world directional gain patterns are problematic for RSS-based localization algorithms. In RSS-based algorithms, a model relating RSS and path length is assumed [8] or estimated from training measurements [9]. When the RFID antenna gain pattern is no longer isotropic, the distances estimated from the log-distance model [10] will not be the same even if the RFID transmitter is in the middle of two receivers. Model-based localization algorithms will infer that the transmitter is closer to the receiver that measured larger RSS and will thus produce estimates that are biased towards directions of high gain in the gain pattern [3].

To deal with the non-isotropic antenna gain pattern and improve model-based RFID localization algorithm, we need to build a model for the directionality of a transmitter RFID badge when it is worn by a person or attached to an object. We present measurements and models for a transmitter badge worn by a person. However, RFID tags attached to large objects will also experience non-isotropic gain patterns, and thus extensions to other types of tagged objects are feasible. As presented in the study of Zhao et al. [3], the variation of RSS was modeled as a function of people's orientation (i.e., facing direction). The study also proposed (1) a first-order model to capture most of the variation in the gain pattern as a function of people's orientation, (2) a method to estimate people's orientation and directionality from ordinary RSS measurements, and (3) an algorithm to estimate the position, orientation and gain pattern of the RFID badge called alternating gain and position estimation (AGAPE) algorithm. We apply the AGAPE algorithm together with a 2D maximum likelihood estimation (MLE) algorithm [8] and 4D MLE algorithm [3] to three sets of experiments performed at different environments: outdoor, indoor and through-wall. Experimental results show different levels of improvement from including the first-order gain pattern model at those different environments.

It is not obvious that a non-isotropic gain pattern can benefit RFID localization because additional model parameters must be estimated together with the RFID locations. In addition to experimental results, we provide theoretical results that show that the existence of a directional gain pattern can actually reduce position error for localization algorithms. The Bayesian Cramer-Rao bound (Bayesian CRB) was derived in Ref. [3] for joint estimation of orientation and position, while the CRB for position estimation was derived in Ref. [8] with an isotropic gain pattern assumption. Comparison between the Bayesian CRB [3] and the CRB [8] shows that joint estimation of orientation and position may outperform (result in lower mean squared error) estimation of position alone in the isotropic case.

In summary, in this book chapter, we present the latest research progress in the effort to include RFID antenna gain pattern in model-based RSS localization algorithms. We show that real-world non-isotropic gain pattern of RFID badge is not a problem to be ignored, but a means to improve localization accuracy. We present measurements, models, estimation algorithms and estimation lower bounds for RSS-based localization in wireless sensor networks. Experimental results from three sets of experiments show that position estimates are improved with the inclusion of orientation estimates from the first-order gain pattern model and the RSS measurements.

2. Models

Statistical models based on real-world measurements are important for model-based RSS localization algorithms. In this section, a measurement-based model is presented for the gain pattern of a transmitter badge worn by a person. A transmitter in close proximity to a human body is strongly affected by human tissue, which absorbs power and distorts the gain pattern of the transmitter [11, 12].

The log-distance model [10] is a general model for the power P_i received at anchor node *i from the transmitter badge t*. We include the transmitter gain pattern in the log-distance model, and the dBm power P_i is modeled as

$$P_i = P_0 - 10n_p \log_{10}\left(\frac{d_i}{d_0}\right) + g(\alpha_i) + \eta \quad (1)$$

where P_0 is the received power in dBm at a reference distance d_0, n_p is the pathloss exponent, d_i is the distance between anchor node i and transmitter badge t, α_i is the angle between anchor node i and the badge, $g(\alpha_i)$ is the gain pattern of the transmitter badge at angle α_i, and η is the model error plus noise. Note that the log-distance model parameters P_0 and n_p can be estimated using the received RSS measurements between pairs of anchor nodes. Assuming known anchor node coordinates, these two model parameters can be estimated via linear regression, as in Ref. [8].

Naive model-based localization algorithms use $g(\alpha_i) = 0$ for all α_i. We propose to include a nonzero $g(\alpha_i)$ in Eq. (1). Any real-world gain pattern will depend on the person and the badge and will look somewhat random; however, we hope to capture the major features of $g(\alpha_i)$ that will be largely accurate for the average person.

2.1. Measurements

The recent study in Ref. [3] quantifies the effect of the orientation of a human body on the RSS measurements using datasets from several experiment campaigns. In their experimental study, two Crossbow TelosB nodes [13] operating at 2.4 GHz were used with one node (node 1) placed on a stand and the other one (node 2) hung in the middle of a person's chest. The person wearing node 2 turned 45° every 20 s, with the distance between these two nodes kept the same. Meanwhile, the RSS at node 1 was recorded on a computer. Node 2 transmitted about 20 times per second, thus about 400 RSS measurements were recorded for each of the eight different orientations made by the person. The described experiments were performed by five people in the student building as well as an empty parking lot at University of Utah. Eight experiments were performed with various distances between the two nodes from 1.5 to 5.0 m. Therefore, a total of 25,600 measurements were recorded.

Experimental results from two different experiments are shown in **Figure 1(a)**. The minimum RSS of Experiment 1 (red) and Experiment 2 (blue) are 145° and 180°, respectively, whereas the maximum RSS are 315°and 0°, respectively. **Figure 1(b)** shows the mean gain pattern, which is averaged across all experiments, and indicates that if the person's orientation is 180°, i.e., the human body blocks the line-of-sight (LOS) path between nodes 1 and 2, the gain pattern is close

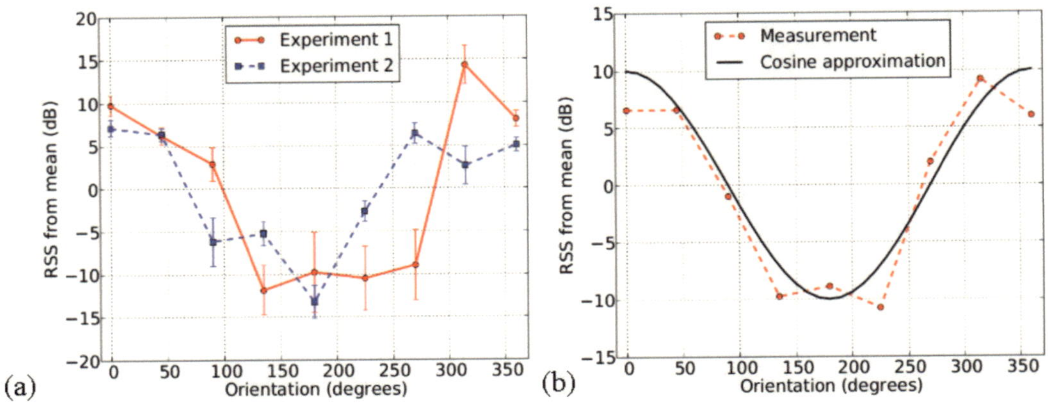

Figure 1. The effect of the human body on the RFID antenna gain pattern (RSS from mean). (a) Measured gain patterns with the error bars in two different experiments. (b) Average over all measured data.

to the minimum. In contrast, if the person's orientation is 0°, i.e., facing the node1, then the gain pattern is about 20 dB higher as compared with its lowest point [the red curve in **Figure 1(b)**]. The average gain pattern in **Figure 1(b)** closely resembles a cosine function (black curve) with period 360° and amplitude 10 dB. It is worth to note that the variation in RSS as a function of orientation due to the presence of a person is similar to other experimental studies [7, 14].

2.2. Gain pattern model

Based on the results of the measurements described above, a model for the gain pattern is proposed as a cosine function with period 360°:

$$\hat{g}(\alpha) = G_1 \cos(\alpha - \beta) \tag{2}$$

where β is the orientation (direction of maximum gain) of the badge, and $G_1 \geq 0$ is the magnitude of the cosine function in dB, which we also refer to as the directionality, and $G_1 = 0$ indicates no directionality, i.e., the RFID badge is an isotropic radiator.

As explained in Ref. [3], the model of Eq. (2) represents the two most important characteristics observed in the measurements. First, regardless of path length or person wearing the badge, the gain is higher in the direction the person is facing and lower in the opposite direction. In a wireless sensor network with several anchor nodes, a person with a badge stands halfway between node j and node k so that the distance between the badge and these two nodes are the same, as shown in **Figure 2**. Given that the person is facing node k, the mean RSS value of node k would be greater than that of node j.

Second, Eq. (2) is a first-order model for any periodic function. The measurements for this particular set of data showed a single order captures the vast majority of the angular variation. Any function with period 2π has a Fourier series representation as the follows:

$$g(\alpha) = \frac{1}{2\pi} \sum_{k=-\infty}^{\infty} G(k) e^{j2\pi k\alpha} \tag{3}$$

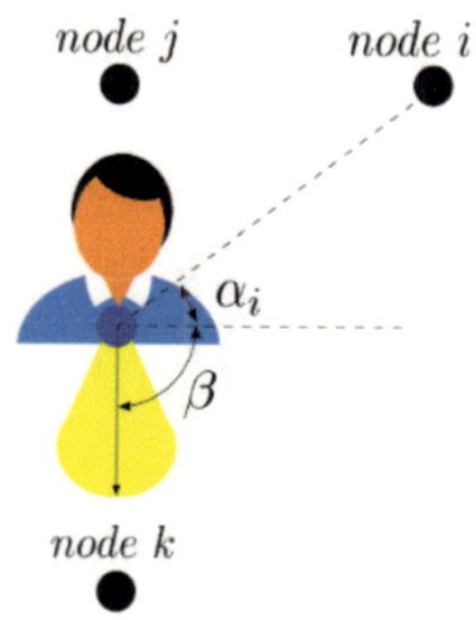

Figure 2. Gain pattern of a badge in a wireless sensor network.

where $G(k)$ are the complex-valued Fourier series components. Note that the model of Eq. (2) is simply the first harmonic of an arbitrary gain pattern measurement. That is, we include only the $k = 1$ term in Eq. (3).

3. Localization algorithms

3.1. Problem statement

This chapter focuses on 2D position estimation using RSS measurements. For a wireless sensor network which has N anchor nodes and one badge, the position estimation corresponds to the estimation of the coordinates of a badge: $z_t = [x_t, y_t]^T$. Note that one badge is used to simplify notation in the chapter. However, extension to multiple badges is possible.

If we only use the log-distance model in Ref. [10] to estimate distances between the badge and anchor nodes, our unknown model parameter $\theta = z_t$, since the other model parameters n_p and P_0 can be determined using pairwise RSS measurements between N anchor nodes.

However, if the gain pattern model is included, two parameters in the gain pattern model must be estimated from Eq. (2). So, we include these two parameters as nuisance parameters, and the unknown parameter vector θ becomes:

$$\boldsymbol{\theta} = [\mathbf{z}_t^T, \beta, G_1]^T \tag{4}$$

where β is the orientation of the RFID badge, and G_1 is the directionality of the RFID antenna gain pattern.

3.2. 4D MLE algorithm

To estimate both the badge position and the gain pattern, a baseline algorithm - 4D maximum likelihood estimation (MLE) algorithm is introduced here as the counterpart of the 2D MLE algorithm [8] with an isotropic antenna gain pattern assumption.

As discussed in Section 2, the received dBm power P_i is modeled as Eq. (1). Assuming the RSS values P_i are independent Gaussian with variance σ^2 and mean $\mu(\theta) = P_0 - 10n_p\log_{10}\left(\frac{d_i}{d_0}\right) + g(\alpha_i)$, one can show that the MLE of the badge position is as follows:

$$\hat{\boldsymbol{\theta}}_{MLE} = \underset{\theta}{\text{argmax}} \sum_{i=0}^{N-1} \left(P_i - \mu(\boldsymbol{\theta})\right)^2 \quad (5)$$

As mentioned in Ref. [3], grid search method was used for finding the MLE solution. For instance, in the isotropic gain pattern case, the TICC2431 used a 2D grid search method to find the 2D coordinate. However, when the dimension of the estimation parameter vector increases, the computation time of a grid search increases exponentially. In addition, the high computation cost of a multi-dimensional gird search also prevents it from real-time applications. To better estimate the position and the gain pattern in real-time, we use signal processing techniques and first-order approximation to develop a different algorithm.

3.3. Gain pattern estimator

Before we propose the algorithm to jointly estimate the position and the gain pattern, we first introduce a gain pattern estimator, assuming we know the badge position z_t. The gain pattern estimator was first proposed in Ref. [3], and we present their work in this section.

When measuring the gain pattern at discrete values of α_i, $i = 0, 1 \cdots N-1$, we require the discrete Fourier transform (DFT) instead of the Fourier series. However, the same principle applies—the cosine with period 2π is the first-order approximation of the gain function. Specifically, for the gain pattern at angle α_i, the discrete-time exponential representation is given by

$$g(\alpha_i) = \frac{1}{N}\sum_{k=0}^{N-1} G(k)e^{j\alpha_i k} = \frac{1}{N}G(0) + \frac{2}{N}\sum_{k=1}^{M} |G(k)| \cos\left(\angle G(k) + \alpha_i k\right) \quad (6)$$

where $M = \frac{N}{2}$, and $\alpha_i = \frac{2\pi i}{N}$, for N equally spaced measurements. In the measurement experiments, we had $N = 8$.

The mean gain $G(0)$ is simply the average of all of the differences (which we call the model error) between P_i and the log-distance path loss model, that is, $P_0 - 10n_p\log_{10}\left(\frac{d_i}{d_0}\right)$. Because n_p and P_0 are determined by linear regression, they tend to make the model error zero mean. Thus, we assume that $G(0) = 0$ dB because any mean model error would have been removed by the linear regression.

Then, the gain pattern from an M order model can be estimated as:

$$\hat{g}_{M(\alpha_i)} = \frac{2}{N}\sum_{k=1}^{M} |G(k)| \cos\left(\angle G(k) + \alpha_i k\right) \quad (7)$$

The first-order model including only the $k = 1$ term in (7) is

$$\hat{g}(\alpha_i) = \frac{2}{N}|G(1)|\cos(\angle G(1) + \alpha_i) \tag{8}$$

By comparing Eqs. (8) and (2) in Section 2.2, we find the two model parameters β and G_1 of the gain pattern can be calculated as:

$$\beta = -\angle G(1)$$

$$G_1 = \frac{2}{N}|G(1)| \tag{9}$$

Thus to estimate the gain pattern, we only need to calculate the DFT term $G(1)$. In the measurement experiments discussed in Section 2.1, it was possible to measure the gain at equally spaced angles. In real deployments, anchor nodes will make measurements at a variety of non-equally spaced angles α_i, depending on badge and anchor node positions. The most common way to estimate the spectral content in a signal using non-equally spaced samples is simply to apply the DFT to the available samples [15]. Thus, we estimate $G(k)$ as:

$$G(k) = \sum_{i=0}^{N-1} g(\alpha_i)e^{-j\alpha_i k} \tag{10}$$

where $g(\alpha_i)$ can be calculated from Eq. (1), knowing the received power and the angle between the badge and anchor nodes.

Note, we need only $G(1)$ for the first-order model of Eq. (2). This calculation of $G(1)$ requires only N complex multiplies and adds, where N is the number of RSS measurements received for a badge. This low complexity is important to minimize the computational complexity of the localization algorithm.

3.4. Alternating gain and position estimator

In the gain pattern estimation, the badge position is assumed known. But in a localization algorithm, the badge position needs to be estimated. For joint position and gain pattern estimation, an alternating gain and position estimation (AGAPE) algorithm has been developed in Ref. [3] to efficiently estimate both the position and orientation of a person in a wireless sensor network.

As described in Ref. [3], the algorithm includes (1) the initial estimation of the position of the badge using isotropic gain assumption, (2) calculation of the gain pattern parameters using the first-order sinusoidal model, (3) re-estimation of the badge position using the RSS-distance model with the estimated gain pattern. The algorithm iterates until a misfit function is minimized. Note that the proposed AGAPE algorithm is a kind of alternating minimization method [16]. **Figure 3** shows the flowchart of the AGAPE algorithm. For the first step, given that the gain pattern is isotropic, the naive MLE method is used to estimate the badge position. The MLE solution can be derived from a conjugate gradient algorithm. However, a 2D grid

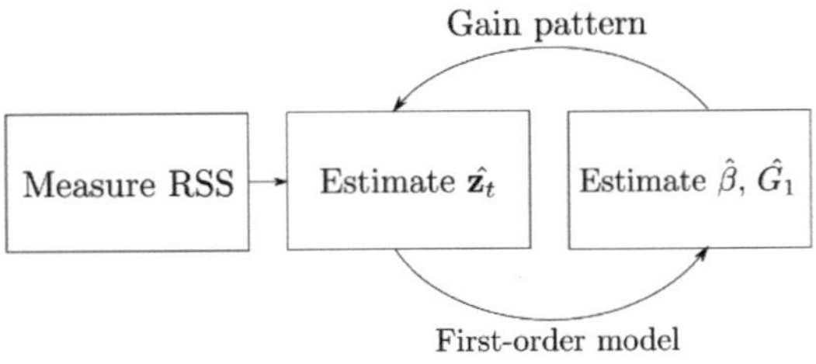

Figure 3. Flowchart of the AGAPE algorithm.

search method was used to avoid the local minima problem here, in the position estimation step. Note that the 2D MLE grid search can be accomplished quickly in hardware. The output of the position estimation step is referred to as $\hat{z}_t$.

For the orientation estimation step, given an estimated position, we calculate the gain pattern $g(\alpha_i)$ from the RSS-distance model Eq. (1), and then, the DFT term $G(1)$ is calculated from Eq. (10). The gain pattern model parameters orientation β and directionality G_1 are then estimated from $\angle G(1)$ the phase angle of $G(1)$ and the magnitude of $G(1)$, respectively, as given in Eq. (9). Finally, the position of the badge is estimated using the RSS-distance model with estimated orientation and directionality again. The steps of position and orientation estimation repeat until the following misfit function is minimized:

$$\mathbf{\Phi} = \sum_{i=1}^{N} (P_i - \widehat{P}_i)^2 \tag{11}$$

where $\widehat{P}_i$ is the RSS estimate at anchor node i, which is calculated from the RSS-distance model Eq. (1).

4. Estimator lower bounds

One might think that the lower bound of the variance of an estimator will increase due to the introduction of an additional unknown gain pattern model. In this section, the Bayesian CRB [17] is derived by including the gain pattern model parameters as nuisance parameters, as derived in Ref. [3]. The Bayesian CRB is used because the prior knowledge of the gain directionality G_1 is available a priori. In this book chapter, we show that the CRB derived in Ref. [8] is a special case of the Bayesian CRB derived here. We also show that the lower bound on the variance of a position estimator is decreased by the introduction of a gain pattern model.

4.1. Bayesian CRB

To derive the Bayesian CRB, we assume that the orientation of the badge β is uniformly distributed in the range of 0–2π because the orientation of the person wearing the badge is arbitrary.

http://dx.doi.org/10.5772/65069

The gain pattern model expressed in Eq. (2) can be rewritten as:

$$g(\alpha_i) = G_I \cos\alpha_i + G_Q \sin\alpha_i \tag{12}$$

where $G_I = G_1 \cos\beta$, $G_Q = G_1 \sin\beta$. Here, we assume the in-phase component G_I and quadrature component of G_Q are i.i.d. Gaussian distributed with zero means and variance σ_G^2. Components G_I and G_Q are affected by many different factors, such as the person's shape and size, and also the badge location on the human body. Thus, their distributions are close to Gaussian, by a central limit argument. This assumption is equivalent to a Rayleigh distribution [18] assumption for G_1, which matches the prior knowledge of G_1: (1) G_1 must have a nonnegative value; (2) G_1 is unlikely to be exactly zero and also unlikely to have very large values, since the gain pattern is related to human size.

The Bayesian CRB is also called the Van Trees bound or the MSE bound [17], it is given by:

$$\text{var}(\boldsymbol{\theta}) \geq (I_D + I_P)^{-1} \tag{13}$$

where $\theta = [z_t^T, G_I, G_Q]^T$, I_D represents the Fisher information matrix, and I_P represents the prior information matrix [17]. Note that the prior information only contains information of the gain pattern, no prior information about the badge position is included. The detailed derivation of the Bayesian CRB is presented in Ref. [3], we compare it with the CRB derived with an isotropic gain pattern assumption next.

4.2. Comparison with CRB

For an estimator with deterministic parameters, a CRB is often used. With an isotropic gain pattern assumption, a CRB for position estimation using RSS is derived in Ref. [8]. When the gain pattern term in the RSS-distance model approaches zero, that is, $g(\alpha_i) = 0$, the Bayesian CRB should be the same as the CRB derived in Ref. [8]. We show this next.

With the additional parameters in the gain pattern model, the Bayesian CRB not only depends on radio channel parameters, but also depends on gain pattern parameter σ_G^2. Once

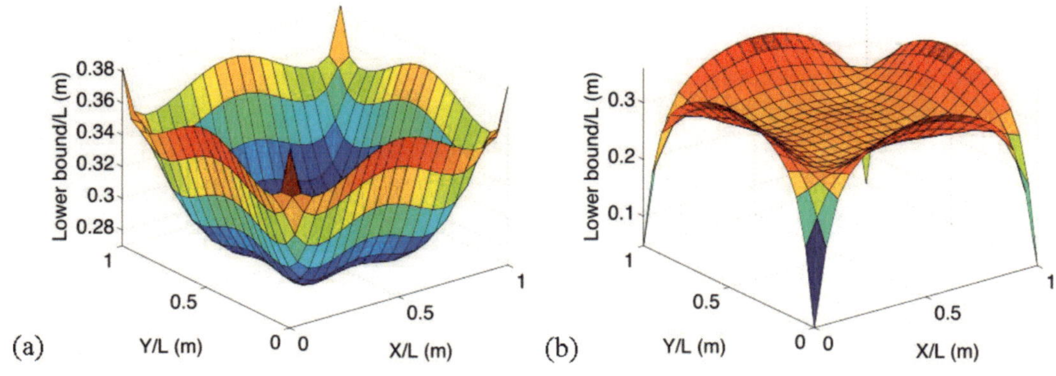

Figure 4. Lower bounds. (a) Lower bound with $\sigma_G^2 = 0.0001$ (minimum value: 0.27, maximum value: 0.38). (b) Lower bound with $\sigma_G^2 = 1$ (minimum value: 0.05, maximum value: 0.36).

these model parameters are calculated, the Bayesian CRB can be calculated for an L m by L m square area with four anchor nodes located at four corners. If we use the same radio channel parameters as [8] and two different σ_G^2 values: $\sigma_G^2 = 0.0001$ and $\sigma_G^2 = 1$, the two Bayesian CRBs are shown in **Figure 4**. For very small σ_G^2, *e.g.*, $\sigma_G^2 = 0.0001$, the Bayesian CRB is shown in **Figure 4(a)**, which is identical to the CRB derived in Ref. [8]. For $\sigma_G^2 = 1$, the Bayesian CRB is shown in **Figure 4(b)**. To obtain a lower bound for the overall area, we introduce the *average RMSE bound*, which is defined as the average value of the square root of the Bayesian CRB bounds over the area. The average RMSE bound for $\sigma_G^2 = 1$ is 0.29 m, which is lower than the 0.30 m average RMSE bound with a gain pattern close to isotropic, *e.g.*, $\sigma_G^2 = 0.0001$.

5. Experiments and results

5.1. Experiment description

We present experimental datasets from three experiment campaigns in this book chapter. These experiments were performed at outdoor, indoor and through-wall scenarios, which cover a variety of multipath effects and environmental noise conditions.

- *Experiment 1*: The first experiment was performed in a 6.4 m by 6.4 m area outside the Merrill Engineering Building of the University of Utah. The area is surrounded by 28 TelosB nodes [13] deployed at known locations on stands at 1 m height, near trees and 3 m away from the building wall. A person worn a TelosB node in the middle of his chest and walked around a marked path at a constant speed of about 0.5 m/s. This outdoor experiment dataset was first reported in Ref. [3], and details can be found there.
- *Experiment 2*: The second experiment was an indoor experiment performed inside the Warnock Engineering Building of the University of Utah. A 6.1 m by 6.1 m area was surrounded by 20 TelosB nodes with an interdistance of 0.91 m between each two anchor nodes. A person wearing a TelosB node walked clockwise twice around a 2.7 m by 2.7 m square, as shown as the purple line in **Figure 9**. The experiment was performed in the building lounge area, during which students occasionally walked outside the peripheral area of the sensor network. This experiment is first reported in this book chapter.
- *Experiment 3*: The third experiment was a through-wall experiment, in which 34 TelosB nodes were deployed outside the living room of a residential house, as shown in **Figure 5 (b)**. A person wearing a transmitter walked four times around a 3.6 m by 3.6 m square in the living room. The experiment was performed in a dynamic environment, where wind caused tree branches and leaves to sway. This experiment dataset is first reported in Ref. [19].

5.2. Experiment test bed and procedure

All three experiments use the same radio hardware, network protocol and follow the same procedure. TelosB nodes were used as network anchor nodes and also mobile node. In all

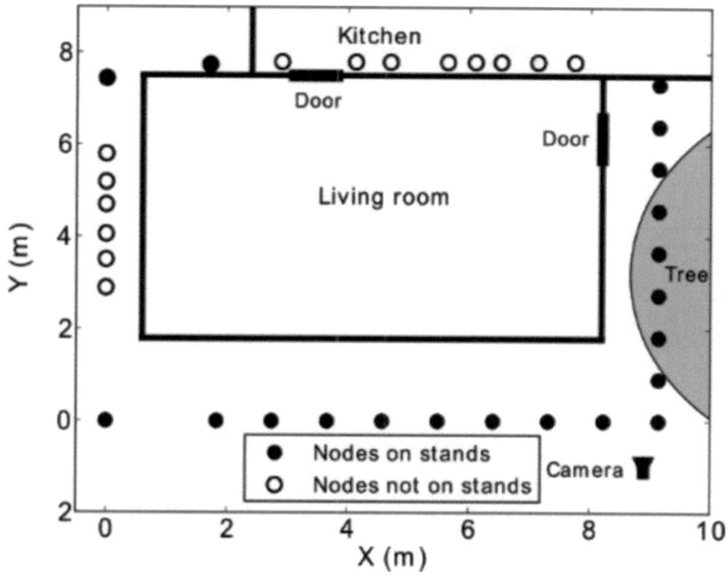

Figure 5. Experiment layout of Experiment 3 (through-wall).

experiments, anchor nodes were deployed at fixed locations, and one mobile node (transmitter badge) was worn by a person in the middle of their chest. All TelosB nodes were programmed with TinyOS program Spin [21] SPAN Lab. Spin protocol, and a base station connected to a laptop was used to collect RSS measurements received by all the anchor nodes.

Before people started walking in the area, a calibration was performed with no people in the experimental area. Since the locations of the anchor nodes are known, we use the measured RSS and the link length to estimate the n_p and P_0 parameters of the log-distance model. During the experiment, a person wearing the radio transmitter on their chest walked around a marked path a few times. A metronome and a metered path were used to keep the walking speed constant so that the position of the person at any particular time was known. The actual positions and orientations of the badge during these experiments are both known, so we can compare them with the position and orientation estimates from the AGAPE algorithm.

5.3. Experimental results

A unique feature of modeling RFID antenna gain pattern is that it enables estimating the orientation of the person, in addition to the person's location. We show the orientation estimation results from the AGAPE algorithm using data from Experiment 1, which was first reported in Ref. [3]. The estimated orientations are shown in **Figure 6**, together with the actual walking directions. The orientation estimates generally agree well with the actual orientations. As mentioned in Ref. [3], "the deviations from the actual orientations are generally less than 30°. However, sometimes when the person is turning, the bias is larger than 30°. This may be due to the fact that the algorithm uses RSS measurements from 28 anchor nodes to estimate the person's orientations, and at the turning points, RSS measurements may be a mix of those

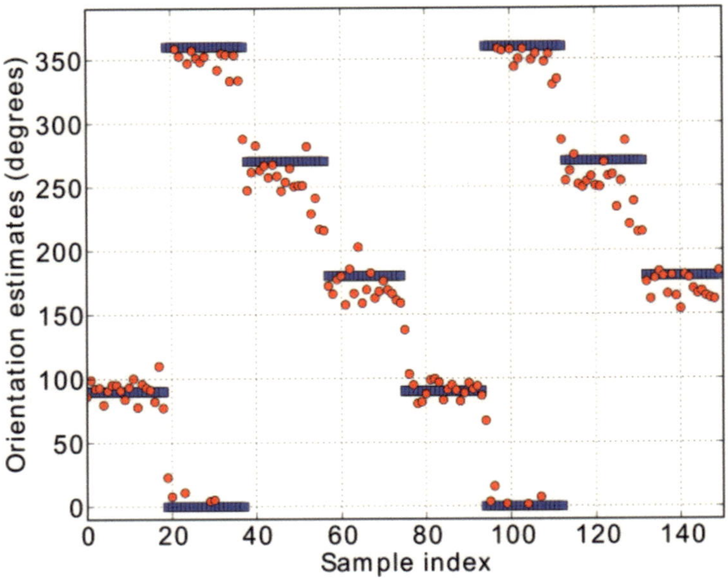

Figure 6. Mobile's actual orientations (■) and orientation estimates (O) (time for each sample is about 0.4 s).

recorded before, after and during turning." The median error from the AGAPE algorithm is about 10°, and more than 90% errors are below 30°. The 4D MLE algorithm can also estimate orientation, but it takes much more computing time. As mentioned in Ref. [3], the 4D MLE implementation uses "10 times more than the AGAPE algorithm in the Python implementation, and the estimates are not more accurate than those from AGAPE." In addition to the orientation of the badge, another model parameter G_1 is also estimated. For Experiment 1, G_1 has an averaged value of 12, which suggests that "the directionality of the gain of the transmitter badge worn by this particular person in this particular environment is about 12 dB."This value is consistent with our experiments in the antenna gain pattern modeling discussed in Section 2.

For the performance of position estimation, the CDF of the position estimation error from Experiment 1 is shown in **Figure 7**. We see that the median estimation error is about 0.61 m, and the 90th percentile estimation error is 1.22 m. However, the 2D MLE method has a median error of 2.60 m, which is about 4.3 times larger than that from AGAPE. From the comparison of the CDFs, we see that significant improvement is made if we include the orientation estimate in the localization.

In Experiment 1, a wireless sensor network with 28 anchor nodes is used to locate a badge in a 6.4 m by 6.4 m square area. However, not so many anchor nodes may be available in some applications. The following tests are performed using RSS measurements from a fraction of all anchor nodes to investigate the effect of node number on the localization accuracy.

As mentioned in Ref. [3], "in the first test—Test 1, we use RSS measurements from different numbers of equally spaced anchor nodes to locate the badge. For example, we first choose the RSS measurements from four anchor nodes at each corner of the square area. As expected, the

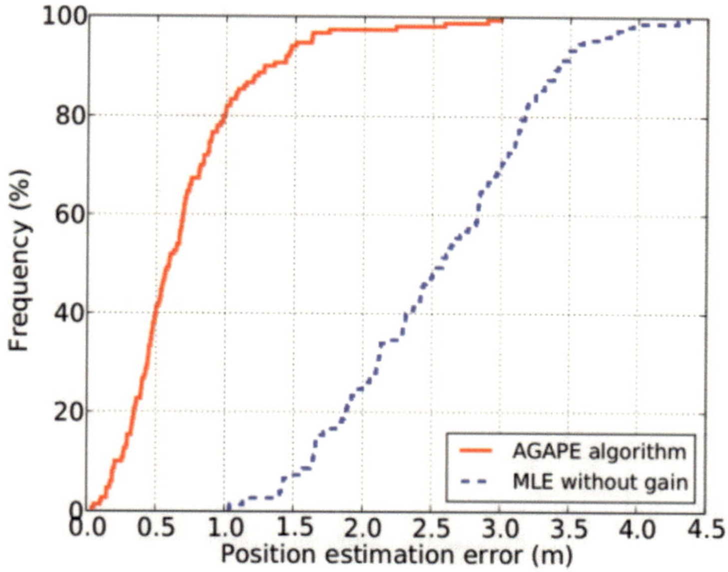

Figure 7. CDFs of position estimation errors from AGAPE and 2D MLE.

localization is not very accurate, the RMSE of the position estimate is 3.36 m, and the RMSE of the orientation estimate is 40°. Next, we use the RSS measurements from those anchor nodes whose ID numbers are multiples of 1, 2, 3 and 4 (since the anchor nodes are placed in a numerically increasing order around the experimental area, these anchor nodes are equally spaced). The RMSEs of the position and orientation estimates are shown as dots in **Figure 8(a)** and **(b)**, respectively. We see that as the node number increases, the RMSEs of position and orientation estimates both decrease. When the node number increases to fourteen, the RMSE of the position estimate decreases to 1.30 m, and the RMSE of the orientation estimate decreases to 18°. Further increase in anchor nodes will continue to decrease the RMSEs, however, there are diminishing returns."

(a)
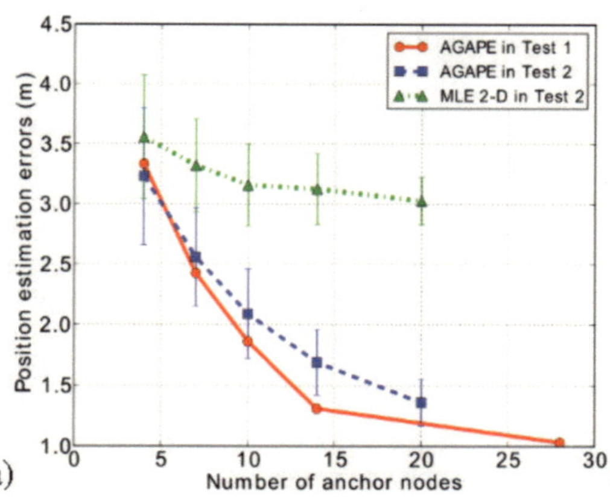

(b)
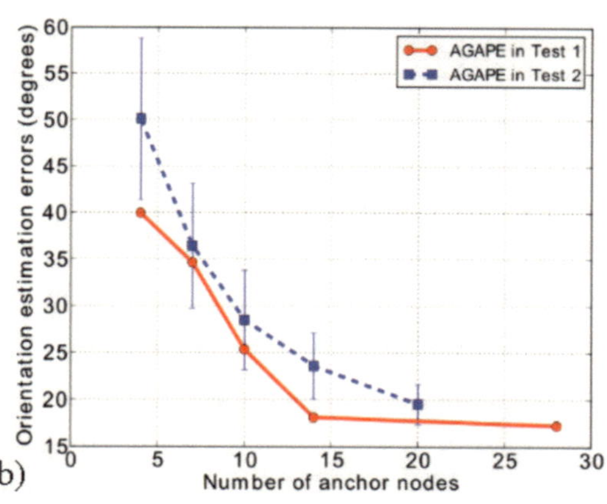

Figure 8. Effect of node number on (a) position estimation error and (b) orientation estimation error. (Test 1 uses equally spaced anchor nodes and Test 2 uses randomly chosen anchor nodes).

"In practical scenarios, anchor nodes may not be equally spaced. Thus, in Test 2, we use RSS measurements from randomly chosen anchor nodes. For example, we randomly choose four anchor nodes and run AGAPE using the RSS measurements from these nodes. We repeat the above procedure 100 times, and each time calculate the RMSEs of the position and orientation estimates. Similarly, we randomly choose seven, ten, fourteen and twenty anchor nodes. The average RMSEs are shown as squares, and the RMSE standard deviations are shown as error bars in **Figure 8**. From **Figure 8(b)**, we see that the average orientation RMSEs in Test 2 are all larger than the RMSEs in Test 1. For position RMSEs shown in **Figure 8(a)**, the average RMSEs in Test 2 are generally larger than the RMSEs in Test 1, except for the extreme case when the number of anchor nodes is four. Thus, the AGAPE algorithm generally performs better if the anchor nodes are equally spaced. However, the AGAPE algorithm is not very sensitive to the effect of anchor nodes being non-equally spaced. In fact, the differences between the position RMSEs in Test 1 and the average position RMSEs in Test 2 are always less than 0.4 m. Finally, we compare the performance of the naive MLE 2D method with the AGAPE algorithm using randomly chosen nodes. As shown in **Figure 8(a)**, the MLE 2D method is not very sensitive to the number of anchor nodes. However, the average position RMSEs from the MLE 2D method are always larger than those from the AGAPE algorithm for different numbers of anchor nodes."

For Experiment 1, we see that the AGAPE algorithm can estimate both the orientation and location of a person wearing an RFID badge with good accuracy for an outdoor environment. However, its performance degrades at the indoor and through-wall experiments, i.e., in Experiments 2 and 3. The position estimates from AGAPE and 2D MLE at a particular time in Experiment 2 are shown in **Figure 9**, together with the likelihood function of MLE. We see the MLE location estimate is biased towards the walking direction of the person, as it does not include the human body effect on the transmitter gain pattern in its model. We also see that the AGAPE algorithm is able to estimate both position and orientation of the person, and the position estimate is closer to the actual location than the 2D MLE estimate. However, AGAPE is not as accurate as in the outdoor experiments, because the modeling error in the first-order gain pattern model increases at an indoor environment due to multipath effects.

For the through-wall experiment Experiment 3, we see that due to the attenuation of walls, the path-loss model parameter $n_p = 3.22$, which is much larger than those from the first two experiments. The AGAPE algorithm can still estimate both the position and orientation of the person with reasonable accuracy, but there are several position estimate errors that are larger than 4 m (not shown in the figure). This is due to the ambiguity problem of AGAPE since AGAPE has orientation β and gain pattern parameter G_1 to estimate, in addition to position estimate. That is, AGAPE can converge to an incorrect position with an incorrect estimate of orientation due to the noisy RSS measurements and the modeling error.

We compare the root mean squared error (RMSE) of the position estimates for the above three sets of experiments. The RMSEs from the AGAPE, 2D MLE and 4D MLE algorithms are listed in **Table 1**. We see that for Experiment 1, the RMSE from the AGAPE algorithm is 0.87 m, which is similar to the 4D MLE algorithm. However, the MLE 4D algorithm uses grid search method and is not a real-time algorithm due to its computational complexity. The RMSE from

http://dx.doi.org/10.5772/65069

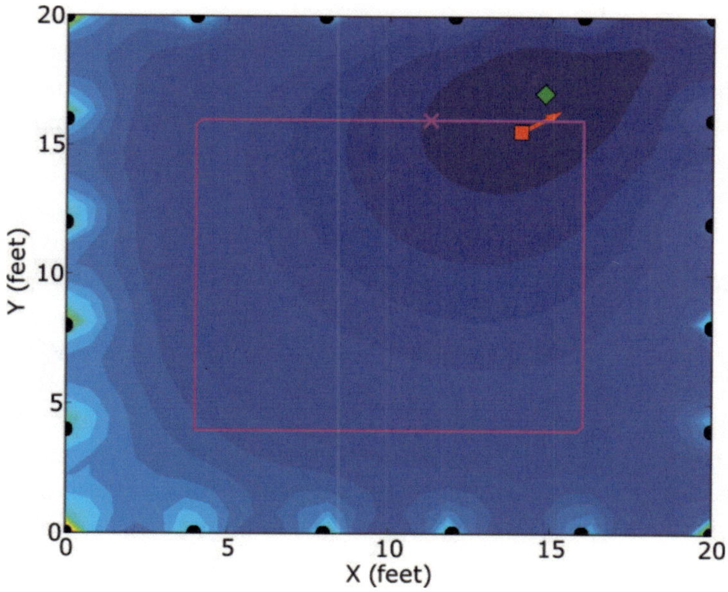

Figure 9. MLE likelihood and position estimates from 2D MLE and AGAPE algorithms in Experiment 2. Marked walking path (purple line); actual person position (×); 2D MLE position estimate (◊); AGAPE position estimate (▪) and AGAPE orientation estimate (→).

Experiment	Model parameters		RMSE from MLE (2D) in meter	RMSE from MLE (4D) in meter	RMSE from AGAPE in meter
	n_p	P_0			
Experiment 1	1.67	48.6	2.64	0.98	1.03
Experiment 2	2.28	19.8	1.86	1.65	1.69
Experiment 3	3.22	30.5	2.10	2.02	2.05

Table 1. Experimental localization results: RMSEs from MLE (2D), MLE (4D) and AGAPE.

the 2D MLE algorithm is 2.64 m. So for Experiment 1, the RMSE from AGAPE is reduced by 67.2% compared to the 2D MLE algorithm. For Experiment 2, the 2D MLE has an RMSE of 1.86 m, while the RMSEs from 4D MLE and the AGAPE are 1.65 and 1.69 m, with 11% and 9% improvement, respectively. Finally, for Experiment 3, AGAPE does not have much improvement compared to MLE. Both MLE and AGAPE have RMSEs of about 2 m.

From the above comparison, we see that the 4D MLE and AGAPE algorithms are significantly more accurate than the 2D MLE algorithm for outdoor environments. The 4D MLE takes much more time than the AGAPE algorithm, but both algorithms can estimate the position and orientation of a person wearing an RFID badge in front of her chest. The benefit from the modeled directional gain pattern reduces at indoor and through-wall environments, since the first-order gain pattern model becomes much noisier due to the increased multipath effects.

The AGAPE and 4D MLE algorithms may suffer from the ambiguity problem, that is, they may converge to a wrong position with a wrong orientation estimate. This ambiguity problem is observed when a person wearing an RFID badge presents in close proximity to walls. This problem may be resolved using orientation estimates from inertial measurement unit (IMU). However, RF device-free localization [19, 20] may provide a simple way to solve the ambiguity issue without adding more sensing modalities.

6. Conclusion

In this book chapter, we present measurements and models of active RFID antenna gain pattern due to the human body effect. We find that a wireless sensor network-based RFID localization system can actually benefit from the non-isotropic gain pattern due to the attenuation and reflection of the human body. We present three estimation methods of RFID localization using received signal strength (RSS) measurements from a wireless sensor network: 2D maximum likelihood estimator (MLE), 4D maximum likelihood estimator (MLE) and alternating gain and position estimator (AGAPE). The 4D MLE and AGAPE algorithms can both estimate user orientation in addition to position, with the first-order gain pattern model and the assumption that the user is wearing the RFID badge in front of her chest. However, the AGAPE algorithm significantly outperforms the 4D MLE algorithm in computational time using discrete Fourier transform (DFT) and first-order approximation. We also derive theoretical estimation lower bound for joint orientation and position estimation problem. The Bayesian Cramer-Rao bound (CRB) shows that the lower bound on the variance of a position estimator decreases with the inclusion of a gain pattern model to the RSS log-distance model. Finally, we present three sets of experiments performed at outdoor, indoor and through-wall environments. The experimental results show that the 4D MLE and AGAPE algorithms outperform the 2D MLE algorithm in localization accuracy in all datasets.

Author details

Yang Zhao[1*] and Neal Patwari[2]

*Address all correspondence to: yang.zhao@ge.com

1 General Electric Global Research Center, Niskayuna, NY, USA

2 Department of Electrical and Computer Engineering, University of Utah, Salt Lake City, UT, USA

References

[1] GE Healthcare. AgileTrac [Internet]. 2012. Available from: http://www3.gehealthcare.com.au/en-au/solutions/hom/agiletrac

[2] G. Mao, B. Fidan, and B.D.O. Anderson. Wireless sensor network localization techniques. Computer Networks. 2007;**51**:2529-2553

[3] Y. Zhao, N. Patwari, P. Agrawal, and M. Rabbat. Directed by directionality: benefiting from the gain pattern of active RFID badges. IEEE Transactions on Mobile Computing. 2012;**11**:865-877

[4] P. Bahl, and V.N. Padmanabhan. RADAR: an in-building RF-based user location and tracking system. In: IEEE Infocom; 2000. p. 775-784

[5] A.M. Ladd, K. Bekris, G. Marceau, A. Rudys, L. Kavraki, and D. Wallach. Robotics-based location sensing using wireless ethernet. In: Conference on Mobile Computing and Networking (MobiCom); 2002. p. 227-238

[6] A. Howard, S. Siddiqi, and G. Sukhatme. An experimental study of localization using wireless ethernet. In: The International Conference on Field and Service Robotics; 2003. p. 201-206

[7] K. Kaemarungsi, and P. Krishnamurthy. Properties of indoor received signal strength for WLAN location fingerprinting. In: The 1st Annual International Conference on Mobile and Ubiquitous Systems: Networking and Services (MobiQuitous); 2004. p. 14-23

[8] N. Patwari, A.O. Hero III, M. Perkins, N. Correal, and R.J. O'Dea. Relative location estimation in wireless sensor networks. IEEE Transactions on Signal Processing. 2003;**51**: 2137-2148

[9] T. Roos, P. Myllymki, H. Tirri, P. Misikangas, and J. Sievnen. A probabilistic approach to WLAN user location estimation. International Journal of Wireless Information Networks. 2002;**9**:155-164

[10] T.S. Rappaport. Wireless communications: principles and practice. NJ: Prentice-Hall Inc.; 1996

[11] M. Jensen, and Y. Rahmat-Samii. EM interaction of handset antennas and a human in personal communications. Proceedings of the IEEE. 1995;**83**:7-17

[12] J. Griffin and G. Durgin. Complete link budgets for backscatter radio and RFID systems. IEEE Antennas and Propagation Magazine. 2009;**51**:11-25

[13] Wiki. TelosB [Internet]. 2010. Available from: http://tinyos.stanford.edu/tinyos-wiki/index.php/TelosB

[14] T. King, S. Kopf, T. Haenselmann, C. Lubberger, and W. Effelsberg. COMPASS: A probabilistic indoor positioning system based on 802.11 and digital compasses. In: Proceedings of the 1st International Workshop on Wireless Network Testbeds, Experimental Evaluation and Characterization; 2006. p. 34-40

[15] N. Lomb. Least-squares frequency analysis of unequally spaced data. Astrophysics and space science. 1976;447-462

[16] A. Gunawardana and W. Byrne. Convergence theorems for generalized alternating minimization procedures. Journal of Machine Learning Research. 2005;**6**:2049-2073

[17] H.L. Van Trees. Detection, Estimation, and Modulation Theory, Part I. John Wiley & Sons; New York, Chichester; 1968

[18] S. Miller, and D. Childers. Probability and random processes: with applications to signal processing and communications. Academic Press; 2004

[19] Y. Zhao, and N. Patwari. Robust estimators for variance-based device-free localization and tracking. IEEE Transactions on Mobile Computing. 2015;**14**:2116-2129

[20] J. Wilson, and N. Patwari. Radio tomographic imaging with wireless networks. IEEE Transactions on Mobile Computing. 2010;**9**:621-632

[21] SPAN Lab. Spin protocol [Internet]. Available from: http://span.ece.utah.edu/spin

Chapter 4

A Methodology for Evaluating Security in Commercial RFID Systems

Tiago M. Fernández-Caramés, Paula Fraga-Lamas,
Manuel Suárez-Albela and Luis Castedo

Additional information is available at the end of the chapter

http://dx.doi.org/10.5772/64844

Abstract

Although RFID has become a widespread technology, the developers of numerous commercial systems have not taken care of security properly. This chapter presents a methodology for detecting common security flaws. The methodology is put in practice using an open-source RFID platform (Proxmark 3), and it is tested in different fields, such as public transportation or animal identification. The results obtained show that the consistent application of the methodology allows researchers to perform security audits easily and detect, mitigate, or avoid risks and possible attacks.

Keywords: RFID, security, pen testing, LF, HF, ISO/IEC 14443, ISO/IEC 7816, ISO/IEC 11784, ISO/IEC 11785

1. Introduction

In the last years, RFID has been applied throughout industry and services, thanks to its ease of use and its multiple practical applications, including animal identification, access control, passport verification, transportation and payment cards, car access control, supply chain traceability, logistics, or toll payments. However, despite becoming an everyday technology, many public and private entities have not considered the security of RFID systems as a basic requirement. In fact, it is easy to find many commercial systems that contain critical security flaws and vulnerabilities [1, 2] that allow for cloning tags or for straight signal replaying. Such vulnerabilities let attackers access certain services or facilities, get or alter personal information, and even track people.

Fortunately, secure mechanisms can be applied to prevent the attacks aforementioned, including the use of cryptography, the automatic detection of rogue devices [3], the enhancement of the resistance to cloning [4], the secure storage of critical data in remote databases or the use of secure physical modulations and medium access control (MAC) protocols. Nonetheless, it is common to find commercial RFID systems that have such security features disabled or detect already-broken RFID security systems still in use.

Taking the considerations previously mentioned into account, this chapter describes a methodology that allows researchers to evaluate the most common security flaws and details the necessary tools for applying such a methodology.

The rest of this chapter is organized as follows. Section 2 first reviews the most common security threats that can be used against RFID systems and then describes some of the latest RFID hardware/software security tools available. Section 3 exposes the methodology proposed for analyzing RFID security. In Section 4, the methodology is tested in different commercial systems. Finally, Section 5 is devoted to conclusions.

2. Security in RFID

2.1. Basics on attacks against RFID systems

Information security has been classically governed by what is known as the CIA Triad: confidentiality, integrity, and availability. Confidentiality is related to the importance of protecting the most sensitive information from unauthorized access. Integrity consists in protecting data from modification or deletion by unauthorized parties, and ensuring that when authorized people make changes, they can be undone if some damage occurs. Finally, availability is the possibility of accessing the data when needed. If any of these three principles is not met, then security can be said that it has been broken.

Like other technologies, RFID is exposed to security threats and, specifically, to attacks on the confidentiality, integrity, and availability of the data stored on the tags or on the information exchanged between a reader and a tag.

The term risk refers to the probability of occurrence of an event that causes damage to an informational asset. Two kinds of risks can be basically distinguished:

- Security risks. They are derived from actions able to damage, block, or take advantage from a service in a malicious way. The action is usually carried out with the objective of obtaining a profit or just for damaging the access to certain service. The most common services provided by RFID systems are access control to facilities and payments.
- Privacy risks. These risks affect the confidential information of the users. RFID tags can store data of the payments they performed or the transportation route followed by the user/owner.

In real life, most risks are a mixture of both security and privacy risks: they threaten RFID security in order to get access to the information stored or to the data related to a transaction.

A classification of RFID attacks can be seen in [5]. The following are the most common attacks associated with security risks:

- Tag isolation. It is technically the simplest attack and probably the most common. It consists in blocking the tag communications to avoid sending data to the reader. It is usually carried out by means of a Faraday cage or by jamming RF signals.
- Tag cloning. The unique identifier (UID) and/or the content of the RFID is extracted and inserted into another tag [6]. Cloning is commonly used for accessing restricted areas or for decreasing the price of certain goods in supermarkets.
- Denial of Service (DoS) attacks. The reader is flooded with such a large amount of information that it cannot deal with the signals sent by real tags [7]. Other techniques are based on emitting radio noise at the operating frequency of the RFID system.
- Command injection. Some readers are vulnerable to remote code execution just by reading the content of a tag [8].
- Signal replaying. It consists in recording the RFID signal in certain time instants with the objective of replaying it later.
- Remote tag destruction. There exist RFID zappers that are able to send energy remotely that once rectified, is so high that certain components of the tag might be burned. Researchers have also found that it is possible to misuse the kill password in some tags (Electronic Product Code(EPC) Class-1 Gen-2) with a passive eavesdropper and then disable the tags [9].
- SQL injection. Like in the case of command injection, it has been found that some reader middleware is susceptible to the injection of random SQL commands [8].
- Virus/Malware injection. Although difficult to perform in the vast majority of RFID tags due to their low storage capacity, it is possible in certain tags to insert malicious code that is able to be transmitted to other tags [8].
- Man-in-the-Middle (MitM) attacks. They consist in placing an active device between a tag and the reader in order to intercept and alter the communications between both elements [10, 11].
- Relay/Amplification attacks. They consist in amplifying the RFID signal using a relay; thus, the range of the RFID tag is extended beyond its intended use [12].
- RFID skimming. They consist in the use of portable point of sales terminals to make unauthorized and fraudulent charges on payment cards.

Attacks associated with privacy risks include the following:

- Unauthorized access to personal data. Many systems store private data on the tag or transmit them when a tag and reader exchange information.
- Personal tracking. This is probably the most feared, since an attacker might determine routes, purchases, and habits of a specific person. The information may be even used for marketing purposes.

2.2. Hardware tools for auditing RFID security

In recent years, a number of projects have been developed with the aim of facilitating researchers' low-level access to RFID communications. Some of them are just software tools that can be used with commercial RFID readers (RFIDiot [13]), while others involve specific hardware (Proxmark 3 [14], Tastic [15], OpenPCD [16], OpenPICC [17], Chameleon Mini [18]), or certain firmware (Proxbrute for Proxmark 3 [19]). Hardware developments are specially interesting: some devices can emulate readers (Tastic, OpenPCD); others can emulate just tags (OpenPICC); and a few can emulate both kinds of devices (Proxmark 3, Chameleon Mini).

There are not many academic platforms developed to test RFID security. An example can be found in [20], where a microcontroller and Field-Programmable Gate-Array(FPGA)-based tag platform is presented with the aim of evaluating high-frequency (HF) and ultra-high-frequency (UHF) RFID tags. The latest development as of writing is the Chameleon Mini, which has been promoted by the Ruhr University (Bochum, Germany): it is a versatile RFID tag emulator compliant with ISO/IEC 14443 and ISO/IEC 15693 (for instance, it currently supports MIFARE Classic 1K/4K/Ultralight emulation).

The platform selected in this chapter to analyze RFID security was Proxmark 3, which is an open-source system able to transmit at LF (125–134 KHz) and HF (13.56 MHz). The system contains an Atmel AT91SAM7S256 (256 KB of flash and 64 KB of RAM), an FPGA (Xilinx Spartan-II), and an 8-bit analog-to-digital converter (ADC). It is powered through an USB and has a SV2 connector for the antenna, which contains four pins: two are for the HF antenna, and the other two are for the LF antenna. All these components can be observed in **Figure 1.** Among Proxmark features, it is relevant its ability to sniff the communications between a reader and different tags, and the possibility of emulating a reader or a specific tag.

When the Proxmark acts as an RFID receiver, the signal that comes from the antenna goes through the ADC and is converted from analog to digital. Then, the digital data are sent through an 8-bit bus to the FPGA, where it is demodulated. Finally, the signal is sent from the FPGA to the microcontroller through the Serial Peripheral Interface(SPI) to deal with the RFID protocol. When the Proxmark acts as a transmitter, the same steps are performed but in reverse

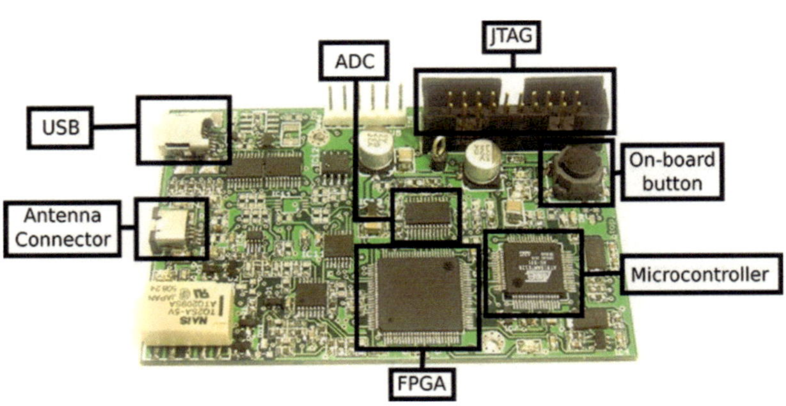

Figure 1. Main components of Proxmark 3.

order. The FPGA modulators/demodulators are developed in Verilog, while the Atmel microcontroller is programmed in C.

3. A methodology for evaluating RFID security

3.1. Methodology proposed

In order to automate the evaluation of security in commercial RFID systems, a methodology has been devised. A reduced flow diagram is depicted in **Figure 2**. It consists of the following main steps:

1. Visual inspection of the tag. Many tags include the name of manufacturer, the model and, sometimes, the RFID standard. With such data, it is usually easy to get more specific information on the way the tags behave and how to perform security tests.

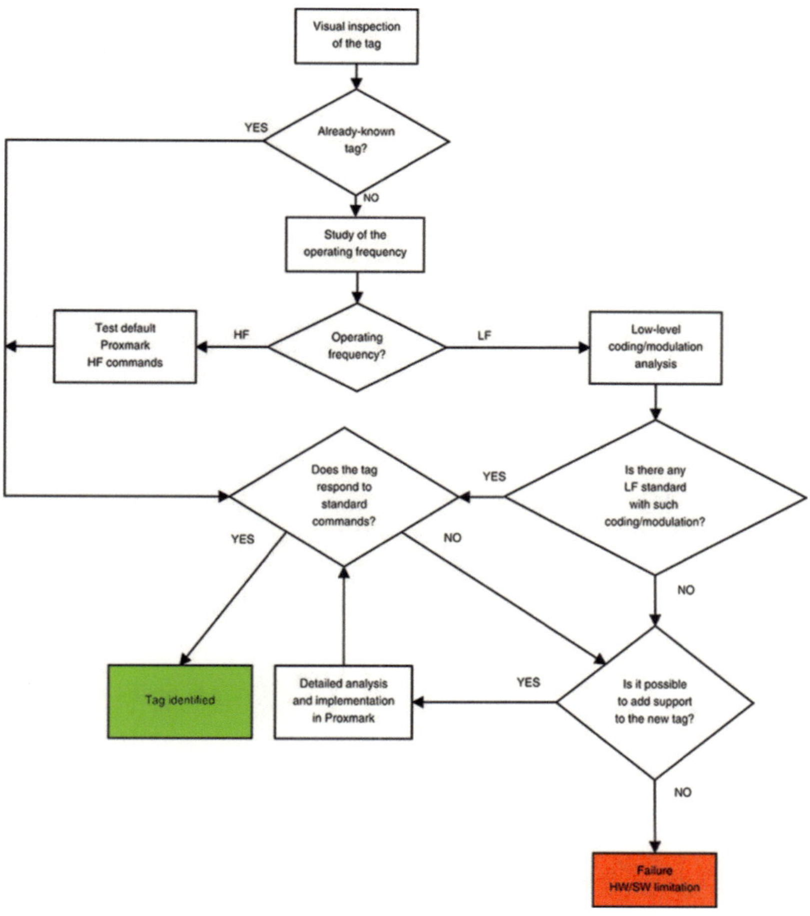

Figure 2. Flow diagram of the methodology.

2. Radio frequency detection. If there are no external signs on the tag, it is first recommended to determine the tag's frequency. In such a case, LF, HF, UHF, and super-high frequency (SHF) tags can be found. There are software and hardware mechanisms to determine which is the operating frequency, like using a spectrum analyzer, or disassembling the tag or the reader to observe the hardware components of the radio interface.

3. Modulation and coding detection.

4. Standard identification. Once obtained the three previous parameters (frequency, modulation, and coding), it is straightforward to determine whether there exists an RFID standard compliant with such configuration. If it is not the case, the research could become tricky, since it might involve a proprietary protocol. However, when working with LF, HF, and UHF tags, standards are usually followed.

5. Sniff and emulate communications to perform security tests.

3.2. Applying the methodology with the Proxmark 3

The methodology presented in this chapter can be easily applied to any unknown HF and LF RFID tags. In the next subsections, the analysis is divided into LF and HF tags, since the way they work varies noticeably. As it will be detailed, it is possible to work at a physical level with LF tags, but that is not easy in the case of HF devices.

3.2.1. Detecting the operating frequency

The first step of the methodology consists in obtaining the operation frequency. For such a purpose, one of the antennas (LF or HF) has to be placed far from any tag and the Proxmark command *hw tune* has to be executed. The command gives us the received voltage in the different supported frequencies. Then, the operation has to be performed next to the unknown tag: if one of the voltages has decreased remarkably for a specific frequency, it means that such a frequency is the operating frequency.

Figures 3 and **4** show an example of the process for an LF tag. First, the voltages are checked with the HF antenna connected (note in **Figure 3** that the LF antenna is said to be unusable), and it can be observed that they almost do not change between tests (i.e., just around 1 V). When the same procedure is carried out with the LF antenna (**Figure 4**), the voltages associated with LF frequencies drop substantially (especially of 134 KHz), and therefore, it is concluded that the tag is indeed LF.

3.2.2. Analyzing LF tags

When determining whether a tag follows an LF standard, the first step consists in figuring out the data modulation and coding. For such a purpose, the following sequence of Proxmark commands has to be executed:

- *LF read* [*h*]: the tag is powered with the selected frequency (125 KHz by default, or 134 KHz using the parameter *h*). The command also records the signal transmitted by the tag.

- *Data sample x*: it downloads *x* of the previously recorded samples to the PC.
- *Data plot*: it allows the user to open a new window to plot the signal. It is useful for evaluating the signal visually.
- Different instructions can be used to modify, amplify, decimate, or normalize signal values to ease signal identification.
- If the signal is clean enough, and its modulation has been recognized, the user can try to demodulate it. For instance, if the signal is modulated in amplitude-shift keying (ASK), the command *data askdemod* can be executed. In the case of frequency-shift keying (FSK) modulated signals, *fskdemod* is the right command.

```
proxmark3> hw tune
#db# Measuring complete, sending report back to host

# LF antenna: 0.00 V @   125.00 kHz
# LF antenna: 0.00 V @   134.00 kHz
# LF optimal: 0.00 V @ 12000.00 kHz
# HF antenna: 9.70 V @     13.56 MHz
# Your LF antenna is unusable.

proxmark3> hw tune
#db# Measuring antenna characteristics, please wait..
#db# Measuring complete, sending report back to host
# LF antenna: 0.00 V @   125.00 kHz
# LF antenna: 0.00 V @   134.00 kHz
# LF optimal: 0.00 V @ 12000.00 kHz
# HF antenna: 8.67 V @     13.56 MHz
# Your LF antenna is unusable.
```

Figure 3. HF voltages for an LF tag when is present (second command) or not in the field.

```
proxmark3> hw tune
#db# Measuring antenna characteristics, please wait..
#db# Measuring complete, sending report back to host

# LF antenna: 12.89 V @   125.00 kHz
# LF antenna: 23.36 V @   134.00 kHz
# LF optimal: 24.98 V @   131.87 kHz
# HF antenna:  0.64 V @    13.56 MHz
# Your HF antenna is unusable.

proxmark3> hw tune
#db# Measuring antenna characteristics, please wait..
#db# Measuring complete, sending report back to host

# LF antenna:  9.40 V @   125.00 kHz
# LF antenna: 13.16 V @   134.00 kHz
# LF optimal: 17.32 V @   139.53 kHz
# HF antenna:  0.68 V @    13.56 MHz
# Your HF antenna is unusable.
```

Figure 4. LF voltages when an LF tag is not in the field (first command) and when it is.

Figure 5 shows an example of the signal obtained after carrying out the first three steps previously mentioned. Such a signal can then be demodulated, as it seems to be modulated either in ASK or FSK.

In this case, when the command *askdemod* was executed, it returned an error indicating that it had not been detected an ASK-modulated signal, and in fact, taking a closer look at **Figure 5** it can be observed that the period of the pulses with less amplitude is different from the others. Therefore, it had to be FSK and *fskdemod* demodulated the signal (**Figure 6**).

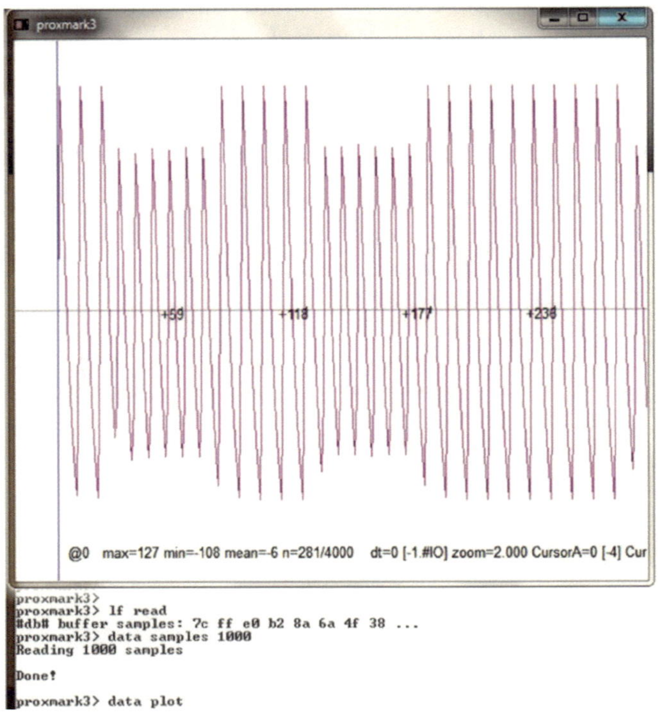

Figure 5. Example of an LF tag signal received.

```
proxmark3> data fskdemod
actual data bits start at sample 6180
length 50/50
bits: '01001010100000101011111111111111111111111111'
hex: 00000950 57ffffff

proxmark3> data fskdemod
actual data bits start at sample 1044
length 50/50
bits: '01001010100000101100110000000000010001001000 1'
hex: 00000950 5980---1
```

Figure 6. LF tag signal demodulated with *fskdemod*.

The next step consists in searching for a bit pattern, which might lead to determine the length of the identifier. Thus, the signal has to be observed during certain periods of time and look for similarities. In order to understand the transmitted data, it can be useful to find the standard that defines and structures them. For instance, in the previous example, the LF tag was an access control card manufactured by HID [21], whose well-known LF data structures can be extracted and then the UID obtained, as it is shown in **Figure 7**.

At this point, the HID tag can be emulated with the Proxmark using the command *lf hid sim*; and it can even be cloned with a rewritable tag like Atmel T5557.

3.2.3. Analyzing HF tags

HF tags behave in a slightly different way than the LF ones: their signal is so fast that it cannot be processed so easily at plain sight. Moreover, in general, HF tags are smarter than LF tags, and they not only transmit an identifier repeatedly but also perform more complex communications with the reader. There exist many HF transmission modes and protocols. Furthermore, HF tags and readers can vary their modulation during the same transmission. For example, a tag can send FSK-modulated data, while the reader responds in ASK.

The steps required to analyze HF tags are not as clear as in LF, so the study becomes more like a trial-and-error process. For instance, the case of a public transportation card whose data were decoded after trying one by one all the possible combinations defined by the most popular standards until the right one was found is shown in **Figure 8**: first, it was tested ISO/IEC 14443-A, then ISO/IEC 15693 and, finally, ISO/IEC 14443-B.

```
proxmark3> lf hid fskdemod
#db# TAG ID: 95059800---1 (1096)
#db# TAG ID: 95059800---1 (1096)
```

Figure 7. Obtaining the tag UID of an access control LF tag manufactured by HID.

```
proxmark3> hf 14a reader
iso14443a card select failed

proxmark3> hf 15 reader
#db# 0 octects read from IDENTIFY request:
#db# 0 octects read from SELECT request:
#db# 0 octects read from XXX request:

proxmark3> hf 14b read
#db# 3 1 e
```

Figure 8. Determining the RFID standard of an HF tag.

```
proxmark3> data hexsamples
50 08 -- -- -- -- 4e 44
4b 33 -- -- -- -- 44 44
```

Figure 9. UID and control bytes from an ISO/IEC 14443-B compliant card.

The command for reading ISO/IEC 14443-B tags sends an Answer to Request Type B(ATQB) command (0x05, 0x00, 0x08, 0x39, 0x73) and records the tag's answer. The second value of the output can be either 0x00000000 or 0x00000001: if it is "1", it means the reply of the tag was received properly. If it is "0", it means that not all bytes (or none) were received.

In the specific case of the previous tag, the answer of the tag is "3 1 e," so the second value ("1") means that the tag is actually compliant with ISO/IEC 14443-B. The Proxmark is able to return the data after issuing the command *hexsamples*, which shows the UID and additional control bytes (in **Figure 9**).

4. Practical evaluation

In order to validate the methodology proposed, three different commercial RFID systems were analyzed and tested. The next subsections first introduce the tags audited and then give details on the analysis and the steps required testing their security.

4.1. M and T cards

In this section, what we have called "M" and "T" cards are analyzed. Please note that such aliases were given to avoid legal issues, since there are still several hundred thousand units of the cards still in use.

In the case of the M card, it has been used in the last years by the city council of a relevant city in Spain for paying different services such as public transportation, museum access, or sport events. It is said that the council has sold more than 200,000 units of the card.

Regarding the T card, it is an RFID card developed by a Spanish regional government that provides public transportation payment to a population of 2.7 million people. It was designed to be compatible with the M card; therefore, in the next subsection a joint analysis of both cards is performed.

4.1.1. Visual inspection

In plain sight, there are no signs or symbols that indicate the frequency band of the RFID cards. It can be assumed that by the reading range and the amount of information stored, they could be HF tags, but a deeper analysis should be performed to verify it accurately.

http://dx.doi.org/10.5772/64844

4.1.2. Operating frequency and modulation

- Radio frequency. Although both cards seem to be HF, the steps described in Section 3.2.1 have to be carried out to determine whether they are LF or HF. Such steps confirm that they are HF tags.
- Modulation. Once the radio frequency is obtained, it has to be decided which of the possible standards the tags follow, and then, the modulation can be determined. A first fast test consisting in sending commands for ISO/IECs 14443-A, 14443-B, and 15693 standards show that the tags only answer correctly to the ones issued following ISO/IEC 14443-B.

4.1.3. Understanding the underlying protocols

ISO/IEC 14443 [22] is a 13.56 MHz-based standard that defines proximity RFID systems that are usually related to payment cards. ISO/IEC 14443 consists of four parts: (1) physical characteristics, (2) RF power and signal interface, (3) initialization and anti-collision, and (4) transmission protocol. It also defines two kinds of tags (type A and type B), which differ in parts (2) and (3). **Table 1** shows the differences in terms of modulation and coding between both types [in such a table, the reader is called proximity coupling device (PCD), and the tag is the proximity integrated circuit card (PICC)].

4.1.4. Security analysis

4.1.4.1. Obtaining communication traces

The first step for the security analysis consisted in obtaining a good set of data samples of the communications carried out between each card and the reader. Note that data samples were taken during real trips in public transportation. Thus, a laptop with the Proxmark was carried in a backpack, while the RFID antenna cable was placed along the sleeve of a jacket until reaching the tester's hand, where the antenna captured the dialog between the card and the reader.

Once the radio signals were captured by the antenna, they were demodulated and decoded with the Proxmark. The main problem with this setup was electric noise: many samples were

	Type A	Type B
PCD to PICC	ASK 100%	ASK 10%
	Modified Miller, 106 kbps	NRZ, 106 kbps
PICC to PCD	Load modulation	Load modulation
	Subcarrier fc/16	Subcarrier fc/16
	OOK	BPSK
	Manchester, 106 kbps	NRZ-L, 106 kbps

Table 1. Modulation and coding used by ISO/IECs 14443-A and 14443-B.

lost because they became corrupted. In fact, none of the first 10 capturing attempts was successful, and it was necessary to perform numerous tests and try three different M/T cards to get a good data set. An example of captured data is shown in **Table 2**.

Timestamp	RSSI	Device	Payload	Additional information
0	142	TAG	50 08 10 2a 1d 53 4e 44 4b 33 81 93 bc 3f	
1398	112	TAG	00 78 f0	
854			05 00 00 71 ff	
11500			05 00 00 71 ff	
11478			06 00 97 5b	
46342			05 00 08 39 73	
1908			1d 08 10 2a 1d 00 08 01 00 94 60	
554	296	TAG	00 78 f0	
3566			02 80 26 4f 11 0a e7 de	
3146	116	TAG	02 00 14 98 70 10 01 01 76 55 72 90 00 73 65	
36188			03 80 32 00 00 18 ea 98	
1852			00 01 00 00 00 00 00 00	**Fail CRC**
480			00 90 00 1d fe	**Fail CRC**
3676			02 80 2e 01 00 20 43 2f	
2870	203	TAG	02 01 01 e0 f5 ff f5 ff 00 00 00 00 01 f4 07 06 a9 8c ff 00 11 03 e8 00 00 b9 0b ff 00 02 00 01 48 90 00 26 57	
48				(SHORT)
3798			03 80 30 00 00 1d 31 f6	
1580			03	(SHORT)
17462			02 80 28 00 00 04 75 39 34 0d 3a 07 d3	
5778				(SHORT)
34972			03 80 2a 01 00 24 00 15 00 4b 00 01 48 41 19 09 01 00 28 01 37 e5 8c 18 21 10 00 c2 01 01 09 23 00 10 01 00 00 4b d4 72 2b eb 04 ca 20	
14542	203	TAG	03 b3 56 ee 2c 90 00 e6 01	
197304			05 00 08 39 73	
804			33 81 93 bc 3f	**FAIL CRC**

Table 2. Example of a M/T trace.

4.1.4.2. Analysis of the traces collected

It is important to emphasize that the communications of the system analyzed were not encrypted. Furthermore, it is first necessary to understand ISO/IEC 14443-B to determine the meaning of the different messages. The following are the steps performed by a regular ISO/IEC 14443-B system:

1. The tag awaits for a Request Type B(REQB) command.

2. The reader sends the REQB.

3. If the application family identifier (AFI) of the REQB is the one expected, the tag answers with the ATQB and waits for an ATTRIB command.

4. The reader sends the ATTRIB command.

5. If the ATTRIB command is the one expected, the tag sends the ATA (also known as the ATATTRIB, answer-to-ATTRIB).

6. Finally, the tag commutes to the active state, where it is able to exchange data commands with the reader until it receives a DESELECT and commutes to a HALT state.

Regarding the messages transmitted when the tag is in the active state, they can be of three types: i-block, s-block, and r-block. The first one is used for transmitting and asking for data from the application layer. The other ones are for protocol operations or are related to data from lower layers. **Table 3** describes the structure of an i-block, which is the only block that appears in the traces of the communications of the M/T cards.

After analyzing a number of traces, it was concluded that the information contained in the i-block was compliant with ISO/IEC 7816 [23], which has been massively used in credit, debit, and other payment cards. Therefore, it is first necessary to describe briefly the structure of the ISO/IEC 7816 requests and answers.

The typical ISO/IEC 7816 application protocol data unit (APDU) follows the structure shown in **Table 4**.

	PCB	CID	NAD	Payload	CRC-B
Length	1 byte	1 byte (optional)	1 byte (optional)	N bytes	2 bytes
Meaning	Protocol control	Card ID number	Node address (for logic addresses)		Cyclic-redundancy check

Table 3. Structure of an i-block.

In **Table 4**, the CLA byte specifies the command class: in case of being equal to 80 or greater (except for FF that is not a valid value), it means that proprietary commands are used. The same happens with the byte INS, which identifies the type of command. The third field on the header is bytes P1 and P2 that in general, refer to memory positions on the card, but they may actually be any parameter(PARAM) of the command.

Field	Description	Length (bytes)
Header	CLA	1
	INS	1
	P1 and P2	2
Lc	Number of bytes transmitted	0, 1 or 3
Data	Payload	Lc
Le	Number of bytes of the response	0–3

Table 4. Structure of an ISO/IEC 7816 APDU command.

Regarding the answers to such commands, they are conformed by two bytes (SW1 and SW2), which are coded according to **Table 5**. The most common answer during a correct sequence of commands is 90-00, but, sometimes, the execution of the sequence can be successful and return a different value.

4.1.4.3. Disassembling the traces

Once the basics of ISO/IECs 14443-B and 7816 are understood, it is possible to process the traces generated by the system.

Contrary to what was illustrated in **Table 2**, the messages "**FAIL CRC**" and "(SHORT)" should not be present, since they are related to data corruption. In the same way, a good trace should have alternating messages from the tag and the reader, instead of containing two consecutive messages from the same device (except from the case when the reader is looking for tags). Taking these facts into account, **Table 6** indicates the relationship between the standard

	SW1–SW2	Meaning
Normal processing	90 00	Ok
Warning processing	61 XX	XX bytes are still pending to be sent
	62 XX	State of nonvolatile memory is unchanged
	63 XX	State of nonvolatile memory has changed
Execution error	64 XX	State of nonvolatile memory is unchanged
	65 XX	State of nonvolatile memory has changed
	66 XX	Security-related issues
Checking error	67 00	Wrong length
	68 XX	Not supported functions in CLA
	69 XX	Command not allowed
	6A XX	Wrong P1–P2 parameters
	6B 00	Wrong P1–P2 parameters
	6C XX	Wrong LE field. There are XX bytes available
	6D 00	Instruction code not supported or invalid
	6E 00	Class not supported
	6F 00	No precise diagnosis

Table 5. Common answers to ISO/IEC 7816 commands.

commands and the trace shown in **Table 2**. As it can be observed, the sequence of messages is not correct: some are missing, and others have not been received in the correct order.

First, at timestamp 12350, the reader sends different REQB commands to wake up tags that are in its surroundings. The first byte of the command is always set to 05, while the second one is the AFI, that is, equal to 0 (i.e., every tag should respond to the request). The byte PARAM varies between both commands, being 00 in the first case and 08 in the second one (they are aimed at waking up tags in different states). Finally, the last two bytes conform the CRC-B field, which checks the integrity of the message.

The second command is the ATQB:

- It always begins with 50.
- The next four bytes are 08 10 2a 1d, which are the pseudo-unique PICC identifier (PUPI, which is fixed for each tag of the system analyzed, but it might be random in other systems).
- Then, the command continues with another four bytes (53 4e 44 4b) that indicate the applications of the tag.

Timestamp	RSSI	Device	Payload	Additional information	Message
0	142	TAG	50 08 10 2a 1d 53 4e 44 4b 33 81 93 bc 3f		ATQB
1398	112	TAG	00 78 f0		ATATTRIB
854			05 00 00 71 ff		REQB
11500			05 00 00 71 ff		REQB
11478			06 00 97 5b		
46342			05 00 08 39 73		REQB
1908			1d 08 10 2a 1d 00 08 01 00 94 60		ATTRIB
554	296	TAG	00 78 f0		ATATTRIB
3566			02 80 26 4f 11 0a e7 de		i-Block
3146	116	TAG	02 00 14 98 70 10 01 01 76 55 72 90 00 73 65		
36188			03 80 32 00 00 18 ea 98		
1852			00 01 00 00 00 00 00 00	** Fail CRC **	
480			00 90 00 1d fe	** Fail CRC **	
3676			02 80 2e 01 00 20 43 2f		
2870	203	TAG	02 01 01 e0 f5 ff f5 ff 00 00 00 00 01 f4 07 06 a9 8c ff 00 11 03 e8 00 00 b9 0b ff 00 02 00 01 48 90 00 26 57		
48				(SHORT)	
3798			03 80 30 00 00 1d 31 f6		
1580			03	(SHORT)	
17462			02 80 28 00 00 04 75 39 34 0d 3a 07 d3		
5778				(SHORT)	
34972			03 80 2a 01 00 24 00 15 00 4b 00 01 48 41 19 09 01 00 28 01 37 e5 8c 18 21 10 00 c2 01 01 09 23 00 10 01 00 00 4b d4 72 2b eb 04 ca 20		
14542	203	TAG	03 b3 56 ee 2c 90 00 e6 01		
197304			05 00 08 39 73		REQB
804			33 81 93 bc 3f	**FAIL CRC**	

Table 6. M/T trace messages analyzed.

- Next, three bytes (33 81 93) specify different aspects of the communications protocol. Their description and use are beyond the scope of this chapter, but the interested reader can obtain such details in ISO/IEC 14443-3.
- The last two bytes contain the CRC-B.

Another imperfect trace is shown in **Table 7**. However, this trace is useful for illustrating the sequence of commands executed during the exchange.

After the ATQB, at timestamp 1104, the reader sends the ATTRIB command. The command is composed by a first byte (1d) that identifies the command, four bytes that indicate the PUPI from the previous command (08 10 2a 1d), three bytes that determine the communications protocol, a byte (00, the Card Identifier(CID)) that selects a tag and two final bytes that contain the CRC-B.

Timestamp	RSSI	Device	Payload	Additional information	Message
0			05 00 00 71 ff		REQB
804	138	TAG	50 08 10 2a 1d 53 4e 44 4b 33 81 93 bc 3f		ATQB
936			50 08 10 2a 1d 7f cf		
464	178	TAG	00 78 f0		ATATTRIB
12350			05 00 00 71 ff		REQB
11472			06 00 97 5b		
46082			05 00 08 39 73		REQB
804	214	TAG	50 08 10 2a 1d 53 4e 44 4b 33 81 93 bc 3f		ATQB
1618			00 00	(SHORT)	
3578			02 80 26 4f 11 0a e7 de		
3050			02 00 16 98 70 10 01 01 76 55 00	** FAIL CRC **	
8198			03 80 32 00 00 18 ea 98		
2334	186	TAG	03 0b 09 87 00 00 10 00 00 00 01 00 00 00 00 00 00 00 00 00 00 00 00 00 00 90 00 1d ce		
3540			02 80 2e 01 00 20 43 2f		
1708			02 01 01 e0 f5 ff f5 ff	** FAIL CRC **	
1162	275	TAG	02 00 00 b2 90 00 d3 b4	** FAIL CRC **	
3846			03 80 30 00 00 1d 31 f6		
2124				(SHORT)	
840	93	TAG	04 34	(SHORT)	
13524			02 80 28 00 00 04 17 67 7f 16 3a 81 41		
6012	230	TAG	02 e7	(SHORT)	
33958			03 80 2a 01 00 24 00 17 00 4b 00 00 b2 41 19 09 01 00 28 01 30 ed 8c 17 36 10 00 c2 01 01 09 23 00 10 01 00 00 4b 99 76 da 3b 04 46 49		
14544	162	TAG	03 79 a0 ac 57 90 00 1a 0d		
218628			05 00 08 39 73		
804	138	TAG	50 08 10 2a 1d 53 4e 44 4b 33 81 93 bc 3f		
1104			1d 08 10 2a 1d 00 08 01 00 94 60		ATTRIB
554	206	TAG	00 78 f0		ATATTRIB

Table 7. Second example of M/T trace.

Then, the tag answers with an ATATTRIB command, which consists in 3 bytes: the first one is the CID (as indicated by the previous command: 00), while the two last bytes are the CRC-B of the message.

After the ATATTRIB, the RFID session is established and the tag is in the active state, ready for transmitting data.

After analyzing a great deal of traces of the M/T system, it was found that a sequence of six pairs of commands was repeated constantly. Since this is just an example of what can be done with the methodology proposed, we will not deepen into the details, but it will be mentioned briefly the structure of the first two pairs of commands.

The first command is always the same: "02 80 26 4f 11 0a e7 de." The standard ISO/IEC 14443-B indicates that it is an i-block, whose first byte means that it is block number 0 and that it does not contain CID or NAD. The last two bytes of the message are the CRC-B, so the transmitted data are composed by five bytes (80 26 4f 11 0a). These bytes follow ISO/IEC 7816: the first one is the CLA byte (80, proprietary command); the second one is the field INS (26); the third and the fourth (4f 11) are P1 and P2 (parameters of the command); and the fifth (0a) is the field LE, which indicates the number of expected bytes to be received from the tag (i.e., 10 bytes are expected).

This first command is followed by the first response of the tag. As it can be observed in **Table 8**, it is almost the same for every tag. Its structure is as follows:

- Byte 1 (02): it indicates that it is an i-block 0.
- Bytes 2–13: ISO/IEC 7816 data. For instance, bytes 2–3 indicate the total number of trips carried out with the card and bytes 12–13 contain the state of the execution of the command (90-00, successful execution).
- Bytes 14–15: CRC-B.

The second request is also always the same: 03 80 32 00 00 18 ea 98.

- Byte 1 (03): i-block 1.
- Bytes 2–6: ISO/IEC 7816 data. Since CLA is 80, the command is proprietary. INS is equal to 32; P1 and P2 are 00 and 00; and LE (expected length of the answer) is 24 bytes.
- Bytes 7–8: CRC-B.

Trace\#Byte	1	2	3	4	5	6	7	8	9	10	11	12	13	14	15
Card1-Trace 1	02	00	14	98	70	10	01	01	76	55	72	90	00	73	65
Card1-Trace 2	02	00	15	98	70	10	01	01	76	55	72	90	00	e2	30
Card1-Trace 3	02	00	17	98	70	10	01	01	76	55	72	90	00	c0	9b
Card2-Trace 1	02	01	40	98	70	10	01	02	07	90	31	90	00	65	ac
Card2-Trace 2	02	01	42	98	70	10	01	02	07	90	31	90	00	47	07
Card3-Trace 1	02	00	0c	98	70	20	01	01	69	87	97	90	00	ba	6a

Table 8. Responses collected for the first command.

The second answer is related to the use of special fares during a trip. **Tables 9** and **10** show examples of traces for different cards. The data are structured as follows:

- Byte 1 (03): i-block 1.
- Bytes 2–27: ISO/IEC 7816 data. For instance, bytes 12–13 and 14–15 indicate the activation and expiration dates of a special fare, and byte 11 the type of fare (e.g., "1" for standard, "3" for reduced fare).
- Bytes 28–29: CRC-B.

The rest of the pairs answer-response contain other interesting information such the balance of the card, the place where the card was recharged (e.g., ATM, bank) or the data about each trip performed (i.e., cost, date, time, line, and vehicle number).

After all the analysis, it was not found a severe security threat in the system, but there are several issues regarding data privacy that developers should consider.

The main problem is that the RFID communications are performed in plain text, without any kind of ciphering, what leads to the possibility of snooping and emulating them. Thanks to that, an attacker can emulate an unauthorized reader and obtain private data such as the credit balance or the specific characteristics of the trips of a user. Note also that many smartphones currently support NFC (near-field communication), which is partially compatible with ISO/IEC 14443-B tags, and it is straightforward to develop an Android application to read the data (there have already been attacks to ISO/IEC 14443-A tags using mobile phones [24]).

The complete disassembling of the protocol opens the possibility to perform MitM attacks, where a third device might alter the data on the RFID transactions in order to get certain benefits (e.g., for instance, to avoid discounting credit on the card).

Trace\#Byte	**1**	**2**	**3**	**4**	**5**	**6**	**7**	**8**	**9**	**10**	**11**	**12**	**13**	**14**	**15**
Card 1-Trace 1	03	0b	89	87	00	00	10	00	00	00	01	00	00	00	00
Card 1-Trace 2	03	0b	89	87	00	00	10	00	00	00	01	00	00	00	00
Card 2-Trace 1	03	0b	89	87	00	00	10	00	00	00	03	b5	8c	f5	8d
Card 3-Trace 1	03	0b	89	87	00	00	20	00	00	00	01	00	00	00	00

Table 9. First half of different responses to the second commands.

Trace\#Byte	**16**	**17**	**18**	**19**	**20**	**21**	**22**	**23**	**24**	**25**	**26**	**27**	**28**	**29**
Card 1-Trace 1	00	00	00	00	00	00	00	00	00	00	90	00	1d	ce
Card 1-Trace 2	00	00	00	00	00	00	00	00	00	00	90	00	1d	ce
Card 2-Trace 1	00	10	30	00	00	00	00	00	00	00	90	00	a8	0c
Card 3-Trace 1	00	00	00	00	00	00	00	00	00	00	90	00	08	7d

Table 10. Second half of the responses to the second command.

http://dx.doi.org/10.5772/64844

4.2. Public transportation card of Santiago de Compostela

This RFID card was used until recently in the city of Santiago de Compostela (Spain) to pay for public transportation.

4.2.1. Visual inspection

Like M/T cards, there is no external sign that identifies the underlying RFID technology. We can only see the contacts of traditional smart card interfaces, so there are at least two interfaces: one wired and another wireless.

4.2.2. Operating frequency and modulation

- Operating frequency. Like the previous cards, it is fair to assume that due to its use for public transportation, there is a high likelihood that it is an HF card. And this fact was confirmed by following the verification steps described in Section 3.2.1.
- Modulation. Once determined the frequency band, it is possible to test the commands for the different ISO/IEC standards. After testing, the ones for ISO/IEC 14443-B and ISO/IEC 15693, it was found that the tag responded correctly to ISO/IEC 14443-A commands that indicated that the tag was a MIFARE Classic 1K.

4.2.3. Understanding the underlying protocols

MIFARE is a contactless smartcard technology from NXP Semiconductors [25] that has sold more than 5 billion tags and fifty million RFID readers. It started to be manufactured around 1994–1995, being its first major deployment performed in Seoul's city transportation.

MIFARE is compliant with the first three parts of ISO/IEC 14443-A at 13.56 MHz, although there are certain differences depending on the version of the tag, which has been evolving during the last years.

MIFARE Classic is probably the most popular version of MIFARE cards. These tags use a really simple application-specific integrated circuit (ASIC) that basically stores data. Their memory is divided into sectors and blocks that are protected with a simple access control system. Each sector is divided into four blocks: three of them contain data, while the other one stores the data access permissions and the access keys.

There is not a fixed data format, although there is a special format called *value block* with specific operations for incrementing and decrementing values. Sectors use two keys (A and B). Each key allows for managing different permissions: a key could be valid only for reading data, while the other one could be dedicated to modify them. The first 16 bytes of the internal memory are read-only and contain the serial number and other data related to the model and the manufacturer. Data are coded in Crypto-1, an already-broken cryptographic protocol [26–28].

There are different MIFARE Classic versions:

- MIFARE Classic 1K. Its name derives from its 1024-byte internal storage, which is divided into 16 64-byte sectors.

- MIFARE Classic 4K. It has 4096 bytes for data divided into 40 sectors.
- MIFARE Classic Mini. It stores 320 bytes in 5 sectors (the actual useful data space is 224 bytes).

After MIFARE Classic, NXP created other versions: Ultralight, Ultralight C, DESFire (whose security was broken in 2011 [29]), Plus, DESFire V1 and V2, etc.

4.2.4. Security analysis

As it was explained in the previous subsection, MIFARE Classic cards implement a security system that prevents reading or writing the internal data. However, this system is outdated and has already been broken.

To get the access keys to read and write the different internal blocks, the Proxmark official firmware offers several options. For instance, the command *hf mf mifare* executes the darkside attack [28] to obtain a valid key. Such an attack usually takes from 30s to half an hour (sometimes it has to be executed several times). An example of the output of the system is shown in **Figure 10**, where the A key of the first block is obtained. Then, another attack called "nested authentication" [30] can be performed: it allows remote attackers to obtain the keys of all the other blocks (in **Figure 11**). Once all the keys have been obtained, a dump of the memory can be extracted.

With the dump, it is possible to study the different parameters (e.g., detect memory changes as more trips are carried out) or save it to restore it later and recover the previous credit balance.

```
...............................................................
isOk:01

uid(329c0b0e) nt(76d9cec2) par(6c7494bcc47cbcc4) ks(0a0a0007040d0204)

|diff|{nr}     |ks3|ks3^5|parity          |
+----+---------+---+-----+----------------+
| 00 |00000000| a |  f  |0,0,1,1,0,1,1,#db# COMMAND mifare FINISHED
0|
| 20 |00000020| a |  f  |0,0,1,0,1,1,1,0|
| 40 |00000040| 0 |  5  |0,0,1,0,1,0,0,1|
| 60 |00000060| 7 |  2  |0,0,1,1,1,1,0,1|
| 80 |00000080| 4 |  1  |0,0,1,0,0,0,1,1|
| a0 |000000a0| d |  8  |0,0,1,1,1,1,1,0|
| c0 |000000c0| 2 |  7  |0,0,1,1,1,1,0,1|
| e0 |000000e0| 4 |  1  |0,0,1,0,0,0,1,1|
---------------------------------------------------------------
Key found:721205421911

Found valid key:721205421911
proxmark3> _
```

Figure 10. Obtaining access key A from a MIFARE Classic card with Proxmark.

http://dx.doi.org/10.5772/64844

Iterations count: 8

sec	key A	res	key B	res
000	721205421911	1	b0b1b2b3b4b5	1
001	721205421911	1	b0b1b2b3b4b5	1
002	721205421911	1	b0b1b2b3b4b5	1
003	721205421911	1	b0b1b2b3b4b5	1
004	721205421911	1	b0b1b2b3b4b5	1
005	721205421911	1	b0b1b2b3b4b5	1
006	721205421911	1	b0b1b2b3b4b5	1
007	721205421911	1	b0b1b2b3b4b5	1
008	7712f5411e53	1	b0b1b2b3b4b5	1
009	7712f5411e53	1	b0b1b2b3b4b5	1
010	7712f5411e53	1	b0b1b2b3b4b5	1
011	7712f5411e53	1	b0b1b2b3b4b5	1
012	7712f5411e53	1	b0b1b2b3b4b5	1
013	7712f5411e53	1	b0b1b2b3b4b5	1
014	7712f5411e53	1	b0b1b2b3b4b5	1
015	7712f5411e53	1	b0b1b2b3b4b5	1

Figure 11. Access keys cracked for every sector.

4.3. Animal identification tags

Pet identification has been carried out throughout Europe since the late 1990s. RFID tags are generally implanted subcutaneously. The main purpose of this identification was animal health of the most common pets, including cats, dogs, and ferrets (European Regulation 998/2003). The same system is used in Europe for breeding and production of equidae (European Regulation 504/2008), and for public health in ovine and caprine animals (European Regulation 21/2004).

4.3.1. Visual inspection

In this case, a visual assessment to detect any sign of the underlying technology is not necessary, since these kinds of tags are regulated and specified by the different European regulations previously mentioned.

4.3.2. Detailed analysis

In the case of pet identification, European Regulation 998/2003 specifies that tags have to be compliant with ISO/IEC 11784 [31] and ISO/IEC 11785 [32]. They both describe LF tags, existing two different versions: half-duplex (HDX) and full-duplex (FDX and FDX-B). In Spain, most pets wear FDX-B tags, which use biphasic coding.

- Operating frequency. It was verified with the Proxmark that a sample tag (already implanted on a dog) was LF, as it was expected from the information given in the previous section.
- Modulation. In this case, it was not straightforward to recognize the modulation used, because the signals captured had a lot of noise (the tag had been implanted on the dog a

year before these tests were performed). An example of the signals received is shown in **Figure 12**. It was usually required to filter the signal to reduce the noise, obtaining a figure like the one shown in **Figure 13**, which resembles a biphasic coding.

When these experiments were carried out, the official Proxmark firmware did not support FDX-B, so it was necessary to implement it. Such an implementation first filters and demodulates the signal, and then decodes it.

4.3.3. Understanding the underlying protocols

ISO/IEC 11784 and ISO/IEC 11785 are international standards that regulate RFID for animal identification. Each animal transponder contains 64 bits with the information shown in **Table 11** (the data values included were generated randomly).

The system works at 134.2 KHz, and there are two different transmission modes: half-duplex (HDX) and full-duplex (FDX or FDX-B). In HDX mode, the tag is not able to send data and receive power at the same time. Thus, reading consists in powering the tag for a short interval and then waiting for the tag to transmit the data. In this mode, an 8-bit header (always "01111110") and a 16-bit cyclic-redundancy check (CRC) are sent. An additional chunk of 24 bits is also sent and includes information on the application. Data are modulated in FSK and coded with non-return-to-zero (NRZ).

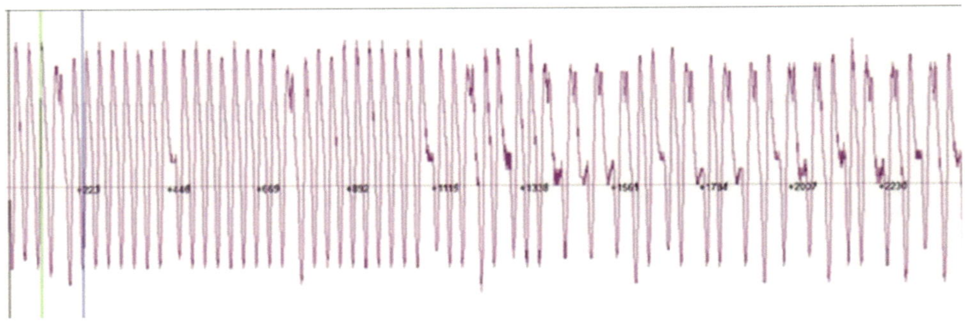

Figure 12. Noisy signal from an animal identification tag.

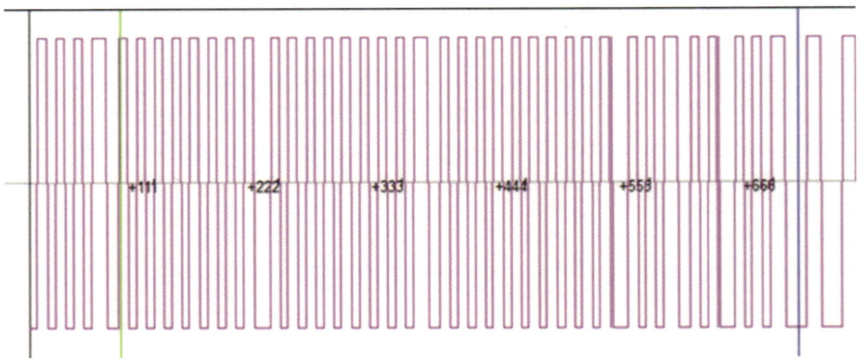

Figure 13. Animal identification tag signal after filtering it.

http://dx.doi.org/10.5772/64844

The tags that operate in FDX-B mode are able to transmit data and be powered at the same time. As it can be seen in **Table 11**, this kind of tags transmits an 11-bit header ("10000000000"), 50 bits of data, 24-bits with the application information and a 16-bit CRC. Moreover, every 8 bits (except for the header) a control bit is added (always "1"). Data are sent in less-significant bit (LSB) order, so, when the reader receives the bits, it can reconstruct them just using simple binary shifts. The bits are modulated in Amplitude-Shift Keying(ASK) and are coded in differential biphase (DBP).

4.3.4. Security evaluation

By making use of the functions implemented, it was straightforward to read data from any FDX-B tag. The software extracts the two main parameters: the country code and the national code (the actual identifier). **Figure 14** shows an example where two consecutive readings were performed: the first one is successful, while the second one shows errors related to a bad reading.

Field\#bit	11	10	9	8	7	6	5	4	3	2	1
	(msb)										(lsb)
Header	1	0	0	0	0	0	0	0	0	0	0
National Code (38 bits)			1	1	0	1	0	0	0	0	0
			1	0	1	0	0	1	1	1	1
			1	0	1	0	0	1	0	0	1
			1	0	1	0	1	0	1	0	1
Country Code (10 bits)			1	1	1	0	0	0	0	0	0
			1	1	1	0	0	0	1	1	1
Data Block Status Flag (1 bit)			1	-	-	-	-	-	-	-	1
Animal Application Indicator (1 bit)			1	1	-	-	-	-	-	-	-
Checksum (16 bits)			1	1	1	0	1	1	1	1	0
			1	0	0	1	0	1	0	1	1
Optional Extra Data (24 bits)			1	0	1	1	1	0	1	1	0
			1	1	1	1	1	0	0	0	1
			1	0	1	0	0	1	0	0	0

Table 11. Internal memory structure of an animal identification tag.

```
Header found, starting data in pos 161
Animal APP
National code: 098104131364
Country code: 981
Obtained CRC: d28d
Calculated CRC: d28d

Header found, starting data in pos 292
Bit control error CC in bit 345
Bit control error in bit 354
Bit control error in bit 372
Bit control error in bit 381
Animal APP
National code: 183524829156
Country code: 249
Obtained CRC: 3ab1
Calculated CRC: 7d8b
```

Figure 14. Example of readings from an animal identification tag.

Security is almost nonexistent in this kind of tags: although writing is not allowed, the tag continuously sends the stored data without any authentication requirement. It may seem that the scenario is not susceptible for including high-security mechanisms, since the objective is to identify the clinical records and the owner of a dog, but in terms of privacy and uniqueness of the identifier, the current system is not effective. Note that, using a device such as Proxmark, it is not only easy to read the data, but also to emulate tags and clone them.

This security problem is even worse when tags are attached to animals aimed at producing human food (e.g., ovine and caprine animals). Cloning or erasing the data breaks traceability, which is the way to determine where an epidemic outbreak was originated.

5. Conclusions

The methodology proposed in this chapter for evaluating security in commercial RFID systems has allowed for detecting relevant flaws in real-world developments, including the following:

- Ability to clone animal identification information.
- Possibility of altering data of certain payment cards.
- Extraction of private information from different transportation cards.
- Possibility of capturing tag-reader communications.
- Possibility of emulating both readers and tags.

Most of the flaws detected were reported to the respective companies, and they have taken the proper measures to mitigate them: in some cases, the system was redesigned to increase security, but most companies had to replace the whole hardware with updated and more secure devices.

The final conclusion is that although RFID systems can implement sophisticated security measures, certain developers have adopted the technology without taking such mechanisms into account. A methodology like the one proposed in this chapter can help to perform audits and determine the security level of an RFID system before taking it from a test environment to a real situation.

Acknowledgements

This work has been funded by the Spanish Ministry of Economy and Competitiveness under grants TEC2013-47141-C4-1-R and TEC2015-69648-REDC.

Author details

Tiago M. Fernández-Caramés*, Paula Fraga-Lamas, Manuel Suárez-Albela and Luis Castedo

*Address all correspondence to: tiago.fernandez@udc.es

University of A Coruña, A Coruña, Spain

References

[1] H. Li, Y. Chen and Z. He. The survey of RFID attacks and defenses. In: 8th International Conference on Wireless Communications, Networking and Mobile Computing (WiCOM); 2012; Shanghai, China. p. 1–4. doi:10.1109/WiCOM.2012.6478720

[2] M. T. Pandian and R. Sukumar. RFID: an appraisal of malevolent attacks on RFID security system and its resurgence. In: IEEE International Conference in MOOC Innovation and Technology in Education (MITE); 2013; Jaipur, India. p. 17–20. doi: 10.1109/MITE.2013.6756297

[3] L. Avanco, A. E. Guelfi, E. Pontes, A. A. A. Silva, S. T. Kofuji and F. Zhou. An effective intrusion detection approach for jamming attacks on RFID systems. International EURASIP Workshop on RFID Technology (EURFID); 2015; Rosenheim, Germany. p. 73–80. doi:10.1109/EURFID.2015.7332388

[4] J. Abawajy. Enhancing RFID Tag resistance against cloning attack. In: Third International Conference on Network and System Security; 2009; Gold Coast, Australia. p. 18–23. doi:10.1109/NSS.2009.101

[5] A. Mitrokotsa, M. R. AU. Rieback and A. S. Tanenbaum. Classifying RFID attacks and defenses. Information Systems Frontiers. 2010;12(5):491–505. doi:10.1007/s10796-00 9-9210-z

[6] K. Bu, X. Liu, J. Luo, B. Xiao and G. Wei. Unreconciled collisions uncover cloning attacks in anonymous RFID systems. IEEE Transactions on Information Forensics and Security. 2013;8(3):429–439. doi:10.1109/TIFS.2012.2237395

[7] Y. Fu, C. Zhang and J. Wang. A research on Denial of Service attack in passive RFID system. In: International Conference on Anti-Counterfeiting Security and Identification in Communication (ASID); 2010; Chengdu, China. p. 24–28. doi:10.1109/ICASID.2010.5551848

[8] A. Suliman, M. K. Shankarapani, S. Mukkamala and A. H. Sung. RFID malware fragmentation attacks. In: International Symposium on Collaborative Technologies and Systems; 2008; Irvine, United States. p. 533–539. doi:10.1109/CTS.2008.4543975

[9] T. L. Lim and T. Li. Exposing an effective denial of information attack from the misuse of EPCglobal standards in an RFID authentication scheme. In: IEEE 19th International Symposium on Personal, Indoor and Mobile Radio Communications; 2008; Cannes, France. p. 1–6. doi:10.1109/PIMRC.2008.4699588

[10] T. Halevi, H. Li, D. Ma, N. Saxena, J. Voris and T. Xiang. Context-aware defenses to RFID unauthorized reading and relay attacks. IEEE Transactions on Emerging Topics in Computing. 2013;1(2):307–318. doi:10.1109/TETC.2013.2290537

[11] S. Guizani. Implementation of an RFID relay attack countermeasure. In: International Wireless Communications and Mobile Computing Conference (IWCMC); 2015; Dubrovnik, Croatia. p. 1318–1323. doi:10.1109/IWCMC.2015.7289273

[12] A. Francillon, B. Danev and S. Capkun. Relay attacks on passive keyless entry and start systems in modern cars. In: NDSS Symposium 2011: 18th Annual Network & Distributed System Security Symposium; 2011, San Diego, California.

[13] RFIDiot official webpage [Internet]. Available from: www.rfidiot.org [Accessed: June 2016].

[14] Proxmark 3 Community webpage [Internet]. Available from: www.proxmark.org [Accessed: June 2016].

[15] Tastic official webpage [Internet]. Available from: http://www.bishopfox.com/resources/tools/rfid-hacking/attack-tools/ [Accessed: June 2016].

[16] OpenPCD Reader [Internet]. Available from: http://www.openpcd.org [Accessed: June 2016].

[17] OpenPICC tag emulator [Internet]. Available from: http://www.openpicc.org [Accessed: June 2016].

[18] Chameleon Project [Internet]. Available from: https://github.com/skuep/ChameleonMini/wiki [Accessed: June 2016].

[19] McAffe's Proxbrute webpage [Internet]. Available from: http://www.mcafee.com/es/downloads/free-tools/proxbrute.aspx [Accessed: June 2016].

[20] M. Feldhofer, M. Aigner, T. Baier, M. Hutter, T. Plos and E. Wenger. Semi-passive RFID development platform for implementing and attacking security tags. In: International Conference for Internet Technology and Secured Transactions (ICITST); 2010; London, Great Britain. p. 1–6.

[21] HID webpage [Internet]. Available from: http://www.hidglobal.com [Accessed: June 2016].

[22] ISO/IEC. ISO/IEC 14443:2000, Identification cards—Contactless integrated circuit(s) cards—Proximity cards.

[23] ISO/IEC. ISO/IEC 7816:1999, Identification cards—Integrated circuit(s) cards with contacts.

[24] Michael Weiß. Performing relay attacks on ISO 14443 contactless smart cards using NFC mobile equipment [thesis]. 2010.

[25] NXP's official webpage [Internet]. Available from: http://www.nxp.com [Accessed: June 2016].

[26] Gerhard de Koning Gans. Analysis of the MIFARE Classic used in the OV—Chipkaart project [thesis]. 2008.

[27] F. D. Garcia, P. van Rossum, R. Verdult, R. W. Schreur. Wirelessly pickpocketing a Mifare Classic card. In: IEEE Symposium on Security and Privacy; 2009; Oakland, United States.

[28] N. Coutois. The dark side of security by obscurity and cloning Mifare Classic rail and building passes, anywhere, anytime. In: International Conference on Security and Cryptography; 2009; Milan, Italy.

[29] D. Oswald, C. Paar. Breaking Mifare DESFire MF3ICD40: Power analysis and templates in the real world. Lecture Notes in Computer Science. 2011; 6917:207–222.

[30] F. D. Garcia et al. Dismantling MIFARE card. In: European Symposium on Research in Computer Security; 2008; Torremolinos, Spain.

[31] ISO/IEC. ISO/IEC 11784:1996, Radio frequency identification of animals—Code structure.

[32] ISO/IEC. ISO/IEC 11785:1996, Radio frequency identification of animals—Technical concept.

Chapter 5

Definition, Characteristics and Determining Parameters of Antennas in Terms of Synthesizing the Interrogation Zone in RFID Systems

Piotr Jankowski-Mihułowicz and Mariusz Węglarski

Additional information is available at the end of the chapter

http://dx.doi.org/10.5772/intechopen.71378

Abstract

The radio frequency identification (RFID) systems are gaining in popularity in automated processes of object identification in various socioeconomic areas. However, despite the existing belief, there is no universal RFID system on the commercial market that could be used in all user applications. All components of a developed solution should be carefully selected or designed according to the specification of objects being recognized and characteristics of their environment. In order to determine parameters of propagation or inductively coupled system, especially when it is dedicated to uncommon applications, a multiaspect analysis has to be taken into consideration. Due to complexity, the problem is reduced to analytical or experimental determination of RFID system operation range and a "trial and error" method is mostly used in the industry practice. In order to cope with the barriers existing in the RFID technology, the authors give the review of latest achievements in this field. They focus on the definition, comprehensive characteristics and determination of the antenna parameters. They also pay attention to the 3D interrogation zone (IZ) that is the main parameter in which multitude technical aspects of the RFID systems are gathered simultaneously, as regards the theoretical synthesis as well as market needs.

Keywords: RFID, antenna, interrogation zone, passive/semi-passive transponder, read/write device

1. Introduction

Radio frequency identification (RFID) refers to modern technology applied to the radio identification of objects of any kind [1]. The RFID systems are gaining in popularity because of their multitude advantages, and today they are frequently used in automated processes in various socioeconomic areas. Usability of this technology is confirmed by a rapidly growing number of innovative practical implementations [2–4]. From an economic point of view, it results from wider availability of RFID devices on the market as well as forecast in terms of their applicability within the next few years [5]. On the other hand, better recognition of the essence pertinent to the operation of these devices as well as methods of determining their parameters constitute the reason in technological terms.

Widely understood processes of automated object identification applied in various areas of life and economy constitute the subject of contemporarily conducted implementation works [1, 6, 7]. RFID devices are, inter alia, increasingly more frequently chosen in security and access control systems, in industrial logistic processes (during shipping of packages, materials or products), and in the course of identification of measurement samples or valuable materials in research processes (in various fields of research, technology or medicine). Significant number of the implementations is carried out in the range of the Internet of Things (IoT) [8]. The RFID system complied with electronic product code (EPC) recommendations is thought to replace barcodes being currently in common use [9]. The development works are conducted to ensure that automatic identification will be effectively and smoothly applied to the fast-moving consumer goods (FMCG) in supply chains [10]. Similar activities are pursued in the areas of reliable and safe identification of moving objects, for example, in the public transport (automatic vehicle identification (AVI)) [7].

It may well be concluded that the observed potential of application use of the radio frequency identification technology justifies the need to conduct intensive research and development works which will constitute a factor of innovative changes in the said framework. The development in this scope is mainly stimulated by highly industrialized countries, but the results obtained by the authors also constitute a contribution to ways of solving many problems in the RFID technology.

Presented works were carried out in many aspects (Chapter 2), including operational effectiveness of single and anti-collision passive and semi-passive RFID systems for perspective frequency bands (HF, UHF). In the course of research, each time it was assumed that it is necessary to achieve essential utility values. Therefore, the majority of published results were positively confirmed experimentally, and then, practical applications were found in the industry, institutions and other places where automated systems were implemented. Considerable part of these works was conducted in the field of definitions, characteristics and determining antenna parameters, which essentially influence the process of synthesis of an interrogation zone (IZ) in RFID systems (Chapter 3).

Overcoming implementation barriers with regard to the RFID technology in various socioeconomic activities constituted the essence of this works. It is worth remarking that determination of RFID system parameters rationally, especially in the aspect of their unusual applications, is only possible by means of a multiaspect analysis of real problems in an automatic identification process (**Figure 1**). It means that despite the existing belief, there is no universal RFID transponder on the market, which could be used to label any object. Such a transponder should be properly selected or—which is more beneficial—designed for the object, in view of many conditions of its performance. Moreover, there is no system that could be used in any automated process. System configuration should be adjusted to the needs of automatic identification of marked objects.

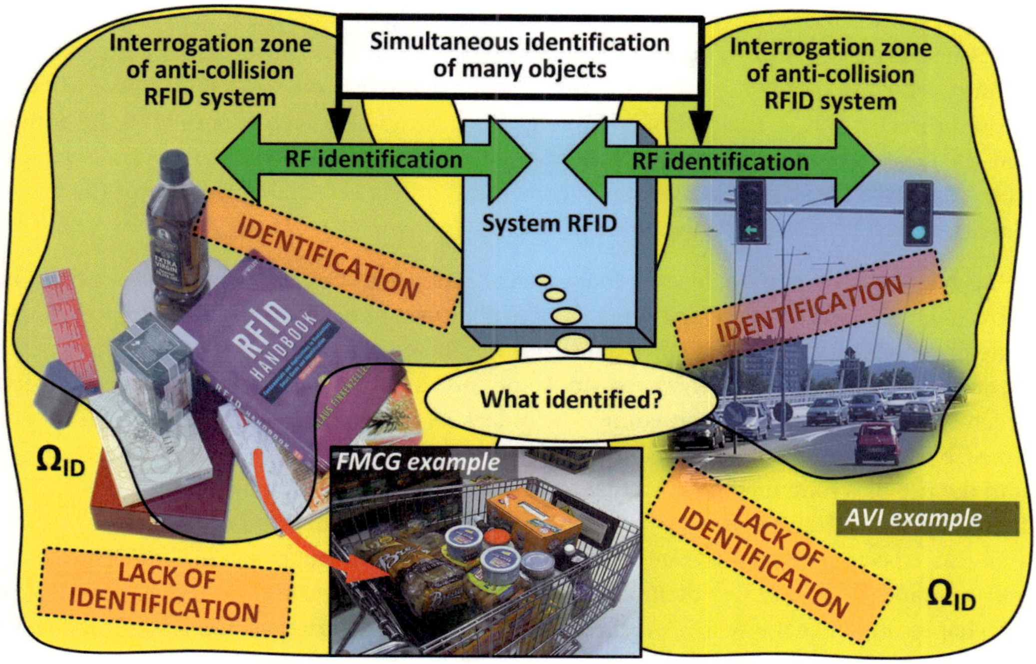

Figure 1. Illustration of RFID automatic identification processes.

The radio communications process in the RFID system can only be conducted in the interrogation zone (**Figure 1**). If only one electronically marked object is assumed to be in it, then this arrangement is called a single identification system. In the case of an anti-collision system, the communications process is conducted simultaneously with many transponders. In this case, radio channel multiaccess algorithms are used, which enable to simultaneously differentiate between many objects. The mechanisms are included in appropriate communication protocols. In the two said examples of RFID systems, it should be assumed that marked objects are located in a three-dimensional $\boldsymbol{\Omega}_{\mathrm{ID}}$ space. Then, one cannot be certain that all these objects will be identified during an automated process since it can also be conducted in a static (permanent spatial location and orientation of objects) as well as in a dynamic manner (changing spatial location and/or orientation of objects).

A properly implemented RFID system is a system in which all objects are successfully marked and—irrespective of the location, orientation or operation status—quickly identified in a planned (anticipated) manner. The solution of the problem consists in predictability of a three-dimensional interrogation zone (3D IZ). The essence of this parameter was pointed out by Klaus Finkenzeller in the monograph [1] where the categorization of aspects in the RFID technology was done for the first time. The importance of the publication and thus validity of the proposed assumptions and solutions is confirmed by the number of its citations. Considerable problems with regard to determining the interrogation zone in a three-dimensional space were noticed, for example, by Nemai C. Karmakar in monograph [11]. Many researchers reduce the IZ synthesis to analytical or only experimental determination of RFID system operation range [12–17]. In industrial conditions, the parameter is usually determined with a "trial and error" method [18, 19] since by definition it means a maximum distance that is necessary to properly conduct a process of read/write data from/into a transponder's memory which is located in an axis of symmetry of a read/write device (RWD) antenna. It can be used directly only in the case of static single identification. In accordance with the definition, the range cannot be utilized to describe a static anti-collision identification or all systems where dynamic changes take place, as it constitutes only a selected parameter of the three-dimensional RFID interrogation zone.

In this context, it should be deemed that some additional parameters should be specified in the practice of designing and validating devices and systems of the RFID technology, in order to determine basic conditions for synthesis of the three-dimensional interrogation zone. In particular, it is related with the necessity to define, characterize and measure parameters, which so far have been: (1) omitted in view of lack of comprehensive recognition, (2) determined by means of an ineffective experimental "trial and error" method, or (3) measured with the use of wrong methods. Among others on the basis of documented R&D works conducted by the authors, it may be deemed that the 3D IZ is a parameter in which multitude technical aspects are gathered simultaneously, as regards the operation of RFID devices, as well as market needs to use them effectively in automated systems. Therefore, the title of this chapter includes the word "synthesis" which—in the determined framework—enabled the authors to present the problem in its entirety, including its many aspects. The factors are already noticeable by leading manufacturers who try to fill the gaps in specifications of their devices and systems based on effects of intensive research and development works conducted throughout the world.

2. The scope of scientific issues

2.1. Frequency bands of RFID systems

Although the performance of RFID systems is pertinent to a radio communication process, many parameters and phenomena should be understood in a nonstandard way. It refers to, for example, a zone in which energy is not radiated but stored in an electric and magnetic field, performance of antennas that are unmatched in terms of waves, phenomenon of impedance matching of a transmitter/receiver and its antenna that is adjusted during wireless data transmission and so on. With regard to the RFID technology, it is necessary to apply many new terms which—in order to be understood—require taking into account construction of RFID devices and their performance.

The scientific investigations in the RFID technology have to be considered according to the used frequency bands (**Figure 2**). In terms of electromagnetic field emission, the RFID systems are placed in a group of radio equipment devices. They use bands (typically LF, HF and UHF) and operating frequencies (f_0) that are commonly available for industrial, scientific and medical (ISM) purposes [20]. Therefore, band and frequency constitute basic factors influencing the differentiation between types of RFID systems, which subsequently determines a different approach in terms of considering the essence of their performance.

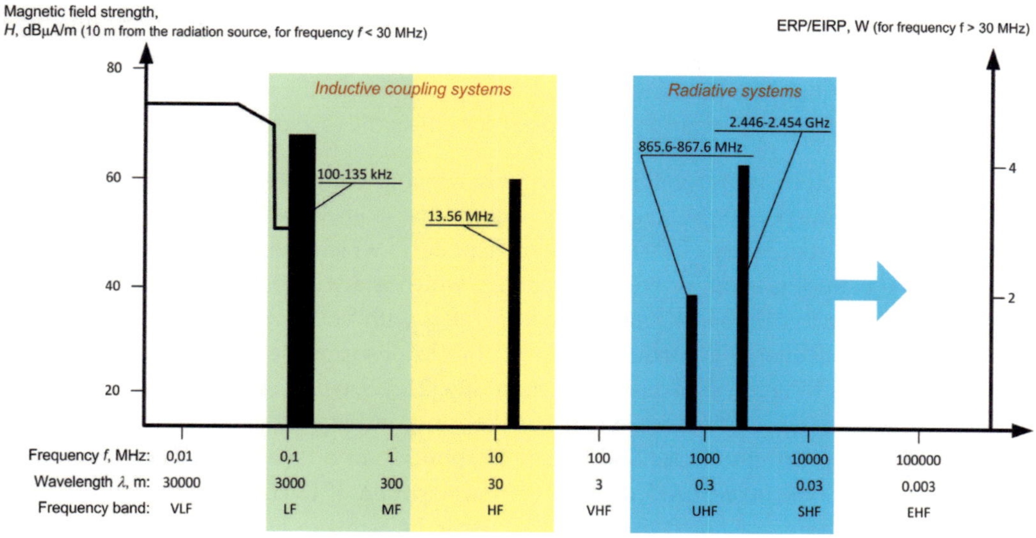

Figure 2. Frequency bands for RFID systems.

2.2. RFID system structure

Irrespective of considered frequency band, a software and hardware component may be distinguished in a radio frequency identification system. The software serves for both direct controlling of individual digital devices and managing the whole system. The second component is composed of two main parts: a read/write device (RWD) with antenna and single or many electronic transponders which are used to mark objects (**Figure 3**).

With regard to the definitions that are used in the RFID technology, the notion of a "reader" can be frequently encountered in the reference literature. Nonetheless, it is worth noticed that the RWD performs a double function in the system (transmitter/receiver) which enables

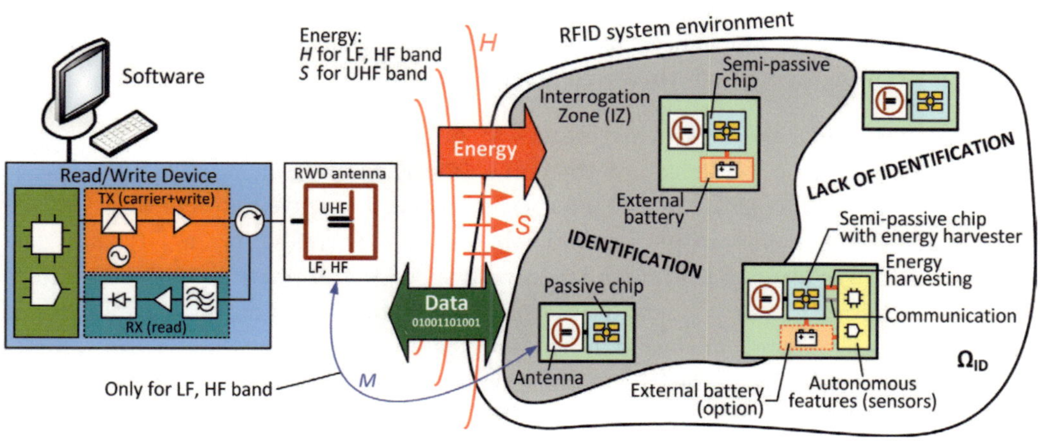

Figure 3. Generalized block diagram of an RFID system.

data transmission in two directions. If in the automated process of object identification, data are not saving into transponders' internal memory, then it may be justified to use the term "reader." In other cases, where information is also written to the transponder memory, a "reader" constitutes an abbreviation which does not reflect the essence of device performance.

The most popular RFID transponder contains only the chip with the connected antenna, so it is called passive transponder, whereas semi-passive type (sometimes called active) has built-in an extra supply source (e.g., lithium disposable battery) which can be exchangeable or not. Generally, the battery is used for enlarging the IZ, which is a very desirable feature for most applications. Moreover, in some new chips integrated with both wired and wireless access ports, the additional energy is used for powering blocks of supplementary autonomous functions, such as measuring physical quantities (humidity [21, 22], temperature [22–24], light intensity [22, 23], pressure [25], acceleration [26], gas [24], etc.), writing gathered data into a built-in memory, managing activity cycles and power distribution in a data acquisition system and so on. These functions are realized without the participation of RWD and give transponders the autonomy. It should be noted that the RWD has to be active in order to conduct the radio communications process, because the extra battery system of transponder is never used for activating the transmission circuit. It means that the transponder antenna does not emit the electromagnetic field as it is in the case of conventional short-range devices (SRDs) [20]. These characteristics help distinguish the semi-passive RFID transponders from the classical active SRDs.

2.3. Inductively coupled systems

According to the main classification of the RFID technology, the first group is composed of inductively coupled systems. The carrier frequency is between 100 and 135 kHz (typically 125 kHz) for the LF band or 13.56 MHz for the HF band. This kind of the systems operates by utilizing zone that is characterized by an inhomogeneous magnetic field (described by the magnetic field strength *H*) and strong coupling (described by the mutual inductance *M*) between antennas of the arrangement components. For the typical operating frequency f_0 = 125 kHz of the LF band, the wavelength λ is 2400 m, and for the f_0 = 13.56 MHz of the HF band, λ is about 22 m. For this reason, the RWD and transponder antennas are made in the form of loop which is small in relation to λ. Hence, the inhomogeneous magnetic field generated into RWD antenna vicinity is the medium for both transferring energy and wireless communications.

A load modulation is the most widespread way of communications with the use of this medium. Thus, in the LF systems, information is transferred by a modulated carrier wave (amplitude shift keying (ASK)). In the range of short waves, inductive coupling between transponder and RWD antenna loops is considerably weaker. Therefore, in the HF band, data are transferred by means of load modulation with subcarrier in order for the energy to be properly transferred to transponders. If a spectrum of a modulated signal is taken into consideration for the LF systems, conveyed information is gathered in sidebands, occurring around the carrier wave, whereas for the load modulation with subcarrier, it has to be regained from precisely defined subcarriers (e.g., 13.56 MHz/16, 32, 64 = 847 kHz, 424 kHz, 212 kHz) [27]. The said communication mechanisms are implemented in appropriate protocols (e.g., ISO/IEC15693, 14443, 18000-3 for an HF band).

The basic parameter that characterizes the interrogation zone and read/write range of the inductively coupled RFID systems is a minimum magnetic field strength H_{min} (or a minimum value of magnetic induction B_{min}) at which the correct data transmission between the RWD and transponder takes place [28]. The minimum value H_{min} that is required in a process of writing data to the transponder's internal memory ($H_{minWrite}$) is bigger by a few percent than a value for readout ($H_{minRead}$). It is the reason why the RFID interrogation zone is depended on the type of operations conducted in communication frame.

The anti-collision systems are even more troublesome in synthesis. Since the several transponders can be simultaneously located in the vicinity of an RWD antenna, it is necessary to provide appropriate power supply for all of them. The influence of their magnetically coupled circuits on the loop impedance of the RWD antenna causes a considerable change of many parameters in the entire system. As a consequence, the phenomenon leads to difficulties in communication with transponders that are located at the zone boundary where the magnetic field strength has a minimum value. In order to assess properly the acceptable borders of spatial distribution for deploying marked objects in a designed system, the correct analysis of the RWD loop impedance with coupled antennas of transponder, and therefore, an analysis of changes in the magnetic field strength has to be performed. The three-directional interrogation zone of an inductively coupled RFID system, independently for a required direction of data transmission, can be determined on the basis of comparison of the H_{min} parameter and a value of magnetic field strength generated in a particular point $P(x, y, z)$. In order to conduct the correct synthesis, apart from fulfilling minimum energy conditions, the efficiency of communication between RFID devices in the anti-collision system with inductive coupling has to be taken into consideration.

2.4. Propagation systems

Operating principles of the RFID devices dedicated to the UHF band (860–960 MHz depending on world regions) are significantly different. In the UHF RFID systems, a far-field region is utilized and the wave locally can be considered as plane. In this region, vectors of electric and magnetic field strength are perpendicular both to each other and to the direction in which the wave disperses. The radiated electromagnetic wave of power density S is energy medium supplying passive or semi-passive transponders (**Figure 3**). The carrier wave of the frequency f_0 is used to transmit energy between matched antennas, but it should be noticed that the impedance matching of a transmitter and a receiver known from classical theory is valid only for the read/write device and its 50 Ω antenna (not for transponders).

The problem with definition, characterization and determination of parameters which essentially influence the synthesis process of the interrogation zone in the UHF band is presented on the basis of the proposed model of a radio communications system (**Figure 4**). The model represents electrical circuits and antenna of the read/write device as well as a single transponder (passive or semi-passive). For simplicity, only the single identification process is considered. But, the same algorithm can be multiplied for all arrangements (RWD and additional transponders in IZ) when the anti-collision system is synthesized.

The electronic chip of a transponder is designed to be supplied by the minimal voltage U_T that is induced at terminals of the connected antenna. As a consequence, the complex impedance

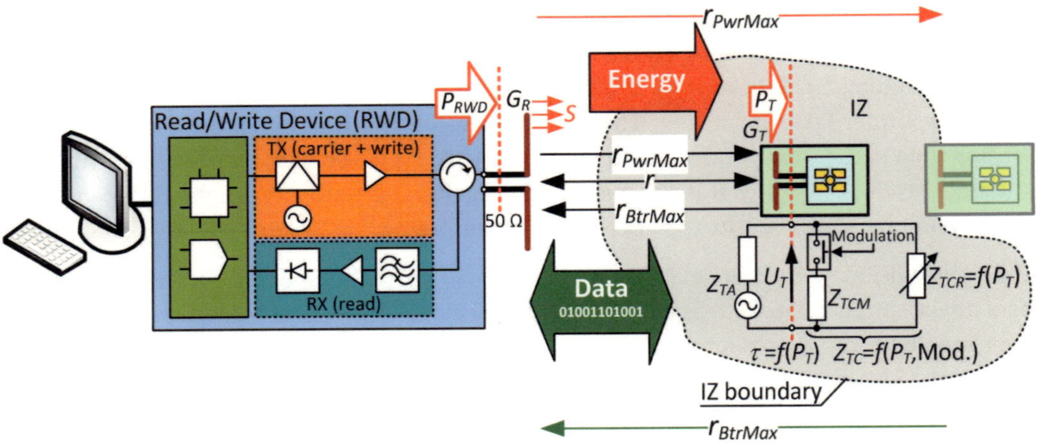

Figure 4. Generalized block diagram of an UHF RFID system.

(Z_{TC}) of the chip front end is continuously changed. The part (Z_{TCR}) of the impedance that represents a rectifier and voltage regulator is strongly influenced by the electromagnetic field. On the other hand, parameters of the electromagnetic field are dependent on the orientation of marked object and its localization in the operating space where both energy and communication conditions have to be established in order to ensure the proper work of the system. The conditions are described by the interrogation zone that constitutes the basic parameter of RFID systems. Since the amount of conveyed energy is very small, the backscatter communications is used for transmitting data in the direction from the transponder to the RWD. In this process, a battery-less device communicates by modulating its reflections of an incident radio frequency (RF) signal. The modulation is realized by step changes of the chip impedance (Z_{TCM} switching). The communication principles are implemented in the protocol of electronic product code (EPC) Class 1 Gen 2 [29], which the latest version is currently standardized in ISO/IEC 18000-63 (formerly ISO/IEC 18000-6).

The Friis transmission equation can be utilized for determining the interrogation zone of a common radio channel [30]:

$$P_T = P_{RWD} \frac{G_R G_T \lambda^2 \tau \chi}{(4\pi r)^2} \tag{1}$$

where P_{RWD} means the power supplied to terminals of the impedance-matched RWD antenna, G_R—the gain of the impedance-matched RWD antenna, P_T—the power received in the transponder antenna, G_T—the gain of the transponder antenna (impedance matching of the antenna and the chip is assumed), χ—the polarization matching factor for a given arrangement of the radio communication antennas, τ—the coefficient of power transfer from the antenna to the chip, λ—the wavelength and r—the distance between the antennas.

The boundary of the interrogation zone, that is, the maximal distance r_{PwrMax} between the axial–symmetrical antennas of a communications system, can be determined by transforming equation (1). The proper conditions for supplying energy to the passive transponder are established in such a defined space. The conditions are characterized by the minimal power P_{Tmin} (chip sensitivity) which is enough for activating internal circuits of the transponder:

$$r_{PwrMax} = \frac{\lambda}{4\pi}\sqrt{\frac{P_{RWD} G_R G_T \tau \chi}{P_{Tmin}}} \tag{2}$$

The transponder sensitivity is dependent on its type (passive or semi-passive) [31, 32] as well as on parameters of radio communication protocol. There is a relation between the sensitivity of passive transponder chip P_{TminP} and semi-passive one P_{TminSP}:

$$P_{TminP} > P_{TminSP} \tag{3}$$

It yields a larger geometrical space of the interrogation zone in semi-passive systems. It is possible due to an extra battery source connected to the chip. But it should be emphasized that the relation (3) is valid when the voltage of internal source is in the range of minimal U_{BatMin} and maximal U_{BatMax} values (**Figure 5**). Therefore, the sensitivity of semi-passive chip should be specified for the given voltage value U_{Bat} of internal supply module.

The maximal distance r_{PwrMax} has to be compared with a r_{BtrMax} value in the process of interrogation zone synthesis. The r_{BtrMax} means the maximal distance between the centers of antennas where proper detection of transmitted signal is possible:

$$r_{BtrMax} = \sqrt[4]{\frac{\lambda^2}{(4\pi)^3}\frac{P_{RWD} G_R^2 \chi \sigma_T}{P_{Rmin}}} \tag{4}$$

where σ_T means the effective reflecting area of the transponder antenna (Radar Cross Section (RCS)) and P_{Rmin}—the minimal power at the RWD input for signal wave reflected off the transponder.

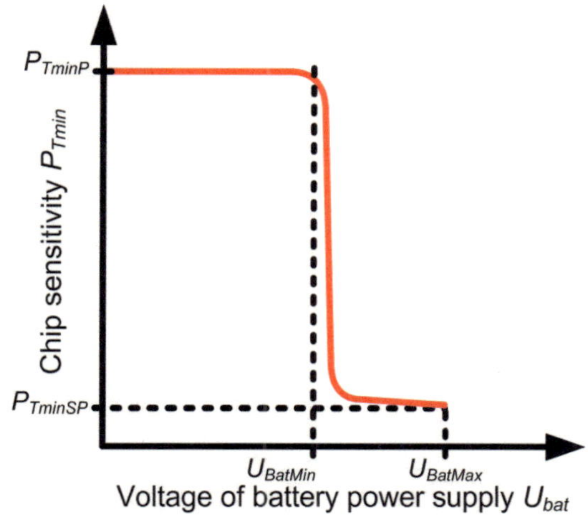

Figure 5. Generalized curve of the sensitivity for a passive and semi-passive chip.

The signal is transmitted by backscatter communications in the direction from the transponder to the read/write device. The process of data exchange can be carried out successfully provided only that the power in antenna circuits of both the RWD and transponder reaches the necessary level. The energy gathered by the transponder located in a point (x, y, z) has to be enough for supplying the chip with a power P_T greater than the minimal value P_{Tmin}. And also the energy of a signal wave reflected back to the RWD antenna has to be sufficient to give a power P_R greater than the P_{Rmin} value:

$$\frac{P_T(x, y, z)}{P_{\text{Tmin}}} \geq 1, \quad \frac{P_R(x, y, z)}{P_{\text{Rmin}}} \geq 1 \tag{5}$$

Eqs. (1)–(5) can be used to determine the interrogation zone in passive or semi-passive RFID systems of the UHF band. It should be borne in mind, however, that many of the listed parameters depend on electrical and geometrical arrangements of RWD and transponder antennas. This is particularly important in dynamic and anti-collision RFID systems which are dedicated to automated processes of object identification. For example, despite the antenna polar diagrams of $G(\theta)$ and $G(\phi)$, the three-dimensional antenna radiation pattern $G(\theta,\phi)$ has to be taken into consideration when orientation of labeled object is changed in all directions. Moreover, the chip sensitivity (i.e., minimal power P_{Tmin}) is the most important in the IZ synthesis process. It describes supply conditions of a transponder [33]. On the base of this parameter, the impedance of the chip placed at IZ boundary, the construction of transponder antenna and the shape of interrogation zone for a given implementation of RFID system are worked out.

The impedance of transmitters or receivers in conventional radio systems is fixed (e.g., 50, 75 Ω) and matched to the antenna at a given frequency. Another situation is in passive and semi-passive RFID systems. The chip impedance Z_{TC} of a transponder varies, while it is working. The impedance matching of chip and antenna Z_{TA} is characterized by the power transfer coefficient τ (**Figure 4**).

The gain G_T in Eqs. (1) and (2) has to be determined at full impedance matching of antenna and chip ($Z_{TA} = Z_{TC}^*$, $\tau = 1$) in order to carry out the interrogation zone synthesis. Thus, the power transfer coefficient is described by equation:

$$\tau = \frac{4\text{Re}(Z_{TA})\text{Re}(Z_{TC})}{\text{Re}(Z_{TA} + Z_{TC})^2 + \text{Im}(Z_{TA} + Z_{TC})^2} \tag{6}$$

In practice, the antenna impedance Z_{TA} is constant at a given frequency, but the chip impedance Z_{TC} varies while the transponder is working (**Figure 4**). This characteristic is crucial in the IZ synthesis, but producers of RFID components do not specify it.

3. Experimental research

3.1. Determining chip parameters in UHF RFID transponder

An attempt to define, characterize and determine parameters of a transponder chip may be found problematic in relation to the considered systems. In the course of preparing research works in this field, the authors observed that both the literature and knowledge on the subject in question are incomplete. Above all, this applies to the UHF band and newly implemented chips with semi-passive functions. In this context, the effective methods of determining parameters for passive and semi-passive UHF RFID chips are presented in the chapter [34]. Elaborated measuring procedures were verified experimentally and discussed in detail. The special untypical laboratory stand was prepared for carrying out the research tasks. Furthermore, the importance of the parameters for the interrogation zone synthesis was described methodically. The special software tools that allow researchers to effectively conduct investigations on protocol parameter modifications in both newly developed and approved standards (e.g., ISO/IEC18000-63) were also designed. These facilities can significantly support many theoretical and simulation works that are developed and described in the branch literature and can improve the reliability and efficiency of designed RFID applications.

Values of impedance Z_{TC} are depended on transponder localizations and orientations according to the RWD antenna. It is because this parameter varies with power P_T that is transferred from the antenna to the chip (**Figure 4**). Power level changes are caused by a rectifier and voltage regulator that are main parts of a transponder RF frontend [35, 36]. Operating modes (e.g., reading or writing operation realized on an internal memory of the chip) also affect the chip impedance, because they can be activated at different power levels ($P_{TminWrite} > P_{TminRead}$). Furthermore, parameters of communications protocols, for example, ISO/IEC18000-63 compatible with EPC requirements [29], have an effect on the Z_{TC}. Unfortunately, the variable chip impedance has significant influence on measurements of the minimal power P_{Tmin} what makes a measuring task very difficult. In order to cope with this problem, a special laboratory stand has to be set in which two methods of chip sensitivity determination can be integrated in the proposed research procedure (**Figure 6**).

The essence of both methods is to determine the minimum power P_{min} at the moment when *16b Random or Pseudo-Random Number* (*RN16*) is identified as a response from the transponder. The number is generated as an answer to the *Query* command according to communication protocols [29] when the condition of $P_T \geq P_{Tmin}$ is met. The power P_{Tmin} is obtained with giving special consideration to the impedance mismatching of chip (Z_{TC}) and 50 Ω measuring channel (Z_0).

In the first method, the real frame with the *Query* command is generated by measuring equipment. An arbitrary waveform generator is used as a simulator of modulated signal source, and a vector signal generator is a source of a carrier signal with adjustable output power. The pattern of real communication frame is generated by *JankoRFIDchip'UHF* program which was designed in the Mathcad environment for the research task. A file with the frame prepared according to the specified protocol (**Figure 7**) is written to the arbitrary waveform generator by a LAN interface.

The pattern signal is integrated with the carrier in the vector generator. The power P_G (**Figure 6**) of output signal with modulated amplitude can be adjusted to a desired level. Generally, the power is transferred with nonmodulated carrier, for example, during *Start* or *Stop* sequences. The frame is sent periodically—it begins with the *Reset* sequence of turning off and resetting internal circuits and finishes with the *Stop* sequence of sending back transponder answer and shutting-down internal blocks. The transmission parameters are synchronized during the header sequence [29].

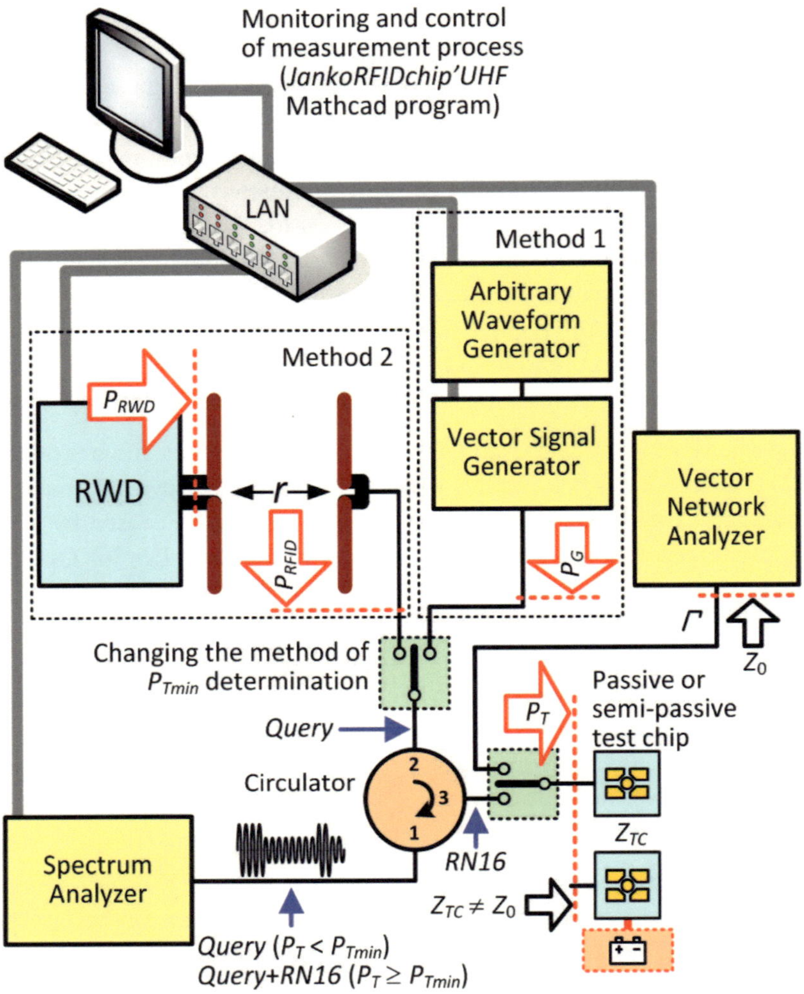

Figure 6. Block diagram of the test stand.

In the second method (**Figure 6**), a long-range read/write device with an antenna is utilized instead of expensive research apparatus. The main advantage of this equipment is the possibility to set up communication protocol parameters according to investigators' tasks. Also, a level of output power P_{RWD} can be adjusted. In this laboratory stand, the power P_{RFID} transferred in a tested RFID application can be also adjusted in the intrinsic way by changing the distance r between antennas of a real arrangement.

Comparing both methods, it should be noticed that the universal and versatile but very expensive generators are used in the first procedure. Thanks to the elaborated special software, an initial process of protocol pattern preparation is very easy and allows designers to control all communication parameters. So, this method can be utilized to conduct all kinds of typical and untypical measurement tasks, even including investigations connected with a synthesis of analytical model. Also, potential environmental disturbances have limited influence on the

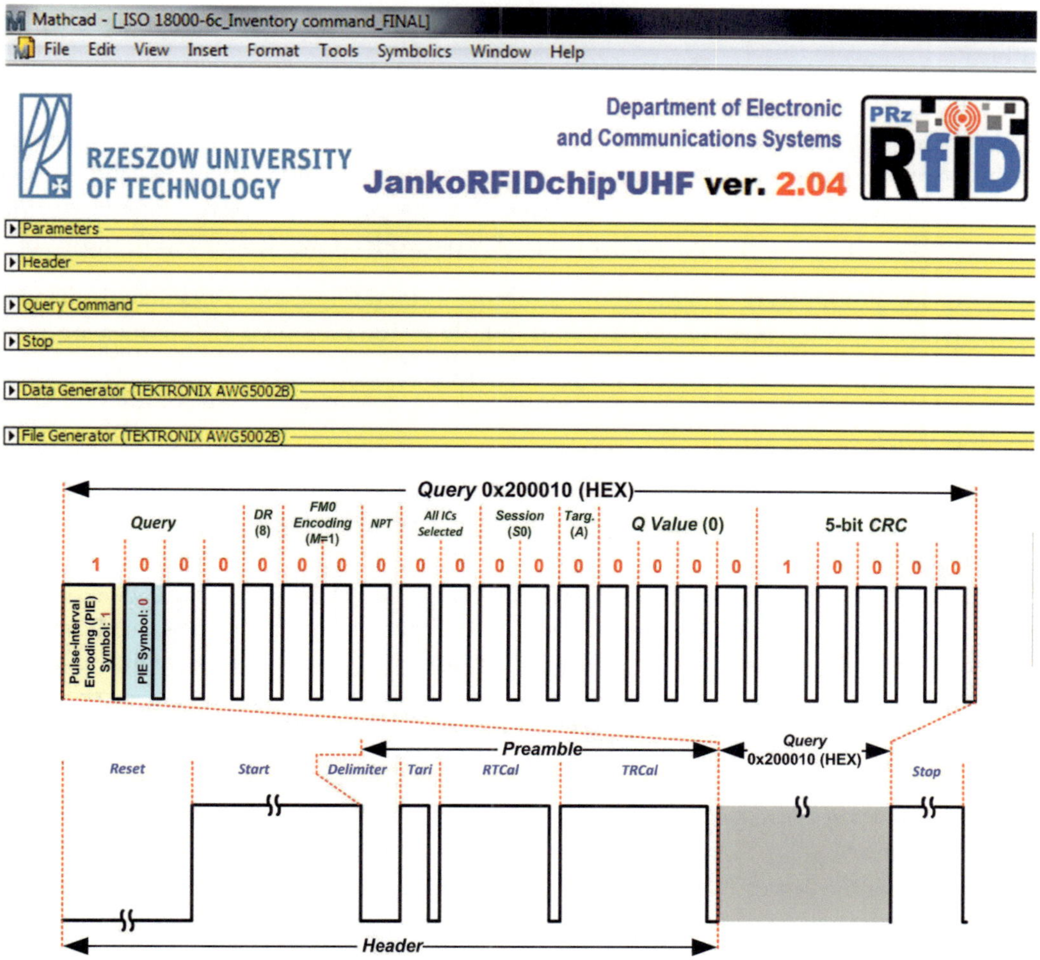

Figure 7. JankoRFIDchip'UHF program (developed in the Mathcad environment).

obtained results. The second method is more time-consuming with regard to the measurement process configuration. Its versatility is restricted by commercial software tools, and it is affected by radio interferences. The main advantage consists in comparatively negligible costs of the laboratory stand.

The command *Query* which is sent in both the procedures is transmitted to the chip by using a ferrite circulator. Since $Z_{TC} \neq Z_0$, the transferred data can be decoded by the spectrum analyzer according to the requirements of [29]. The analyzer can be also utilized to measure the minimal power P_{min}, but losses of measuring channel on the way between the analyzer input and the chip gate have to be taken into account. The sensitivity of tested chip is determined by the relationship:

$$P_{T\min} = P_{\min}(1 - |\Gamma|^2) \tag{7}$$

where Γ means the reflection coefficient which is measured by the vector network analyzer (VNA).

The reflection coefficient is specified at the previously determined value of power P_{min}. Prior to the measuring procedure, the VNA input has to be calibrated with the impedance $Z_0 = 50\ \Omega$. Also the reference plane has to be moved to the junction of chip and its antenna—the method of port extension can be used [37, 38]. The testing stand and all time-consuming measuring procedures can be controlled remotely by the LAN network on the base of TCP/IP protocol.

Selected chip groups were tested in the measurement stand (**Figure 8**). Obtained results [34] are convergent for the methods presented in **Figure 6**. The measured P_{Tmin} values are very close to the information given in producer's documentations. However, it should be noted that the information specified by manufacturers is too perfunctory from the RFID system designer point of view.

The chip sensitivity varies with frequency, communication protocol parameters, etc., but these characteristics are very often suppressed in specifications. Moreover, the conditions of this parameter determination (e.g., what frequency or band was it determined for?) are not described by producers. Also, the same problems are valid for the difference between sensitivity values for the chip working in passive ($U_{bat} = 0$ V) and semi-passive ($U_{bat} > 0$ V) modes (**Figure 9**). So, it is necessary to determine the sensitivity P_{Tmin} of semi-passive transponders with regard to voltage levels of the auxiliary battery supply unit (**Figure 9a**). It has to be taken into consideration by designers on the stage of RFID equipment preparation.

If the chip sensitivity is determined correctly, it is possible to measure the chip impedance by the means of VNA. The results of impedance measurement can be obtained at the sensitivity P_{Tmin} (**Figure 9b**) [34]. Significant differences in the gathered data can be observed for the higher value of the power P_T. It is caused by an internal stabilizer of chip which has to adjust voltage in the input circuits. This effect does not have significant impact on the measuring

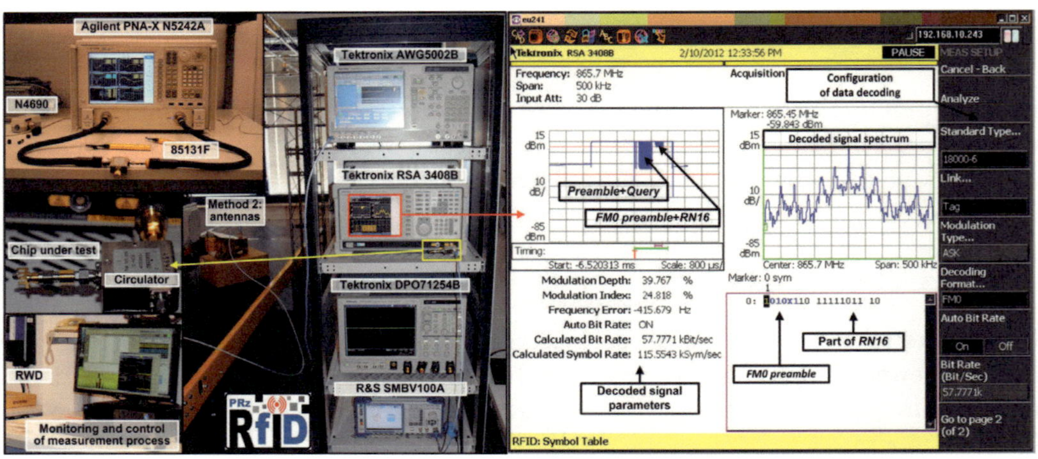

Figure 8. Test stand in the authors' RFID laboratory at the Department of Electronic and Telecommunications Systems (DETS) in Rzeszow University of Technology (RUT).

http://dx.doi.org/10.5772/intechopen.71378

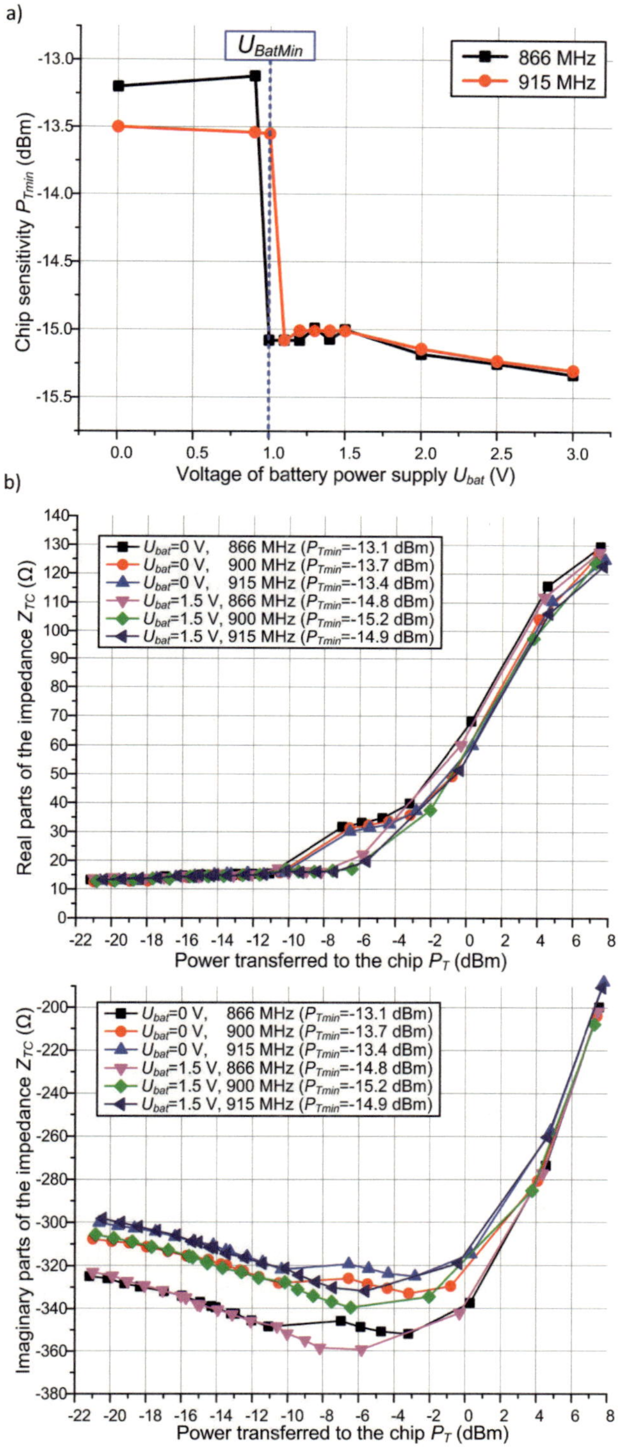

Figure 9. Example results for a passive/semi-passive chip: (a) the sensitivity vs. battery voltage and (b) the impedance vs. power transferred to the chip.

procedure of interrogation zone. It is because the amount of energy which is harvested from the electromagnetic field generated by the RWD antenna is enough for proper operation of the chip. However, it should be noted that the impedance value at the power P_{Tmin} for the semi-passive chip is independent of the supplementary battery source. This fact has essential practical meaning because it allows designers to construct only one type of transponder antenna for both the operating modes (passive and semi-passive).

3.2. Antenna synthesis for UHF RFID transponder

Since the huge progress observed in the RFID technology covered also aspect of antenna constructions, the complement of the knowledge in the field of literature and verification of well-known methods used in synthesis of transponder antennas for various frequency bands is compulsory.

An example problem for the UHF band was discussed in [39]. A novel microstrip antenna dedicated to UHF semi-passive RFID transponders with an energy harvester was presented in this paper. The antenna structure designed and simulated by using Mentor Graphics HyperLynx 3D EM (HL3DEM) software was described in detail. The modeling and simulation results along with comparison with experimental data were analyzed and concluded. The need to eliminate a traditional battery form a transponder structure was the main goal of the project. The energy-harvesting block, which was used instead, converts ambient energy (electromagnetic energy of common radio communication systems) into electrical power for internal circuitry. In order to benefit from the additional function of gathering extra energy, it was necessary to create new designs of antennas.

Typical values of a UHF semi-passive chip resistance R_{TC} equal from a few to tens Ω at the chip sensitivity P_{Tmin}. A value of a chip reactance X_{TC} (typically a few of hundreds Ω) depends mainly on an internal capacitance that accumulates energy which is necessary for supplying the transponder [34]. Impedance matching means that the chip resistance R_{TC} is equal to an antenna resistance R_{TA}, and also an antenna reactance X_{TA} has inductive character;then, the equation $Z_{TA} = Z_{TC}^*$ is met.

In the classical passive UHF chip, there are several ways to obtain highly inductive character of the antenna impedance [40]. The first group of methods consists in modification of a microstrip antenna construction. It can be achieved by adjusting the coupling effect between the antenna and the transponder environment [41] or by modifying chip circuit by utilizing T-matching (**Figure 10a**) [42] or a parasitic induction loop (**Figure 10b**) and others. These methods cannot be applied to same solutions of chips due to their specific internal circuit design [34]. Then, it is necessary to use symmetrical/asymmetrical open-antenna arms (open dipole) which are adjusted by a microstrip and/or SMD elements (**Figure 10c**).

Type of chips considered in [39] has an RF rectifier output for gathering energy from the electromagnetic field of RFID system (**Figure 11**). This output, together with an external battery, is used for powering blocks of supplementary autonomous functions in a semi-passive transponder. The classical passive RFID antennas (utilizing, e.g., T-matching or parasitic induction loop for matching impedance) negatively influence the harvester, and lack of energy blocks the

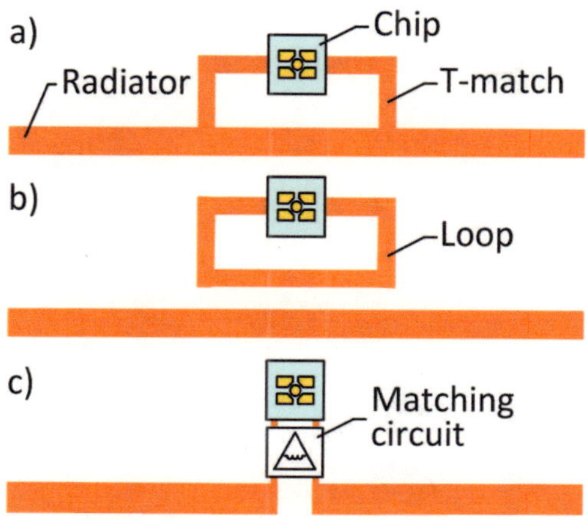

Figure 10. Means of impedance matching in the UHF RFID transponder: (a) T-match, (b) parasitic loop, and (c) other antenna circuit.

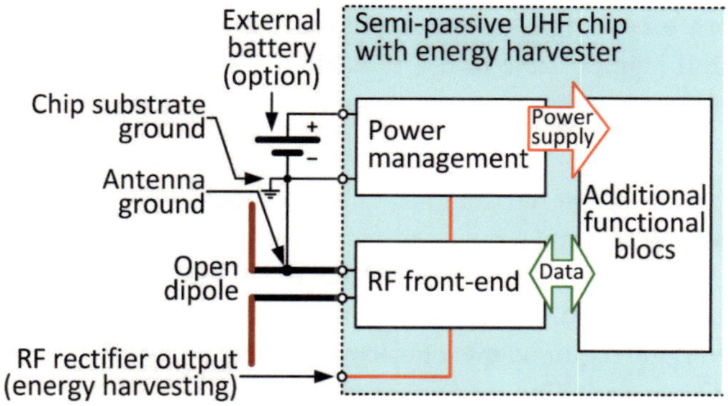

Figure 11. RF frontend in a semi-passive UHF chip with the energy harvester.

whole transmission between the transponder and RWD. It is due to the fact that the antenna and chip have a common ground. So, it is necessary to use the symmetrical/asymmetrical open dipole for the semi-passive UHF RFID transponder with the energy harvester (**Figure 10c**).

The process of antenna designing for the semi-passive UHF RFID transponder with the energy harvester is discussed on the basis of numerical calculations (model HL3DEM) and practical implementations in the PCB technology (**Figure 12**). The investigation is applied to the real RFID passive/semi-passive chip (AMS SL900A in QFN16 package [43]). Additionally, it is assumed that the designed antenna should be resistant to the proximity of metal objects. This assumption stems directly from the fact that the construction of this kind of chips is the most advanced and the most expensive among the currently available solutions on the market. For this reason, only those objects of significant value are marked with such transponders—during freight forwarding processes, it is necessary to guarantee that the valuable products will get to a proper destination by an agreed upon date, and in good condition. Hence, it is a good idea but expensive in practice to control parameters of the surrounding environment

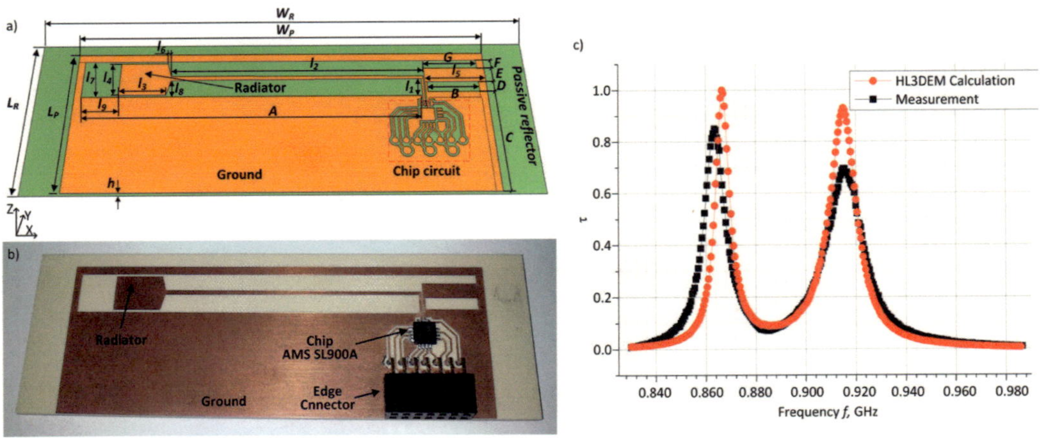

Figure 12. Proposed antenna for a semi-passive UHF RFID transponder with the energy harvester: (a) HL3DEM model, (b) practical implementation and (c) results of the power transfer coefficient.

by means of sensors, for example, embedded in the high-performance transponders [44–46]. On the other hand, it is impossible to use typical low-cost transponders made in a form of pressure-sensitive labels in a disturbing environment (metal or any other object made of electrically conductive materials).

Additionally, it is assumed that the designed antenna should have a directional radiation pattern, a small geometrical size and a power transfer coefficient $\tau = 0.7{:}1$ in the band: 865.6–867.6 and 902–928 MHz. The choice of the frequency band meets the requirement of proper operation in various regions of the world. It is especially important for long-range RFID systems which work complying with the requirements of electronic product code in the UHF band (protocol ISO 18000-63, RWD compatibility: (a) European version of ETSI EN 302 208 – 2W ERP, frequency band 865.6–867.6 MHz, or (b) American version of FCC Part 15.247 – 1 W of transmitter output power with maximal gain of 6 dBi – 4 W EIRP, frequency band 902–928 MHz).

In order to justify the elaborated numerical model (**Figure 12a**), the test samples (**Figure 12b**) were made on low-loss double-sided laminates (ISOLA IS-680-300: thickness of dielectric layer $h = 1.547$ mm, thickness of copper layer 18 μm, $\varepsilon_r = 3$, tg$\delta = 0.003$ at $f_0 = 2$ GHz). The convergence of measurements and calculations is confirmed in **Figure 12c** [39]. It should be mentioned that due to the lack of reliable information about parameters of the dielectric layer for the presumed resonance frequency (866 and 915 MHz), additional tests had to be carried out. The proper value of $\varepsilon_r = 3.08$ necessary in the model calculation is determined on the basis of ring resonators [47]. The proposed solution had provided basis for further development work (e.g., Grant No. PBS1/A3/3/2012) conducted in the scope of the RFID technique.

3.3. Antenna synthesis for HF RFID transponder

The progress in the RFID technology is also pertinent to changes of technological materials that are used in transponder constructions. It substantially influences the process of antenna synthesis and determining operation parameters. In the context of problems described in

Section 3.2, the synthesis of flexible antenna dedicated to semi-passive transponders of a HF RFID system with inductive coupling is presented in the paper [48]. It can be found in this work that the considered matching of an antenna to a chip is completely different than in the UHF band case. Moreover, the possibility of manufacturing the antenna in the inkjet technology is emphasized in it. Impact of the technology on antenna parameters is also discussed as it is important for transponder operation in a target application. The validation study of the synthesis method and sample behavior in the inhomogeneous magnetic field is carried out by the authors of the chapter.

It should be mentioned that planar structures on elastic substrates and their diverse modifications are currently the subject of intensive research in the world's laboratories. The permanent progress is possible due to availability of new materials, technologies and also software tools that significantly support antenna designers. It allows researchers to develop, for example, 3D antennas of RFID transponders [49, 50] or transponder antennas operating in two frequency bands [51] and following to integrate these antennas with very thin objects such as tickets, banknotes, valuable and identity documents and so on [52].

The antenna loop (**Figure 13a**) is represented by a parallel circuit where L_T is the self-inductance and R_T characterizes the resistance of wires that are used for creating the winding and it also includes the ohmic losses (C_{TS} denotes the inter-turn capacitance). R_{TS} and L_{TS} quantities denote respectively the resistance and the inductance of series antenna circuit. The source U_{RT} represents the voltage induced in the antenna loop when the transponder is in the magnetic field of RWD antenna. The maximum value U_T across loop antenna terminals is obtained for the parallel resonance between the inductance L_{TS} and the capacitance C_{TC} of an active chip. This phenomenon is used to supply the chip and also to harvest additional energy from RFID system

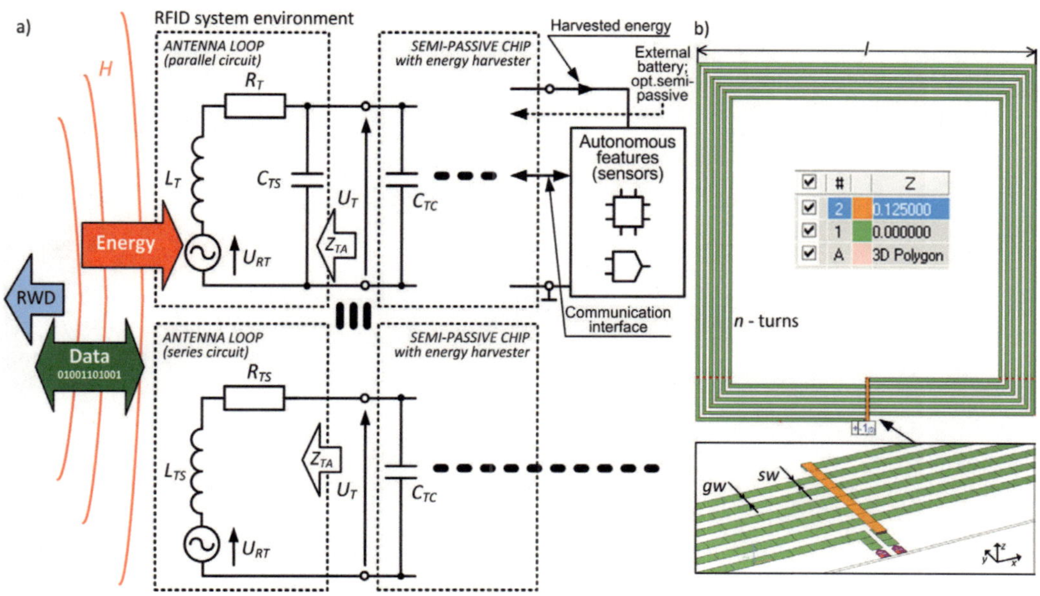

Figure 13. HF RFID semi-passive transponder: (a) diagram of antenna circuit and (b) HL3DEM design model.

environment. These operating principles concern the semi-passive transponders with the extra harvester that recovers energy from the magnetic field of RWD antenna. The harvested energy can be accumulated and used for powering blocks of additional autonomous functions.

The flexible square antenna synthesized in the research is dedicated to the STM M24LR16E-R transponder chip [53]. The selected chip operates according to the communication protocol ISO/IEC15693. The presented design is a development base for flexible construction of autonomous semi-passive transponders dedicated to operation in anti-collision dynamic RFID systems (works conducted as a part of the grant PBS1/A3/3/2012).

The numerical model of loop antenna (**Figure 13b**) was developed in the HL3DEM. The project was prepared for the selected DuPont Kapton HN-500 substrate (thickness 125 μm, relative permittivity 3.5, loss tangent 0.0026) and the Harima NPS-J silver nanoparticle ink (thickness for three layers: 3 μm, resistance: 3 μΩ·cm). The calculation of model parameters were carried out to obtain the parallel resonance between the L_{TS} and the C_{TC} at the f_0 = 13.56 MHz.

The test antenna (**Figure 14a**) was realized practically by using PixDro LP50 inkjet printing system (**Figure 14b**). The results of measurements and calculations were compared, and usefulness of the developed antennas in flexible RFID transponders was confirmed (**Table 1**). The prefabricated samples of antennas can operate correctly in the inhomogeneous magnetic field of RFID system and can be matched to any HF RFID chip in both communication and energy aspects.

3.4. Determining impedance parameters for RFID antennas

Measurements of antenna parameters pose a considerable problem in the RFID technology [39, 45, 46, 48, 54]. For this reason, in the paper [55], the authors were paid particular attention

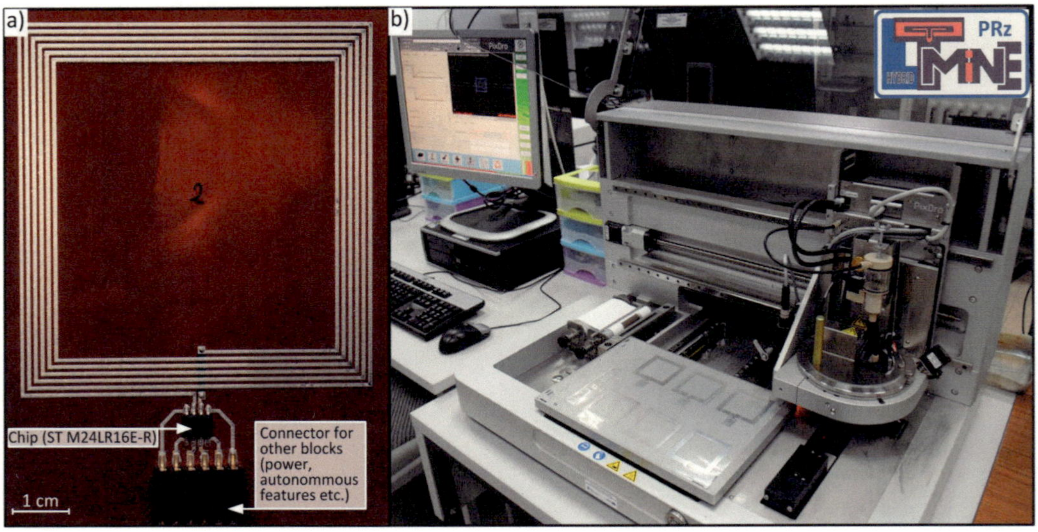

Figure 14. HF RFID semi-passive transponder: (a) sample and (b) inkjet printing stand in the authors' HYBRID laboratory at DETS in RUT.

Calculation/measurement	R_{TS}, Ω	L_{TS}, μH	sw, mm	gw, mm
HL3DEM model (calculation)	39.3	5.04	0.60	0.60
Sample #1 (measurement)	46.5	5.50	0.69	0.65
Sample #2 (measurement)	39.5	5.52	0.73	0.58
Sample #3 (measurement)	35.8	5.48	0.73	0.61
Sample #4 (measurement)	35.3	5.46	0.70	0.63
Sample #5 (measurement)	35.5	5.49	0.75	0.58
Sample #6 (measurement)	41.0	5.48	0.73	0.61
Sample #7 (measurement)	51.1	5.51	0.81	0.52

Table 1. Example results.

to this subject. Such kinds of investigations have to be realized by using two ports of VNA and dedicated passive differential probe (PDP). Since the measuring procedures and estimated parameters are strongly depended on the frequency band (LF/HF/UHF), operating conditions, type of the element (transponder or RWD) and its antenna designs, the appropriate verification on the base of properly conducted experiments is a crucial stage. Accordingly, a systematized procedure of impedance measurements is proposed in [55]. It can be easily implemented by designers preparing antennas for different kinds of RFID applications. It should be emphasized that precise values of antenna parameters are essential for estimating the interrogation zone which is the main parameter that describes an RFID system in its target application and also which is very sensitive to errors made in the design stage.

The RWD antenna together with transponder antennas comprises a radio communication arrangement that has to be wave- and impedance-matched. It should be emphasized that the classical impedance matching of a transmitter and receiver is established only between the RWD output and connected antenna (**Figure 15**).

During antenna synthesis (for both components: transponders and RWDs) in the inductively coupled systems, the measurement problem is mainly related to determining parameters of a symmetrical (with respect to ground) antenna loop with an impedance Z_L which is different from the typical value of 50 Ω. This impedance can be expressed by formula:

$$Z_L = R_S + j\omega L_S \tag{8}$$

where R_S and L_S denote the serial resistance and the inductance of the loop antenna and $\omega = 2\pi f_0$ describes the pulsation.

Correct specification of the loop parameters has significant influence on next stages of the synthesis. In the RWD, the results are necessary for designing a construction of impedance matching circuit [56–60] whereas in the transponders for determining a parallel resonance between an antenna and a chip [45, 61–64].

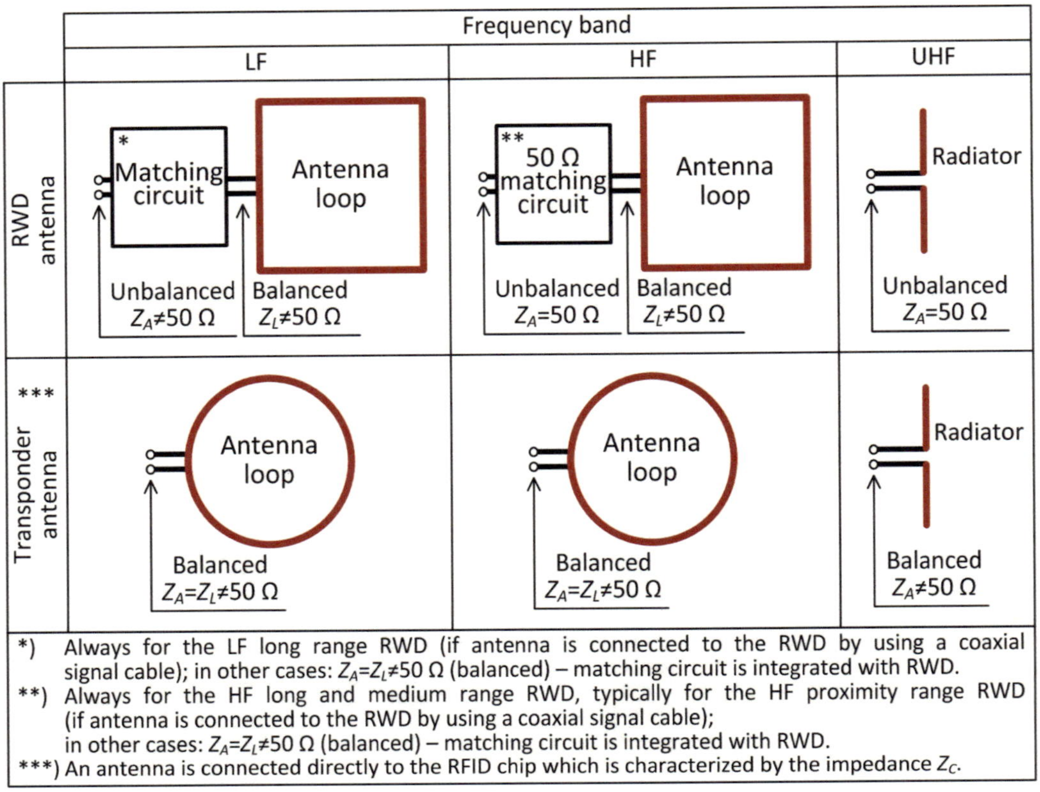

Figure 15. Antenna constructions for RFID devices.

In the RFID systems of the UHF band, the measurement problem concerns transponders and consists in the necessity of determining impedance that is different from the common value of 50 Ω. This impedance can be described as:

$$Z_A = R_A + jX_A \tag{9}$$

where R_A i X_A denote the resistance and the reactance of the transponder antenna.

The impedance parameters mentioned in [55] that are determined in each of described frequency bands (LF, HF and UHF) are essential for estimating energy and communication conditions of RFID systems. The energy conditions influence the amount of energy conveyed from the RWD to transponders. The communications conditions have an effect on efficiency of data transmission by wireless medium.

In LF systems, the typical RLC bridge working at the given frequency band can be used for measuring parameters of antenna loops. The measurement problem is more complicated in the HF and UHF bands. Two nonsymmetrical 50 Ω ports (P1, P2) of a vector network analyzer and PDP probes (**Figure 16**) have to be used in the experimental procedure. The procedure consists in realization of indirect differential measurement of impedance parameters: balanced

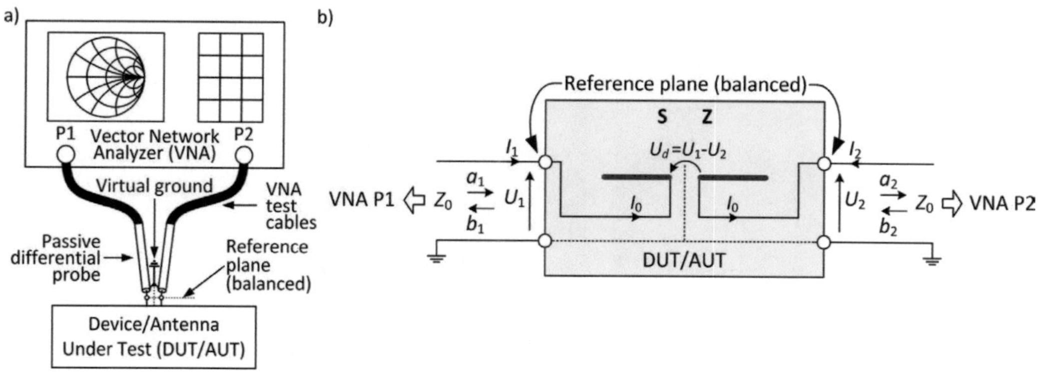

Figure 16. Test stand: (a) block diagram and (b) measurement model.

Device Under Test (DUT) or Antenna Under Test (AUT)—with respect to a kind of device under the test: antenna or its part. The differential measuring technique cannot be applied to RWD antennas of the UHF band because their impedance is matched to the typical value of 50 Ω. In such a case, the tests are realized by using just the one nonsymmetrical port of VNA.

The ports of VNA play function of a signal transmitter or receiver. The function can be distinguished on the basis of estimated scattering matrix **S**. The DUT/AUT separation from connection wires is provided by the differential probe. It makes possible to connect test samples to the measurement equipment. The probes should be matched to tested samples individually because of the diversity types and designs of antennas [39, 46–48, 54].

Measurements of the scattering matrix **S** does not provide immediate readout of the impedance parameters (8) or (9) in DUT/AUT cases. The dependence of the differential impedance Z_d has to be used, and it is discussed in [55]:

$$Z_d = 2\,Z_0 \frac{S_{12}\,S_{21} - S_{11}\,S_{22} - S_{12} - S_{21} + 1}{(1 - S_{11})(1 - S_{22}) - S_{12}\,S_{21}} \tag{10}$$

The problem is crucial in the context of measuring various antenna structures since they work in both transponders and RWD devices and in the LF, HF and UHF bands.

The impedance measurement problem in the RFID technique can be discussed on the basis of practical implementations of various antenna constructions which are made in the PCB technology (**Figure 17**). The investigation can be done for example on the test stand presented in **Figure 18**. The measurement results are compared with numerical data obtained for models in the HL3DEM software. They show a satisfactory convergence, so the presented procedures can be easily implemented during designing new RFID systems.

3.5. Determining the radiation pattern of UHF RFID transponder

The antenna radiation pattern is one of the basic parameters that are required to evaluate the usefulness of a given radio communications system. The typical hardware and software

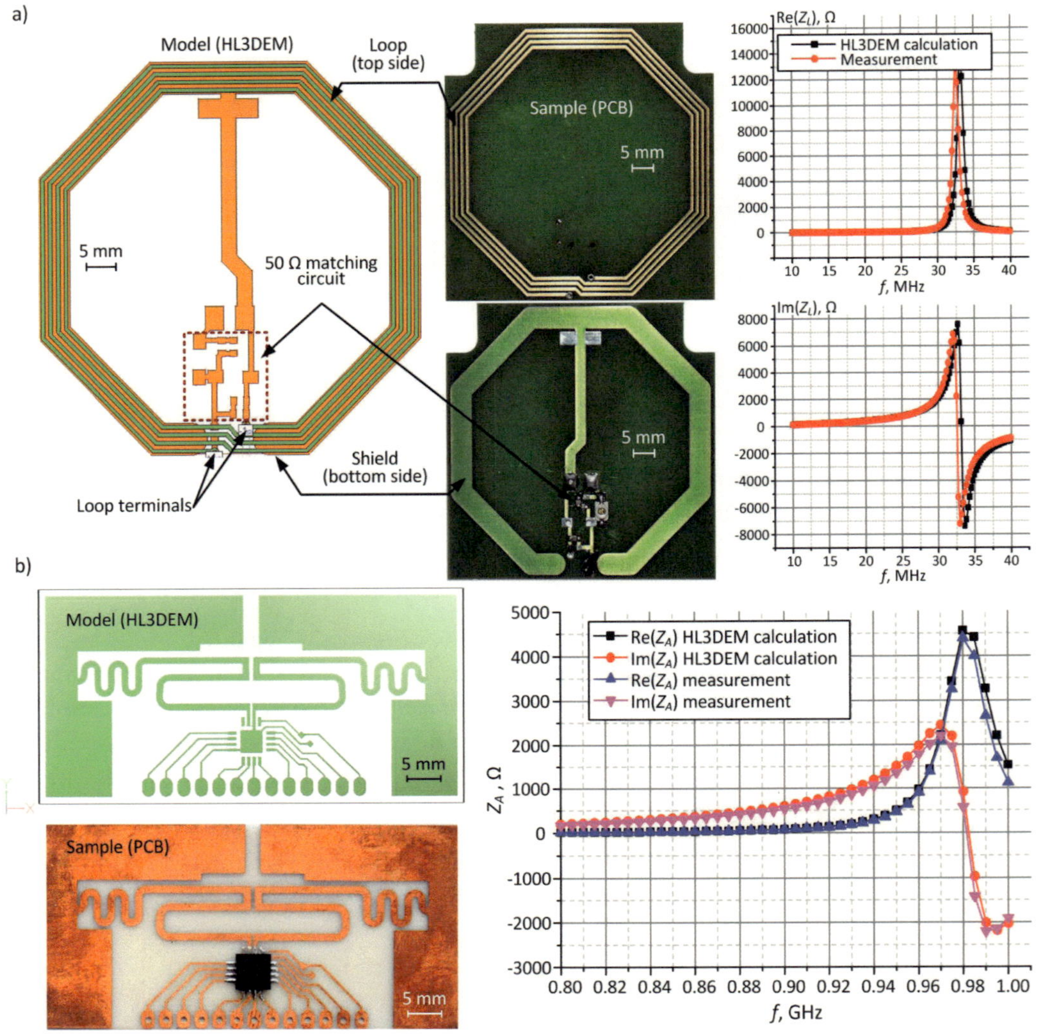

Figure 17. Examples: (a) HF RWD antenna and (b) UHF transponder antenna.

configuration of measurement systems can be applied to determine the radiation pattern of most antennas that are commonly used in DVB-T, GSM, UMTS, LTE or WiFi and others [65]. They can also be adapted to new antenna constructions [66] as well as to new implementations of common antennas in wireless communications [67]. But there is a problem in the case of RFID systems operating in the UHF band. It is impossible to determine the radiation pattern of RFID transponders by using the standard laboratory stands and measurement methods. The problem consists in impedance matching of an antenna and a chip. A complex impedance of RF front end varies, while the transponder chip is working and its value is dependent on the electromagnetic field parameters (the electromagnetic field in RFID systems is influenced by environmental conditions around marked objects).

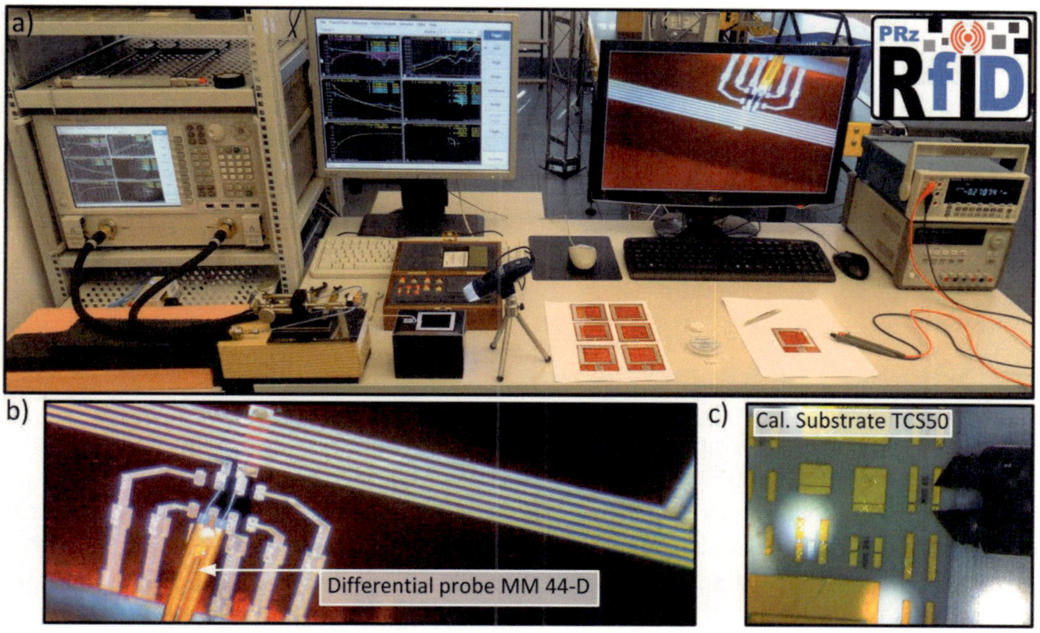

Figure 18. Measurement process: (a) antenna measurement stand in the authors' RFID laboratory at DETS in RUT, (b) differential probe fixed to terminals, and (c) calibration set of test stand.

It is the reason why the classical theory of antennas cannot be applied to solve the matching problem and new measurement methods have to be developed in order to determine the parameters of RFID antennas. A measurement process in which the nature of a UHF RFID transponder (the variable impedance of the chip) is taken into consideration is seldom described in the branch literature. In one of the encountered solutions, authors use very expensive apparatus dedicated only to the intended aim [68]. In another proposal, supplementary (e.g., movable) antennas are implemented [69], but the described experiment is highly complicated and additional measurement uncertainties have to be taken into consideration. With regard to the endeavors made to solve the abovementioned problems, the authors worked out a universal method of the radiation pattern determination and described it in detail in the paper [70]. The elaborated measurement stands are supplemented with cheap and commercially available RFID devices, and some own control and data-acquisition software procedures. The additional benefit of the proposed method is that the radiation pattern can be determined just for a transponder as well as for a whole electronically marked object. The second option is particularly useful when the efficiency of identification process in automated systems and implementation or maintenance costs are considered.

The main requirement for measurements to be carried out in a proper way is to maintain the constant value of the impedance Z_{TC} (Z_{TCR} without modulation), while polar diagrams of the radiation pattern (according to θ and φ angles of the spherical coordinate system) are being determined (**Figure 4**). The measuring procedure has to be conducted when the transponder is placed inside the interrogation zone of an RFID system (when the energy and communication conditions of transponder operation are met). The test conditions can be controlled only at the IZ boundary. In the developed method, the authors propose to perform it by changing the power P_{RWD} supplied to the terminals of the impedance-matched RWD antenna.

Power received in the transponder antenna equals the minimal value P_{Tmin} if the terminals of the impedance-matched RWD antenna are supplied with the minimal energy P_{RWDmin}. It allows the transponder to be properly supplied (in given environmental conditions) according to the relation:

$$P_{T\min} = P_{RWD\min} \frac{G_R G_T \lambda^2 \tau \chi}{(4\pi r)^2} \tag{11}$$

The (11) dependency is crucial for the IZ boundary determination where the impedance Z_{TC} is equal to $Z_{TCR}=f(P_{Tmin})$ [34]. This impedance is obtained on the basis of communication protocol in the task process where the transponder sends its unique identification number (Unique Identifier (UID)) as an answer to a *Query* command from the RWD [29]. The requirement of maintaining the constant value of the chip impedance that is met when the condition $P_T = P_{Tmin}$ is true for any variation of θ and φ angles at constant distance r is fundamental for the authors' method of measuring the radiation pattern (**Figure 19**).

Since the chip impedance is complex (≠50 Ω), the radiation pattern is determined wirelessly. It means that signal paths of measuring devices do not have to be connected to the transponder chip by wires and the radiation plots can also be drawn for electronically marked objects. The test procedure is performed in an anechoic chamber equipped with an AUT positioner, linear polarized RWD antenna with mast and digital controller. A small anechoic chamber can be chosen for the test purposes [71] according to the dimensions of transponders and their operating frequency band. The amount of power conveyed to the tested transponders can be controlled by the RWD and an output attenuator. The normalized radiation pattern (in dB) is determined on the basis of the following dependency:

$$F_{Tn\,dB}(\theta,\phi) = \left[P_{RWD\,dBm}(\theta,\phi)\right]_{\min} - P_{RWD\,dBm}(\theta,\phi) \tag{12}$$

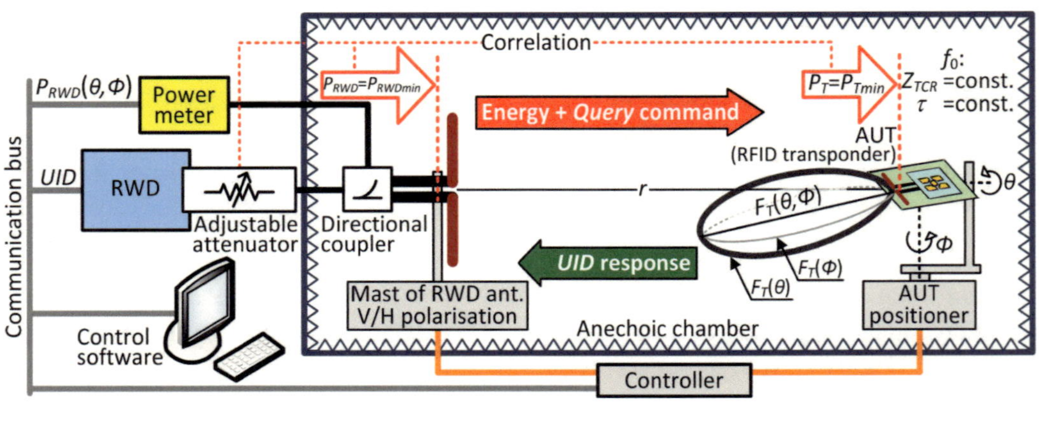

Figure 19. Block diagram of the proposed method for measuring the radiation pattern.

where P_{RWDdBm} means the measured power in dBm (by using a scope probe, spectrum analyzer, etc.), whereas index "min" refers to the minimal value of this parameter.

The elaborated conception can be verified and developed in a typical RFID laboratory (**Figure 20**). The common components of radio communication test sets (anechoic chambers, positioners, etc.) that are typically dedicated to measure radiation patterns of standard antennas can be used to build up the new stands for the method proposed by the authors. In addition, commercially available and relatively cheap RFID devices (in relation to the equipment for common antenna tests) can be implemented in the stand with the aim of adjusting the RF laboratory to the proposed research. Nevertheless, research investigators have to design control procedures in order to adapt the apparatus to the scheduled tests (the special LabView program entitled *RFID(UHF)SysAntPat* was prepared by the authors in their RFID laboratory).

The elaborated conception was verified and developed by the authors in experimental tests on two examples: omnidirectional and directorial antenna, designed especially for commercial RFID chips. In order to evaluate the obtained results, the radiation pattern was measured twice: using the authors' conception and the classical method (**Figure 21**), in the same experimental conditions. The results of measurements and calculations obtained in both the experiments are convergent for the V as well as H planes of the radiation pattern. It confirms the usefulness of the developed method.

3.6. Synthesis of RWD antennas

The synthesis process of the three-dimensional interrogation zone is to a large extent determined by an RWD antenna, since the device generates the electromagnetic field, which constitutes a source of energy and a medium for two-directional data transmission in an RFID system. The authors conducted a synthesis of RWD antennas for the HF [54] and UHF [72] band. The issue was considered in a view of: (1) proximity range (means the transmission distance up to about a dozen centimeters with a separation of the near-field communication scope in the HF band, where the transmission distance is up to about few centimeters), (2) medium range (means the distance ofseveral dozen) and (3) long range (means the distance to a few meters).

The effective synthesis process of a complete RF output circuit in a proximity-range single RFID system with inductive coupling is presented in [54]. The paper also incorporates problems connected with designing read/write devices that are constructed on the basis of integrated circuits (ICs) from different manufacturers. The presented method can be applied to any process of automatic identification requiring the proximity-range RFID system operating at the frequency of 13.56 MHz and using one of the suitable communication protocols (e.g., ISO/IEC 14443, 15693).

In generalized form, the antenna unit can be represented by a combination of: loop- and impedance-matching components as well as an EMC filter and a signal detection circuit for data transmission in transponder—RWD direction (**Figure 22**). This diagram is adequate for any antenna system design solution in which there is a necessity to separate its individual modules by using wire connectors. On its basis, it is possible to synthesize the effective antenna that can work with the integrated circuit such as: TRF7960, CLRC632, EM4094, AT88RF1354, AS3910 and many others.

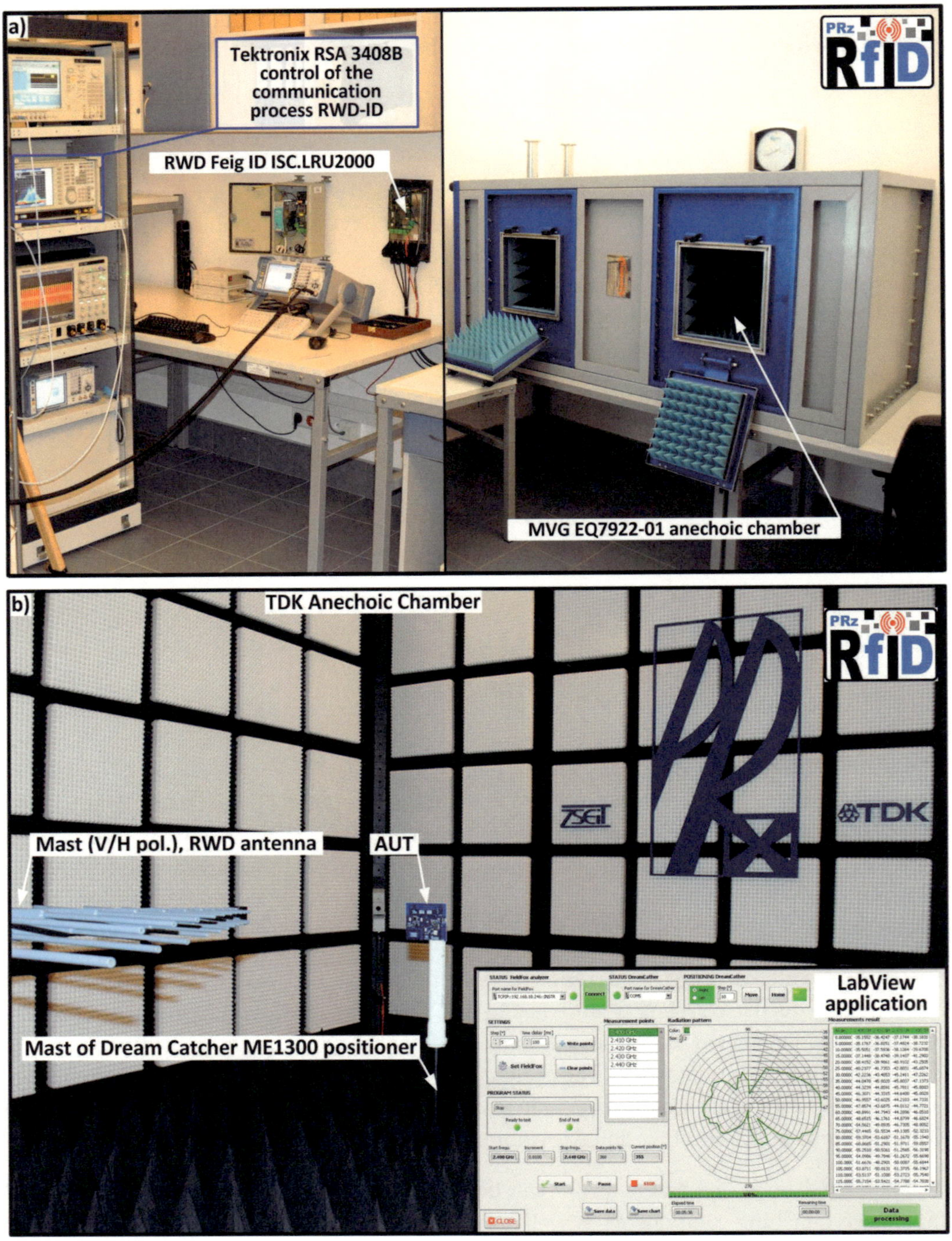

Figure 20. Test stands in the authors' RFID laboratory at DETS in RUT: (a) laboratory room with MVG anechoic chamber and (b) laboratory room with TDK anechoic chamber.

The proper use of the RWD antenna requires a connection of unmatched (in impedance and wave conditions) antenna loop to a symmetric (with respect to ground) input with mismatched impedance in the read/write device (TX1-TVSS-TX2). It is realized by using a coaxial

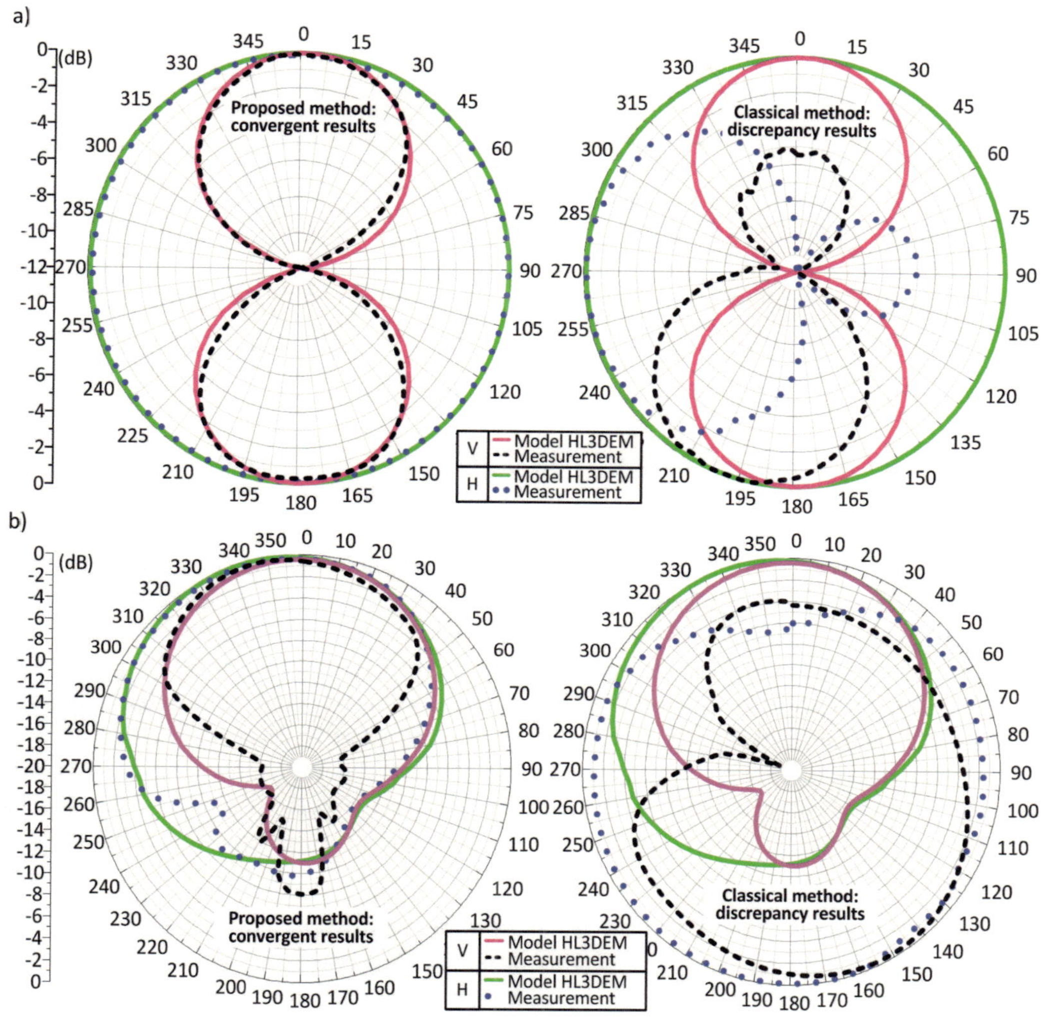

Figure 21. Experimental verification: (a) measurements by using system located in the MVG chamber—Sample #1 and (b) measurements by using system located in the TDK chamber—Sample #2.

signal cable with the wave impedance of $Z_C = 50\ \Omega$ as well as by a symmetric EMC filter on the RWD side and an asymmetric matching circuit on the side of the antenna loop. The both systems can be connected by a balancing transformer with configuration 4:1 (200 Ω / 50 Ω), where a turns ratio is equal $n = 2$.

The impedance matching circuit of the antenna loop consists of a capacitive divider C_{R1}, C_{R2}. It is integrated with a resistance R_{RA} which lowers a Q_R factor of the RWD antenna. The *Q*factor cannot exceed the maximum value Q_{Rmax} which directly results from the data rate required by a communication protocol. If values of the *Q*factor are smaller than the maximum Q_{Rmax}, the RWD device is more resistance to detuning due to, for example, environmental influences. However, it reduces the size of the interrogation zone and thus limits the usefulness of the designed RFID system in which there is usual tendency to obtain the maximum distance for recording or reading information to or from a transponder memory.

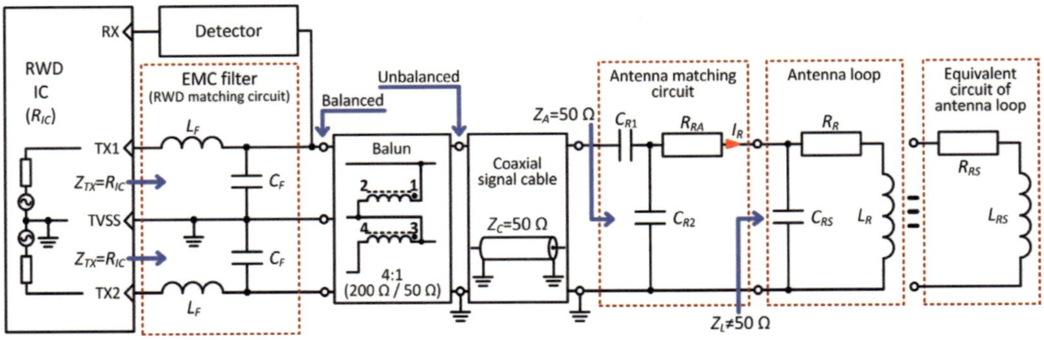

Figure 22. Generalized block diagram of an antenna unit connected to an HF RWD.

A circuit of the symmetric low-pass EMC filter (L_F, C_F) serves an additional function of impedance matching Z_{TX} to an IC input. The impedance value depends on the type of chip and should be only the real part (close to the required value of R_{IC}). It ensures the effective transfer of power from the circuit of RWD to its antenna. Besides the impedance matching, the EMC filter has to ensure an elimination of higher harmonics during energy transmission, improve signal-to-noise ratio for transmission between a transponder and a read/write device and also improve conditions for transferring data to a transponder. The resonant frequency f_{EMC} should be also taken into consideration in design process. The required value of the frequency f_{EMC} results from the signal spectrum for subcarrier modulation. In this process, the transmitted information should be recovered from the side bands. The frequencies of the side bands are strictly defined according to the used communication protocol (e.g., f_0/16, 32, 64 gives approximately 847, 424, 212 kHz, and so on). For example, if the bit rate equals 106 kb/s, the frequency of the filter is f_{EMC} = 14.4 MHz (13.6 MHz + 847.5 kHz).

The circuit of signal detection is the last module presented in the **Figure 22**. It is used for detecting data received from a transponder. This module is characteristic for the IC, and therefore, the detailed electronic diagram is not specified. It must be emphasized that the proper design of the whole circuit connected with energy transfer from the RWD to the transponder is very important in determination of the interrogation zone of a read/write device especially that works in the near field of the HF band. If the specificities of each discussed element are correctly taken into consideration, the proper synthesis of the magnetic field is possible. Then, any implementation process of identifying any object at a distance of several centimeters from the antenna system of RWD is feasible.

The octagonal antenna was synthesized in order to verify the presented experimental method (**Figure 17a**). The antenna is dedicated to a multiprotocol circuit of a read/write device of the proximity-range RFID system in the HF band. The typical two-sided FR-4 laminate is used to prepare the model and test antenna. The shield connected to ground is placed on the bottom layer. The antenna has four terns that are located on the opposite side of the laminate. The shield covers the area of the antenna loop, and its main function is to separate the electronic system from the magnetic field supplying a passive RFID transponder. The distribution of current values that confirms this function is presented in **Figure 23a**. The obtained value of the return loss (**Figure 23b**) confirms the full antenna impedance matching to the designed circuit of RWD.

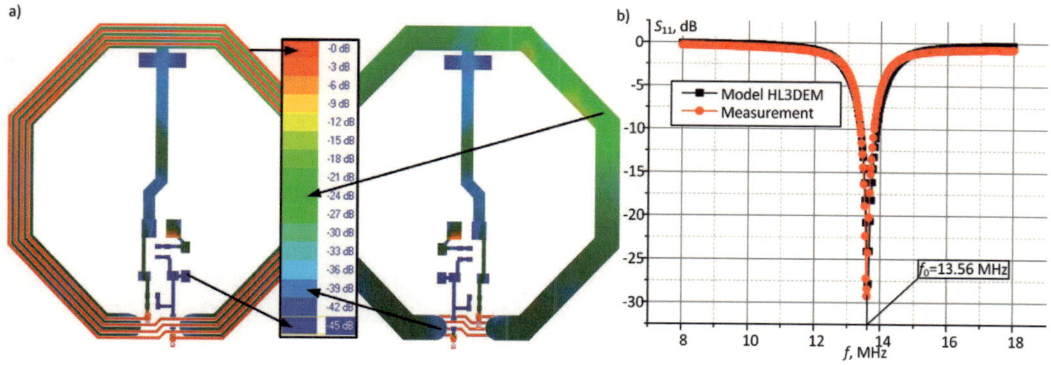

Figure 23. Experimental results: (a) 3D current distribution and (b) return loss.

3.7. Model of antenna radiation pattern

Possibly the best choice of appropriate devices which enable efficient realization of an automated process constitutes an essential stage with regard to implementing an RFID system. However, the devices are selected to the applications with respect to availability in the market and economic aspects. Then, predictability of the three-dimensional interrogation zone comes down to basic analytical or numerical calculations, or sophisticated computer simulations since it is conducted by using a few elementary parameters that are described in product specifications. With regard to selection of UHF transponders or RWD antennas, a radiation pattern constitutes the crucial parameter. From a practical point of view, there is a problem to transform—in easy way—available plots of the radiation patterns (e.g., presented in an antenna datasheet) to analytical dependences or discrete data required for numerical calculations of radio wave propagation.

On the basis of available subject literature, it can be stated that there is the need for developing simple tools by means of which it would be possible to generate a numerical representation of the radiation pattern for a real antenna. For this reason, a numerical model of the directional radiation pattern in which part of energy emitted in side and back lobs is taken into consideration is discussed in the chapter [64]. The authors present the useful software tools (*NmAntPat*) that generate the numerical data on the basis of parameters that can be read from the antenna datasheets. The output file can be easily implemented into an analysis of radio wave propagation phenomenon in any algorithms and numerical calculations. The results of the work are confirmed on the example of real antenna that can be applied in read/write devices working in the UHF band of RFID system.

The essence of the model of directional radiation pattern consists in the power gain diagram G calculation conducted in vertical (θ) or horizontal (φ) plane. It is represented by the function *NmAntPat*:

$$G(\theta, \phi) = NmAntPat\begin{pmatrix} G_0, HPBW, HPBW_{back}, \\ FS, FB, FB_{rest}, n_{side}, n_{back}, \\ ANG, TILT \end{pmatrix} \tag{13}$$

Basic parameters of the modeled antenna are input arguments of the function *NmAntPat*: G_0—maximum value of the gain (dBi), *HPBW*—half-power beam width of the main lobe (°), $HPBW_{back}$—half-power beam width of the main back lobe (°), *FS*—front-to-side ratio (dB), *FB*—front-to-back ratio (dB), FB_{rest}—front-to-back ratio of the back lobes (dB), n_{side}—number of the side lobes (equal distribution in the range from 0° to 180°), n_{back}—number of the back lobes (equal distribution in the range from 180° to 360°), *ANG*—variable θ in vertical or φ in horizontal plane (from 0° to 360°) and *TILT*—tilting of the pattern (°).

The *NmAntPat* program implemented in the Mathcad environment not only visualizes the radiation patterns but also generates files for subsequent data processing (**Figure 24**). A user may select any format that is typical for data of this kind. It is useful during further analysis of radio wave propagation phenomena. So, it can be utilized in any user algorithm, freeware or commercial platform. The main software procedure *NmAntPat* comprises the derived dependences (13). An additional procedure is used for calculating and visualizing values of every lobe levels. It simplifies the approximation of modeled radiation pattern.

A real antenna of read/write device (Feig ID ISC.ANTU250/250 in EU version [73]) working in the UHF band of RFID system can be used to present the problem of radiation pattern

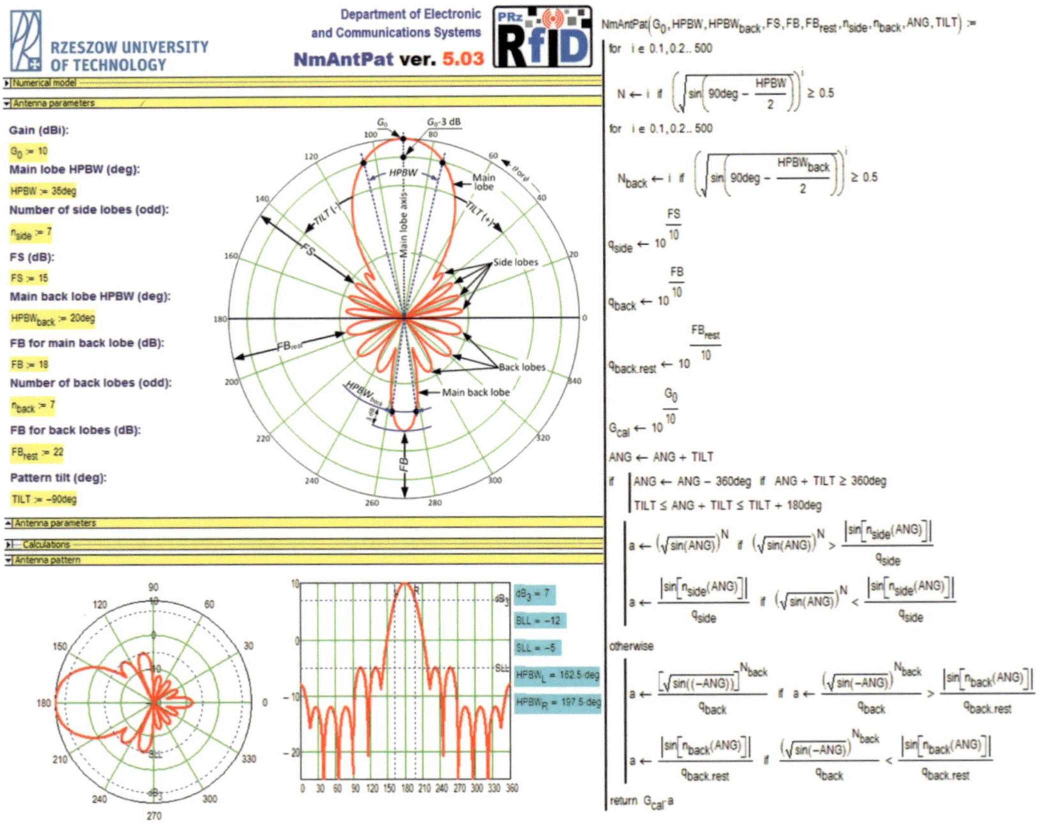

Figure 24. NmAntPat program and its numerical procedure.

synthesis. The comparing chart of directional radiation patterns is presented in **Figure 25**: the first diagram is calculated from producer's datasheet, and the second one—on the basis of measured data. The measurements were carried out in the TDK anechoic chamber by using the MI Technologies antenna system.

The both presented cases give satisfactory results and convergence of the determined radiation pattern. It shows the practical utility of the developed model and software tools. The preparatory studies revealed vagueness of data specification notes published by manufacturers for their products. The lack of important parameter values makes a radio communication system synthesis (e.g., interrogation zone in RFID system) very difficult, and shared information is not sufficient to reproduce the characteristics of the antenna. But an accurate analysis of the specified radiation pattern can lead to determine missing input data for proper implementation of antennas in a real environment.

3.8. Autonomous semi-passive RFID transponder

The problems discussed so far constituted a base for a conception and implementation of a new idea in the field of RFID technology that is presented in publication [44] and partially in [45, 46] (most of this work was supported by the Polish National Centre for Research and Development (NCBR) under Grant No. PBS1/A3/3/2012 entitled "*Synthesis of autonomous semi-passive transponder dedicated to operation in antic-collision dynamic RFID systems*").

A small application area of commercial semi-passive transponders compared to the passive constructions is due to disadvantages of the electrochemical cells. The commonly used batteries have a limited lifetime decreasing in harsh environmental conditions (e.g., in low temperature ambient), restricted ability to supply a load with short high-power pulses, or they have to be replaced after discharge or protected against theft and so on. Because of these drawbacks, the rare semi-passive RFID systems are expensive in production and maintenance, not stable

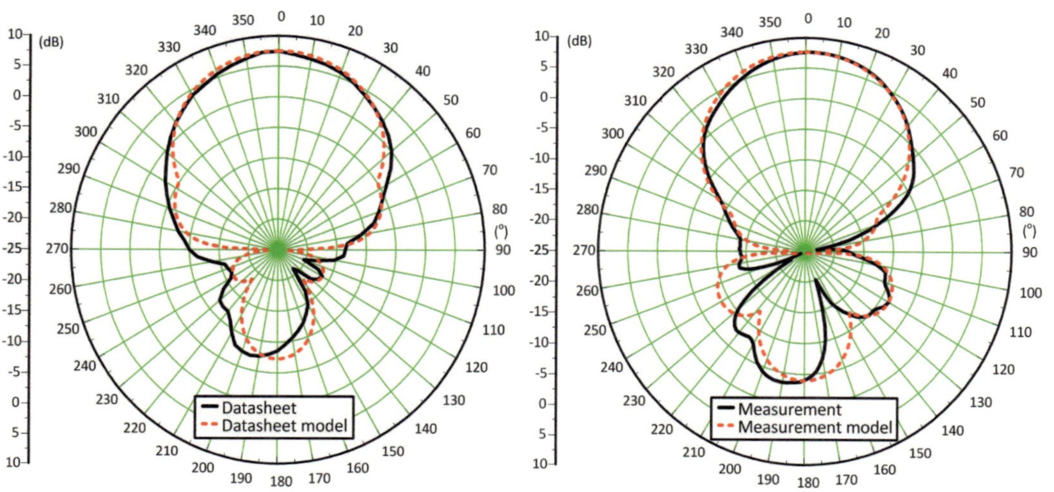

Figure 25. Comparing chart of the directional radiation patterns.

and do not provide a high level of identification efficiency. To cope with these inconveniences, the authors work out the multiband development board dedicated to battery-less autonomous semi-passive RFID transponders in which extra functions of energy harvesting from the electromagnetic field of different radio communication systems as well as a dedicated power conditioner and an energy storage block are implemented. The proposed idea contributes significantly to the development of automatic identification (**Figure 26**).

The beginning stage of the progress in the identification system—optical machine-readable barcodes—provides only basic and unchangeable information about marked objects (**Figure 26**). The recognition process can be realized only with a single object simultaneously, and the barcode has to be visible to a reader. Currently, passive and semi-passive (but not autonomous) RFID transponders are beginning more and more popular and they mark a new stage in the advancement of object identification. They can be not only read, but also it is possible to change stored data during operational use of the systems as well as their configuration or maintenance and so on. Moreover, some user's extension information is written into a tag memory and a read/write process can be realized simultaneously with several transponders (anti-collision identification) without optical visibility.

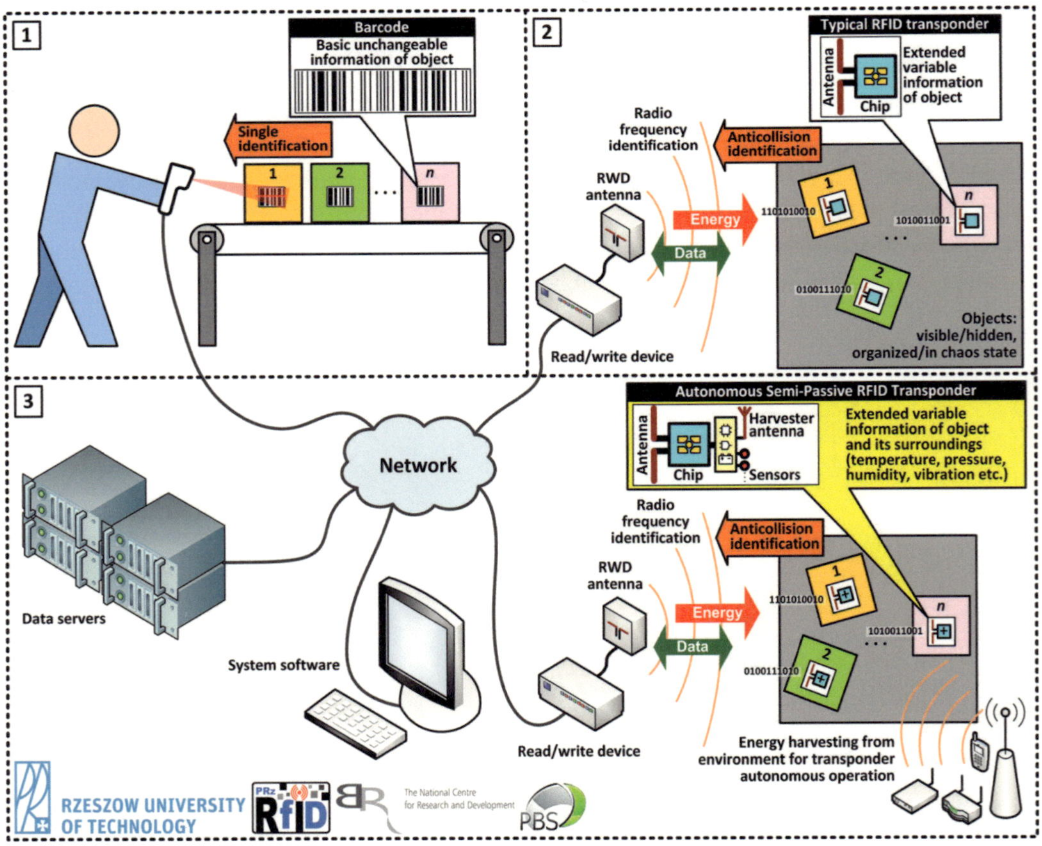

Figure 26. Development stages of automatic object identification systems.

The author's developed idea [44] helps to open a new chapter in the automatic object identification. In the third stage, the RFID transponders provide not only details about marked objects but also extended variable data gathered from surrounding by built-in sensors of different physical quantities. Moreover, the transponders are developed toward the capability of being powered from the electromagnetic field of common radio communication systems. In this case, an internal supply block consists of an energy harvester integrated with an RF frontend and an advanced low-voltage regulator supported by a super-capacitor. The element that stores environmental energy is free of drawbacks and limitations that are inherent for the traditional galvanic cells [74, 75]. The super-capacitors are maintenance free, with low degree of wear. Their high capacity at their small dimensions bridges the gap between possibilities of electrolytic capacitors and rechargeable batteries—significant amount of energy can be released with high volume power [76].

Another important problem is to provide suitable conditions for charging the untypical power source of the autonomous semi-passive transponders. There are examples of effective using electromechanical, thermal or photovoltaic transducers [77, 78] for obtaining energy from the environment. But in the view of RFID system operation principles, the electromagnetic field generated by radio communication systems (e.g., base transceiver stations of the wireless communication technologies like GSM, wireless local loop, Wi-Fi, WiMAX or other wide area networks) that are present almost in every place on the Earth is a more natural source. The choice of electromagnetic waves as the medium of conveying power in the proposed autonomous development board follows the new solutions that appear in RFID chips of semi-passive transponders—a few producers offer the possibility to split energy supplied by the RWD to the chip between the internal communication transceiver and additional blocks, for example, sensors, analog-to-digital converters, external outputs, and so on [34, 46].

The proposed research conception will hopefully make a real contribution toward easing integration of low-power devices in the transponder structure, and it allows the semi-passive transponders to be fully autonomous. In fact, it should be stated that commercial potential of such possibilities is described in the literature, but its practical usefulness in RFID system applications is significantly restricted by the described drawbacks of galvanic cells that are presently in use.

In initially pursued conceptual and designing works, the authors started research that was pertinent to modification and extension of a well-known structure of passive RFID transponders (III stage of a cycle in the advancement of object identification—**Figure 26**) [79]. A particular attention was drawn to characteristics and determining parameters that influence an interrogation zone in RFID systems modified in this way. In this context, in publication [46], a model and practical construction of an HF RFID transponder was put forward, in which new utility functions were implemented (**Figure 27**).

The efficiency estimation of energy transmission from RWD to passive transponder is very complicated for wireless medium—magnetic field in the HF band, especially in proposed solution with autonomous features (e.g., module for measuring physical quantities). Since the extra electronic circuits disturb the proper operation of transponder, the careful study of its impact on main parameters is compulsory. This problem is explained in detail on the elaborated model

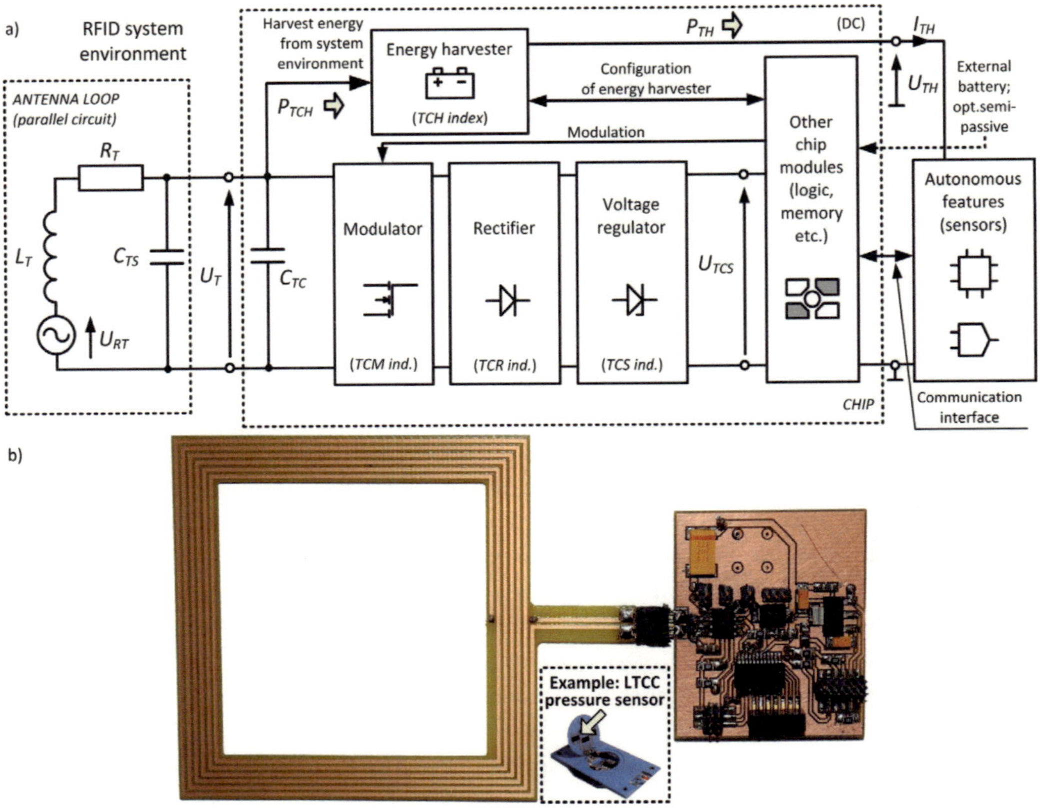

Figure 27. HF RFID transponder with autonomous features: (a) model and (b) practical realization.

of a passive transponder with the active build-in block for harvesting energy from the RFID system environment. It includes all blocks of real solution: loop antenna, chip with extra energy harvester and in addition microprocessor for controlling autonomous features. Since an antenna set of a proximity or long-range RWD device is assumed as an element of the model, the considerations are suitable for the active transponder located in a $P(x, y, z)$ point of the Cartesian coordinate system. System performance and all parameters can be described with appropriate analytical relationships. The correctness of the developed model was confirmed on the basis of calculated and measured (in practical HF RFID application, by control and measurement instruments of RFID laboratory at DETS in RUT) results and presented in [46]. The developed methodology for testing passive and semi-passive transponders with harvester that derives energy from RFID system environment is the key approach to determine the tree-dimensional interrogation zone for both single and anti-collision RFID systems.

A practical flexible construction of an HF RFID transponder in which new usage functions were implemented (**Figure 28**) was proposed in publication [45]. Temperature change is one of the key factors which should be taken into account in logistics during transportation or storage of many types of goods. In this study, a passive UHF RFID-enabled sensor system for elevated temperature (above 58°C) detection was demonstrated. This system consisted

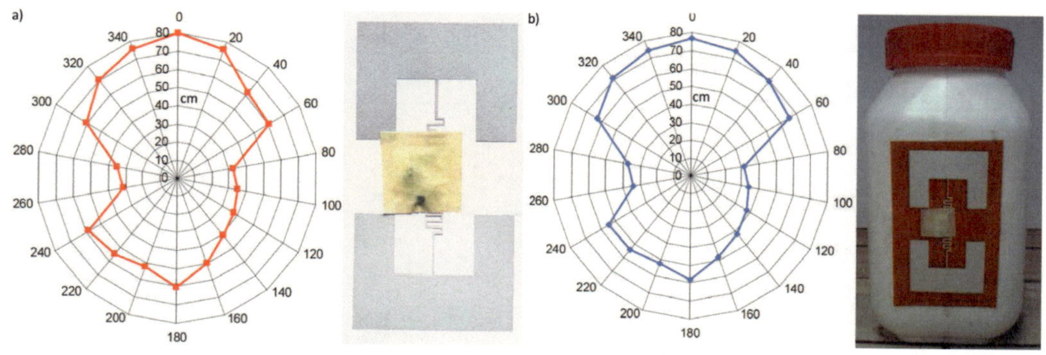

Figure 28. Transponder-sensor with the UHF RFID interface and example results of IZ border: (a) paper substrate and (b) Kapton substrate.

of an RWD and disposable temperature sensor comprising an UHF antenna, RFID chip and temperature-sensitive unit. The UHF antenna was designed and simulated in the HL3DEM software. The properties of the system were examined depending on the temperature level, kind of object package and type of substrate, on which the flexible structure of an UHF RFID transponder-sensor has been prepared.

Finally, the proposed conception was realized under the Polish government project of the PBS1/A3/3/2012 number. The multiband development board of battery-less autonomous semi-passive RFID transponder was elaborated on the basis of worked-out assumptions. The electrical harvester from the electromagnetic field of different radio communications systems, sophisticated low voltage converter and low leakage energy storage were designed especially for the demonstrator (**Figure 29**).

The development board is equipped with two independent RFID interfaces—one of them operates in the HF band (ISOIEC15693 protocol) and the second in the UHF band (EPC Class 1 Gen 2 protocol consistent with ISOIEC18000-63). These blocks are designed on the basis of semi-passive chips that have additional wire serial peripheral buses for communications with a supervising controller (HF band: STM24LR64E chip with I2C bus; UHF band: AMSSL900A chip with SPI bus). Moreover, the both ICs can gather energy from the electromagnetic field generated by antennas of RWD, in their operating frequency bands. It means that the super-capacitor of the supply unit is charged whenever the demonstrator appears in the IZ. Of course, the communications in RFID system can be realized without regard to activities of the extra blocks.

The autonomy of the semi-passive transponder is achieved by applying a harvester that gathers environmental energy derived from radio communications system present in its current location. The antenna of special construction is designed for the presented demonstration board. It operates in the frequency band of 930–975 MHz and is matched to the input circuit of the Powercast P2110B harvester. The block provides the RF harvesting from GSM900, converts RF energy to DC and stores it in a capacitor. Also the power management for battery-free micropower devices is implemented. It is possible to measure the value of power at the input and to adjust how frequently the module is woken up depending on the existing energy

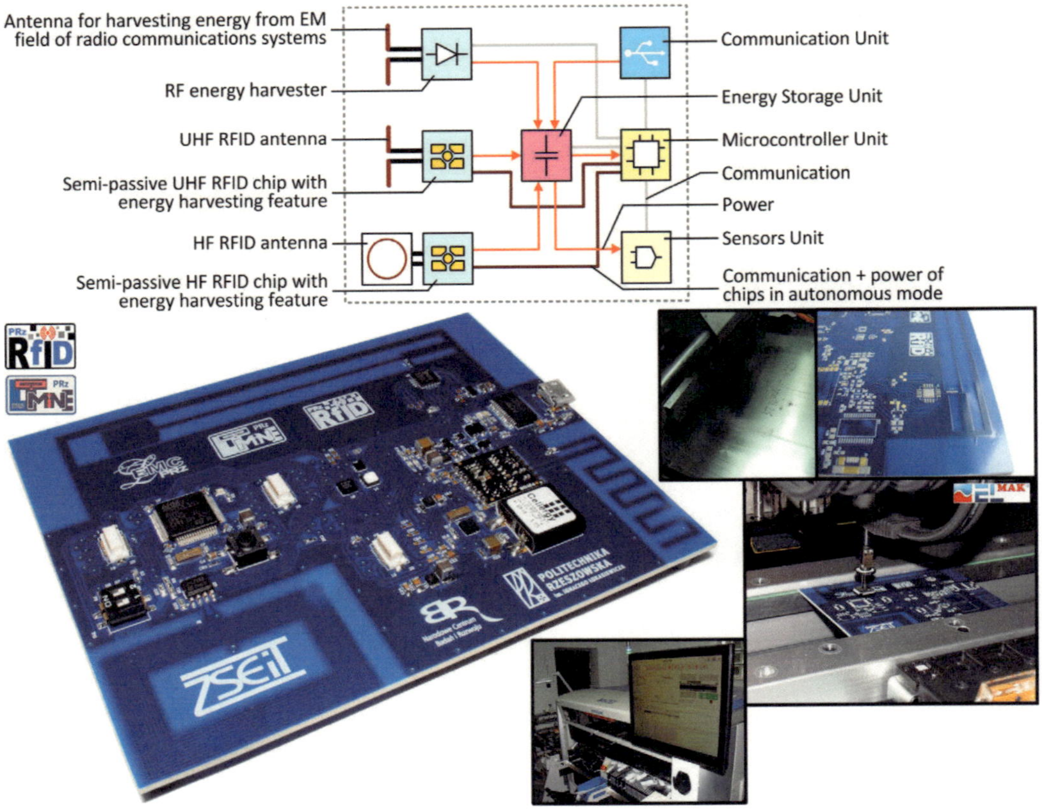

Figure 29. Elaborated development board (Polish government project no. PBS1/A3/3/2012).

conditions. The research and development cooperation with Powercast Company allows the authors to redesign the development board to another radio communication system (e.g., UMTS, LTE and WiFi).

The typical environmental RF energy source is characterized by low capacity, and it causes the necessity to design an ultra-efficient energy storage unit. Stored energy allows the demonstrator to work autonomously, and it is utilized to acquire information about surroundings of electronically market objects. It is achieved by measuring periodically physical quantities and storing results in the data memories of the RFID chips. The block of signal transducers and conditioning circuits is integrated in the module and consists of three-axis MEMS accelerometer (Analog Devices ADXL362), humidity and temperature sensor (Silicon Labs Si7020) and ambient light sensor (Maxim Integrated MAX44009). There is also possibility to connect external intelligent sensors by I2C bus, and it could be useful when the demonstrator is adjusted to future user's applications.

The demonstrator activity is controlled by the digital block that is designed on a basis of 32-bit microcontroller (STM32L151RBT6). The demonstration software is elaborated to support a future user in development works with the presented autonomous semi-passive transponder, and it can be adapted to target application requirements by USB interface.

The worked out development board allows potential users to start investigations and different application projects in the scope of both the object identification and the monitoring of environmental conditions. The undertaken enterprises should quickly lead the users to the product commercialization. In this context, the first preproduction batch was assembled in the production line of ELMAK Company. Also, the project concerning product potential in the market and the possibility of its commercialization as well as the estimation of decision-making determinants in the process of the transponder implementation in the Polish industry was realized [80, 81].

3.9. Synthesis of interrogation zone in RFID systems

The research on definition, characterization and determination of parameters for RFID devices available on the market or new developed designs that are continuously conducted by the authors led to prepare appropriate procedures and synthesis methods useful in the RFID technique. In this context, elements of algorithm for determining the 3D interrogation zone in an inductively coupled anti-collision RFID system are presented in the chapter [60]. The algorithm based on the Monte Carlo (MC) method and the computer program implemented in the Mathcad engineering calculation software is utilized in order to achieve the posed aims.

From a practical point of view of a planned implementation of anti-collision RFID systems, the most useful solution is to look for the interrogation zone with a given shape, position and orientation in space. The essence of its determination by the proposed method is presented in **Figure 30a**. In the conducted research, it is assumed that the demanded volume should be cube-shaped (of side b) and situated at the z_{ID} height, whereas its location should

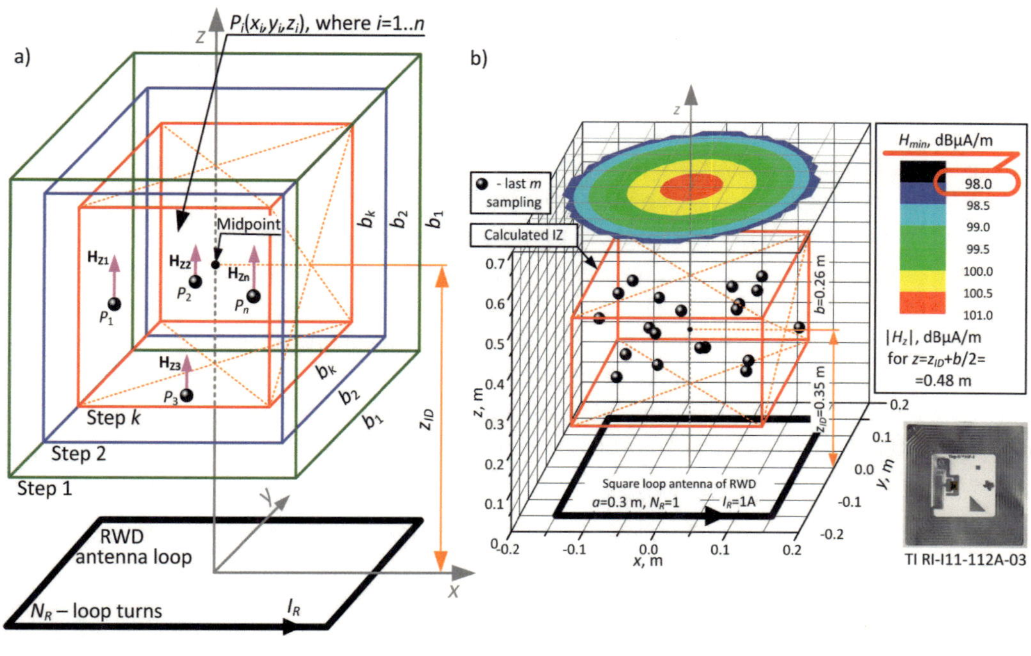

Figure 30. IZ determination by using the MC method: (a) graphic representation and (b) example of measured and calculated results.

be axially symmetrical and parallel to an RWD antenna loop. Such an assumption results from orientation of transponders that are parallel to the symmetrical RWD antenna which has, for example, a circular, square or different polygon shape in inductive coupling RFID systems. The process of the interrogation zone determination is realized according to a proposed algorithm.

A random deployment of n-transponders at P_i points of Cartesian space at (x_i, y_i, z_i) is assumed in steps k considered in a sequence during the search of the RFID system interrogation zone. The random variables x_i, y_i and z_i, for $i = 1 \ldots n$ have a uniform distribution. It results from the fact that the electromagnetic field in any point of the communications space is heterogeneous. The random variables x_i, y_i and z_i are mutually independent. The interrogation zone is determined for a given efficiency of identification η_{ID}:

$$\eta_{ID} = \frac{l_{IDOK}}{n} \cdot 100\% \tag{14}$$

where l_{IDOK} is the number of transponders for which desired read/write operations are properly done.

In order to determine that the RFID system is operating correctly for given locations of transponders, it is not enough to achieve the $\eta_{ID} = 100\%$ for n-transponders and fulfil all energy conditions (absolute value of the z-component of magnetic field strength H_z is greater than H_{min}) in an anti-collision application. It cannot be predicted whether the sampling of coordinates of transponders placed in k area in which all the conditions mentioned above are fulfilled meets the boundary requirements necessary for correct operation of the whole RFID system. The practical use of the law of large numbers for a k-step (in which all conditions of RFID system proper operation are met with a given efficiency) is a solution to this problem. Nevertheless, it can be found that the m-tuple increase of the number of the random variables x_i, y_i and z_i sampling in k-step lengthens the calculation process during the simulation of an antenna unit arrangement. But in accordance with the law of large numbers, the probability of a correct estimation of the interrogation zone increases. This is mainly connected with the examining a larger number of deployed n-transponder cases. If the conditions of correct operation are not fulfilled in any of m multiple sampling of transponders' location for k analyzed area, then the next process of multiple sampling should be stopped, and it becomes necessary to examine the next (k+1) smaller cube ($b_k = b_{k-1} - b_{step}$). The MC solution for the analyzed object completes a procedure which confirms the fulfilment of all conditions for the correct operation of anti-collision RFID system. The procedure is completed for a given efficiency of identification and for the area in which all the m multiple sampling of transponders location leads to a positive calculation result of the antenna unit arrangement consisting of a read/write device and transponders.

The experimental determination of the interrogation zone is divided into two parts: calculation and measurement. In the both parts of the experiment, a laboratory process of anti-collision RFID identification is subjected to verification. For the computational part, a program called *JankoRFIDmc'3D-IZ* is developed in the Mathcad environment by the authors. This program enables a random deployment of n-transponders and to study the effectiveness of an antenna set. The interrogation zone for a given efficiency of identification is the solution of this calculation. The example results of numerical calculations by *JankoRFIDmc'3D-IZ* and the importance of its individual elements are presented in **Figure 30b**.

The convergence of the measurements and calculations confirms a practical usefulness of the presented concept of determining the three-dimensional interrogation zone by using the Monte Carlo method in inductively coupled anti-collision RFID systems. The program *JankoRFIDmc'3D-IZ* developed on the basis of this method is practically used to solve many problems—reported by industry representatives—connected with implementation of RFID systems.

The problem of object identification that changes their location and/or orientation (**Figure 31a**) is encountered by the authors in their research works. It also resulted from the demanded needs of industry partners. In this context, a model of automated identification in the RFID anti-collision system in which communication with groups of transponders entering and leaving interrogation zone (**Figure 31b**) takes place is presented in the chapter [82] as an example. Dynamic location changes of transponders influence RFID system reliability, which is characterized by the efficiency coefficient and the identification probability of objects in the specific interrogation zone. The communication conditions are crucial for efficient exchanging data with all transponders during dynamic process. Presented problem is the base to specify

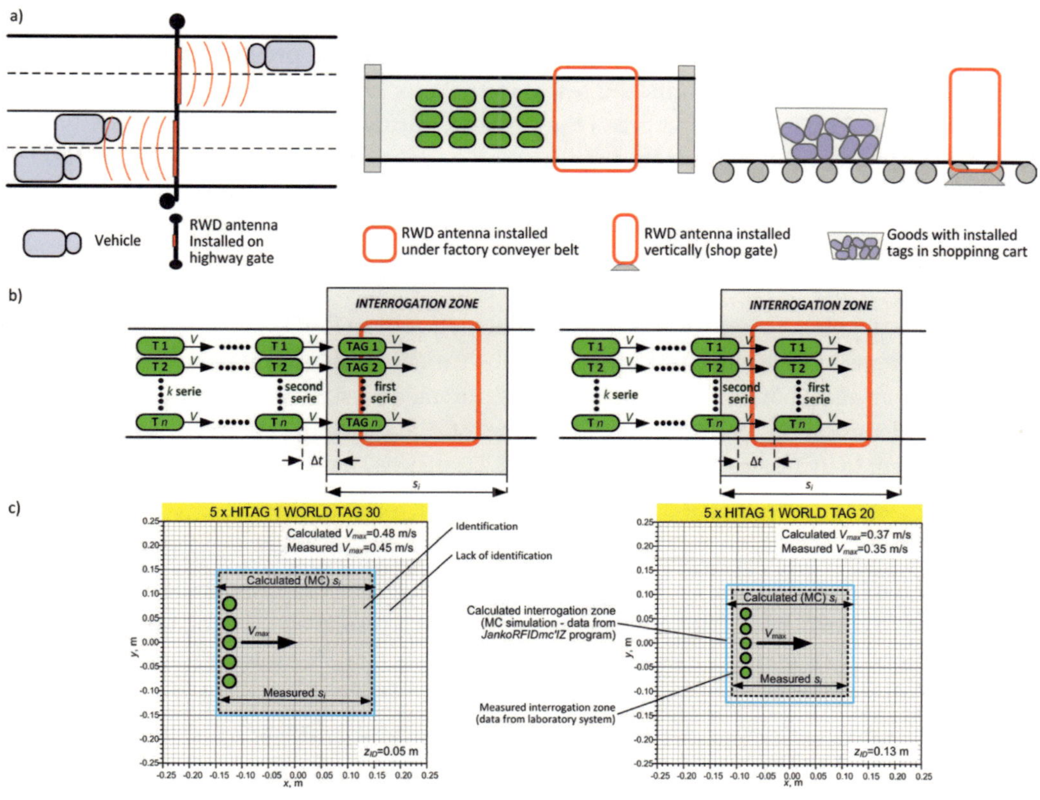

Figure 31. Anti-collision identification with dynamic location change of transponders: (a) selected processes, (b) illustration of considered problem, and (c) example of experimental results.

new application transponder parameters (such as maximum speed of transponder motion) and to synthesize the IZ required for all dynamic anti-collision RFID applications.

The maximum speed of transponders motion V_{max} is the practical parameter that is obviously related to the problem of identified objects that dynamically change their location in anti-collision RFID systems. The maximal value is determined for the speed at which the correct executions of the operations in transponder's internal memories are still allowed. In general case, this parameter can be expressed by the dependence:

$$V_{\max} = \frac{s_i}{t_{i\min}} = \frac{F_s\{IZ\}}{F_t\{D_{UID}, BR, n_{\max}\}} \tag{15}$$

The length of the track s_i that is travelled by transponders crossing the interrogation zonehas to be knownin order to evaluate V_{max}. For the case of anti-collision object identification, the s_i is the function F_s of the *IZ* and it has to be determined with regard to the maximum number of correctly operating transponders n_{max}, which—in critical period of time—may be inside the interrogation zone. The minimum time t_{imin} is necessary to identify all serial numbers of transponders inside of the IZ. This time is the function F_t, which results from a used communication protocol and takes into account the data quantity D_{UID}, required for transmission with a proper bit rate (*BR*).

The example results of calculated (data from the *JankoRFIDmc'IZ* program based on the MC method) and measured (data from the test stand) charts of IZ and V_{max} parameter are presented in **Figure 31c**. The convergence of the curves confirms a practical usefulness of the presented conception of determining the interrogation zone by using the Monte Carlo method in anti-collision RFID systems with dynamic location change of transponders.

3.10. Methods to increase geometric size of the interrogation zone

From a practical point of view (an effective implementation of an RFID system), the interrogation zone should be as large as possible regardless of the variable location and orientation of objects. This parameter also should be appropriate to requirements established for an application of automated identification. With regard to problems of dynamic anti-collision systems, selected issues pertinent to increasing geometric size of the IZ are presented in the publications [83, 84].

The greatest flexibility in developing RFID implementations and shaping the interrogation zone can be achieved using a system with an antenna multiplexer (MUX). In this context, the problem of the IZ determination in HF RFID application with two orthogonal RWD antennas is presented in the chapter [83]. In the paper, the research results are obtained on the basis of theoretical model as well as investigations in an example system configuration. The specialized measuring stand in the common RFID laboratory is used for experimental verification of the identification efficiency. Finally, the authors propose a software tool *JankoRFIDmuxHF* elaborated in the Mathcad environment (**Figure 32**).

The arrangement of two perpendicular antennas connected to the one RWD with the MUX is the problem to solve. The antennas have to be switched, while marked objects are being

http://dx.doi.org/10.5772/intechopen.71378

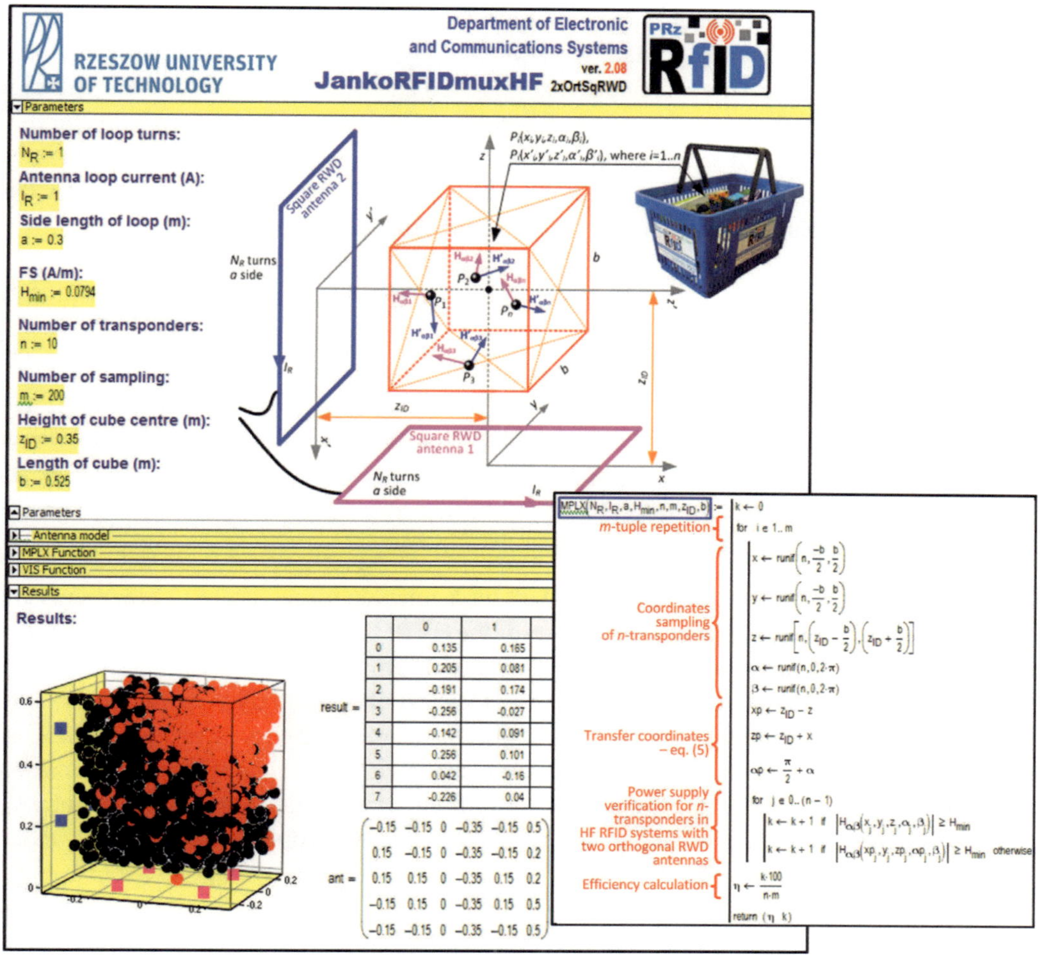

Figure 32. JankoRFIDmuxHF program.

identified in the inside of a cube of side b. The process of energy transfer from the RWD to RFID transponders is subjected to the analysis in the study to be carried out. The energy is conveyed by the inhomogeneous magnetic field of intensity H.

The obtained equations allow designers to calculate values separately for individual components in x, y and z directions (H_x, H_y, H_z). The case of an object orientation in the space $\mathbf{\Omega}_{\text{ID}}$ can be described as a transponder deviation by α and β angles from parallel planes of the RWD-transponder antenna loops. It means that marked objects are in a chaos state, such as in a shopping basket that contains the so-called fast-moving consumer goods (FMCG) (**Figure 1**). In this case, a perpendicular component of the magnetic field strength for a deviated transponder is given by:

$$H_{\alpha\beta} = H_z \cos(\alpha)\cos(\beta) + H_x \sin(\alpha)\cos(\beta) + H_y \sin(\beta) \tag{16}$$

If the condition $|H_{\alpha\beta}| \geq H_{min}$ is met, then a transponder is powered correctly and can exchange data with RWD. The value of $H_{\alpha\beta}$ should be considered separately for each multiplexed antenna and individually for the each transponder that is located and oriented in the point P_i (where $i = 1\ldots n$, and n denotes the number of considered transponders). It means that the condition for correct supplying one of the transponders should be analyzed in two steps, that is, the $H_{\alpha\beta}$ should be calculated in the point $P_i(x_i, y_i, z_i, \alpha_i, \beta_i)$ for the antenna #1, and in the $P_i(x'_i, y'_i, z'_i, \alpha'_i, \beta'_i)$ for the antenna #2. The coordinates in the system (x', y', z') can be calculated from:

$$(x', y', z', \alpha', \beta') = (z_{ID} - z, y, z_{ID} + x, 90^o + \alpha, \beta) \quad (17)$$

It should be emphasized that more antennas and their hypothetic localizations in a space can be considered by using the elaborated model. It is difficult to accurately predict the coordinates of the points P_i in a chaos state. In fact, it is not possible to analyze all potential locations and orientations of a group of n-transponders in the inside of the cube of side b. The described problem has a probabilistic nature, and proposed solution is obtained by simulating a group of given objects by using the MC method [46].

The essence of the model is represented by the *MPLX* function for which input arguments are determined on the basis of primary parameters of the HF RFID system with the two orthogonal and multiplexed RWD antennas. The *JankoRFIDmuxHF* program can be used for calculating the identification efficiency and the RWD antenna localizations for the given input data. Results of identification process are presented graphically along with efficiency effects (correct/incorrect identification). The convergence of measurements and calculations (**Figure 33**) confirms a practical usefulness of the presented concept of interrogation zone determination in anti-collision systems. It also shows the practical utility of the developed model and software tools.

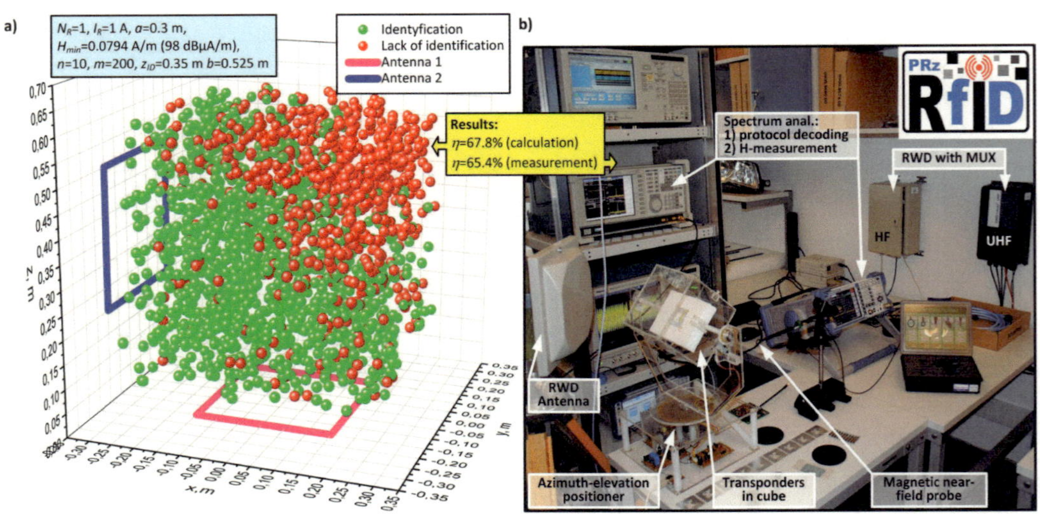

Figure 33. Interrogation zone: (a) example of calculated and measured results and (b) prepared test stand.

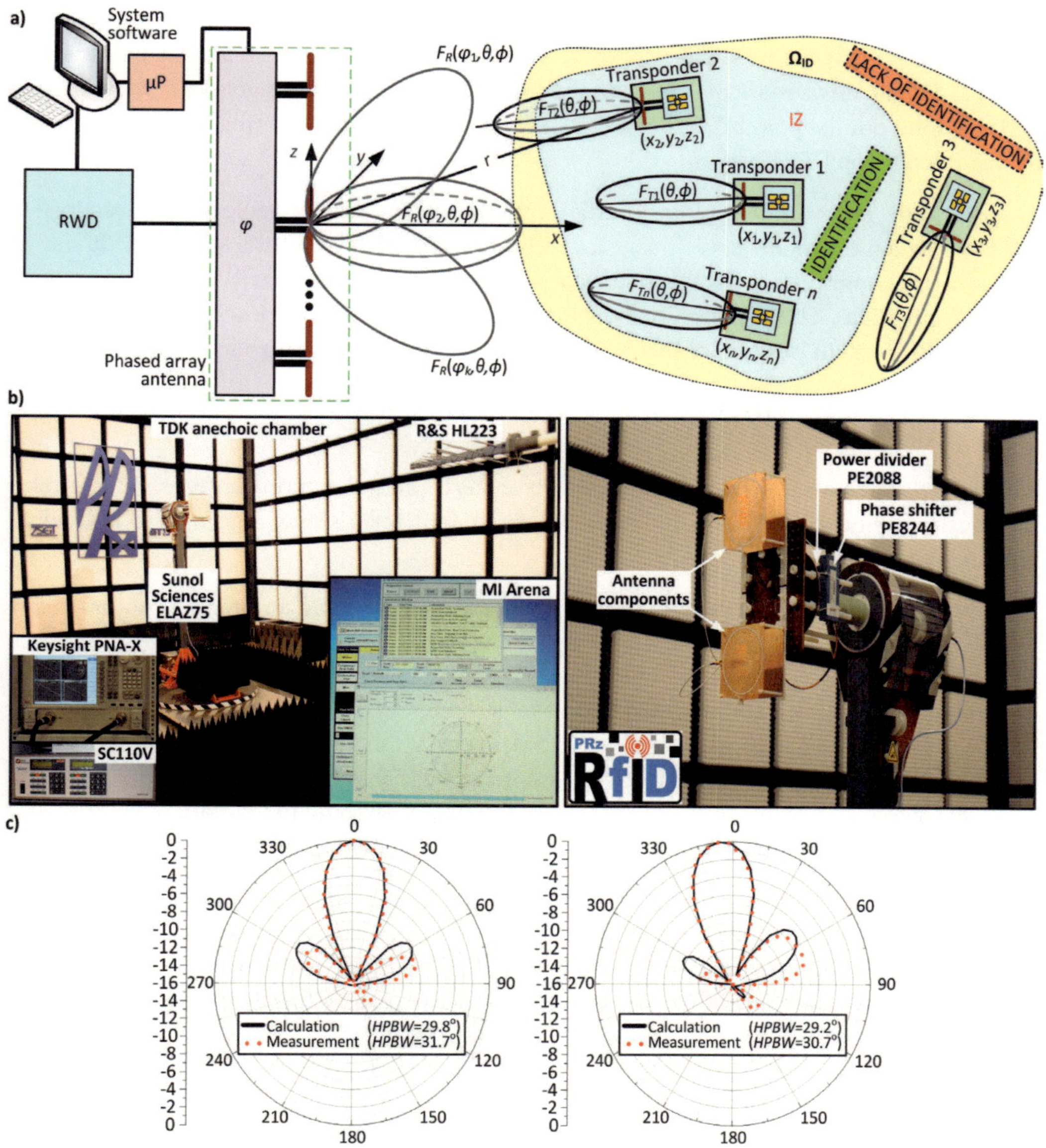

Figure 34. Anti-collision UHF RFID system with the array of phased antennas: (a) idea, (b) test stand and (c) example results.

In the phased antenna array, an interesting solution is an electronic control of the main beam of radiation pattern. Despite the fact that for a long time this function was used only in military applications, now increasingly, its implementations can also be observed in the civilian areas when object identification is based on the shapes of their echoes, for example, in the radio astronomy or weather forecasting [85]. In this context, new opportunities may be sought for the use of the array of phased antennas [86].

Bearing in mind the European (ETSIEN302208) and American (FCCPart15.247) limitations of available energy, the idea and practical solution of the phased antenna array dedicated to UHF read/write devices are presented in the chapter [84]. On the basis of tests carried out, the authors point out the possibility of using developed devices for the synthesis of a determined IZ in anti-collision RFID system.

In analogy to, for example, military radiolocation systems, it is possible to focus energy of the electromagnetic field to variously localized and oriented RFID transponders. It can be obtained by changing/shaping the main beam of the radiation pattern of RWD phased antenna array (**Figure 34a**). The proposed concept of maximizing IZ can be described by a function which includes a *k*th position of the main beam in relation to *n*th transponder in a space $\mathbf{\Omega}_{ID}$:

$$IZ(\mathbf{\Omega}_{ID}) = f\left(F_R(\phi_k, \theta, \phi), F_{Tn}(\theta, \phi), \tau_n, \chi_n, P_{RWD}, P_{Tmin}\right) \tag{18}$$

where $F_R(\phi_k, \theta, \varphi)$ means the radiation pattern of RWD phased antenna array, $F_{Tn}(\theta,\varphi)$—transponder radiation pattern and ϕ—angle of phase shift for a signal feeding the individual antenna of the array.

Assuming constant location and orientation of transponders in an automated process, a key influence on the IZ can be obtained by shaping the radiation pattern $F_R(\phi_k, \theta, \varphi)$. The system with possibility of shifting the main beam can be made even with the simplest set consisting of: power divider, phase shifter, microprocessor system and two antennas (**Figure 34b**). In the read/write device of the proposed solution, the power of the feeding signal is evenly divided on the antennas, but one of them is powered with a phase shift by the angle ϕ. Equal strength of output signal and phase shifting gives the possibility of shaping the radiation pattern without any mechanical changes in the position of the whole antenna arrangement.

On the basis of conducted calculations and measurements (**Figure 34c**), it can be concluded that the effective possibility of changing direction of the main been energy in the range of 14° is feasible in stable phased antenna array system. Results of this work will provide introduction to comprehensive assessment of the interrogation zone in anti-collision UHF band of RFID systems on the basis of the proposed functions (18).

4. Conclusions

An RFID system is properly implemented only when all marked objects are successfully recognized irrespective of their dynamics, location and orientation or operation status. Possibly the best choice of appropriate devices that enable efficient realization of the automated process constitutes the essential stage when new implementations are designed. Usually, the elements of RFID system are selected mainly with respect to availability in the market and economic aspects. An attempt to define, characterize or determine parameters of RFID devices may be found problematic in many practical or theoretical cases, and predictability of the 3D interrogation zone is often reduced to basic analytical or numerical calculations or computer simulations. Since complete characteristics of the devices are not available, the lack of important parameter values makes a radio communication system synthesis (e.g., interrogation zone in RFID system) very difficult. The presented studies revealed vagueness of data specification notes published by manufacturers for their products. Since the literature and knowledge in this field are incomplete, the time-consuming and expensive "trial and error" method is most commonly used especially in the industry practice when new applications are designed. Therefore, the authors prepared the comprehensive review on their efforts to change this state of affairs. These facilities can significantly support many theoretical and simulation works that are developed and described in the branch literature and can improve the reliability and efficiency of designed RFID applications.

The presented works were carried out in many aspects connected with single and anti-collision, passive and semi-passive, static and dynamic RFID systems for perspective frequency of the HF and UHF bands. The authors especially focused on the definition, characteristics and determination of the antenna parameters in propagation and inductively coupled systems, and they proved that the 3D interrogation zone is the most important and practically useful parameter when the RFID system is considered. They also revealed that the classical theory of antennas cannot be applied to solve some problems (e.g., antenna and chip matching, radiation pattern determination, etc.) and new measurement methods have to be developed in which the nature of RFID technology is taken into consideration—it is seldom mentioned in the branch literature. Accordingly, they systematized measuring procedures, elaborated own methods and constructed sophisticated test stands implemented in their common RFID and electronic technology (HYBRID) laboratories that could be useful to characterize the transponder and RWD chips or antennas as well as whole real system applications. They supplement the knowledge in the field of literature and verification of well-known methods used in synthesis of transponder and RWD antennas and the interrogation zone.

It can be found in this work that the considered problems are completely different for the HF and UHF band cases. In this distinction, several of crucial analyses, syntheses and experiments are carried out in relation to: (1) determination of transponders' and RWDs' chip parameters; (2) antenna synthesis for both transponders and RWDs; (3) estimation of antenna impedance and radiation pattern; and (4) simulation, modeling and prediction of the interrogation zone and also possibility of its enlargement. Finally, on the basis of described items, the conceptions of autonomous semi-passive RFID sensor/transponder and system with an antenna multiplexer (phased antenna array) are revealed. Moreover, impact of the material and electronic technology is also discussed as it substantially influences the process of antenna synthesis and determining operation parameters. As an example, the possibility of manufacturing the flexible antenna in the inkjet technology is considered in the discussion.

The proposed ideas contribute significantly to the development of automatic identification. On their basis, the authors point out the third stage of RFID progress in which the transponders provide not only details about marked objects but also extended variable data gathered from surroundings by built-in sensors of different physical quantities. Moreover, the transponders are developed toward the capability of being powered from the electromagnetic field of common radio communication systems.

In order to achieve this level of research, some special software tools (e.g., *JankoRFIDchip'UHF*, *JankoRFIDmuxHF*, *NmAntPat*, *RFID(UHF)SysAntPat*) had to be elaborated in different kinds of design environments (e.g., Mathcad, Mentor Graphics HyperLynx 3D EM, LabView, uVision). Thanks to them, researchers could effectively conduct investigations on antenna synthesis, radio wave propagation phenomenon, system simulations, radiation pattern determinations, and protocol parameter modifications in both newly developed and approved standards and so on.

In the course of research, each time it was assumed that it is necessary to achieve essential utility values. Therefore, the published results were positively confirmed experimentally, and then, practical applications were found in industry, institutions and other places where automated systems were implemented. The special untypical investigation stands were prepared for carrying out the research tasks in the authors' laboratories.

Acknowledgements

Results of Grant No. PBS1/A3/3/2012 from Polish National Centre for Research and Development as well as Statutory Activity of Rzeszow University of Technology were applied in this work. The work was developed by using equipment purchased in Operational Program Development of Eastern Poland 2007-2013, Priority Axis I Modern Economics, Activity I.3 Supporting Innovation under Grant No. POPW.01.03.00-18-012/09-00 as well as Program of Development of Podkarpacie Province of European Regional Development Fund under Grant No. UDA-RPPK.01.03.00-18-003/10-00.

Author details

Piotr Jankowski-Mihułowicz* and Mariusz Węglarski

*Address all correspondence to: pjanko@prz.edu.pl

Department of Electronic and Telecommunications Systems, Rzeszów University of Technology, Poland, Rzeszów, Poland

References

[1] Finkenzeller K. RFID Handbook—Fundamentals and Applications in Contactless Smart Cards, Radio Frequency Identification and Near-Field Communication. 3rd ed. Chichester: Wiley; 2010. 478 p

[2] Ustundag A. The Value of RFID. Benefits vs. Costs. 1st ed. London: Springer-Verlag; 2013. 176 p. DOI: 10.1007/978-1-4471-4345-1

[3] Diorio C. New intelligence for RFID resurgence at item level. ID World Magazine. 2014;Dec.:44-45

[4] IDTechEx. Continued growth as market for RFID exceeds $10bn milestone. ID World Magazine. 2015;Dec.:38-39

[5] Das R, Harrop P. RFID Forecasts, Players and Opportunities 2014-2024 Report. Cambridge: IDTechEx; 2014

[6] Brown DE. RFID Implementation. New York: McGraw-Hill; 2007 466 p

[7] Bartneck N, Klaas V, Schönherr H. Optimizing Processes with RFID and Auto ID. Erlangen: Publicis Publ.; 2009

[8] Giusto D, Iera A, Morabito G, Atzori L, editors. The Internet of Things, 20th Tyrrhenian Workshop on Digital Communications. New York: Springer-Verlag; 2010. 442 p. DOI: 10.1007/978-1-4419-1674-7

[9] GS1. GS1 System Architecture Document—How GS1 Standards fit together. Release 4.0.1. Brussels: GS1; 2015

[10] Traub K, editor. The GS1 EPCglobal Architecture Framework. Ver. 1.6. Brussels: GS1; 2014

[11] Karmakar NC. Handbook of Smart Antennas for RFID Systems. Hoboken: Wiley; 2010 620 p

[12] Ukkonen L, Sydanheimo L, Kivikoski M. Read range performance comparison of compact reader antennas for a handheld UHF RFID Reader. IEEE Communications Magazine. 2007;**45**(4):24-31. DOI: 10.1109/MCOM.2007.348674

[13] Nikitin PV, Rao KVS. Antennas and Propagation in UHF RFID Systems. In: IEEE International Conference on RFID; 16-17 April 2008; Las Vegas, NV, USA. IEEE; 2008. p. 277-288. DOI: 10.1109/RFID.2008.4519368

[14] Dobkin DM. The RF in RFID: UHF RFID in Practice. 2nd ed. Oxford: Newnes; 2012 540 p

[15] Boaventura AJS, Carvalho NB. Extending reading range of commercial RFID readers. IEEE Transactions on Microwave Theory and Techniques. 2007;**61**(1):633-640. DOI: 10.1109/TMTT.2012.2229288

[16] Yojima H, Tanaka Y, Umeda Y, Takyu O, Nakayama M, Kodama K. Analysis of read range for UHF passive RFID tags in close proximity with dynamic impedance measurement of tag ICs. In: IEEE Radio and Wireless Symposium (RWS); 16-19 January 2011; Phoenix, AZ, USA. IEEE; 2011. p. 110-113. DOI: 10.1109/RWS.2011.5725440

[17] Oyeka DO, Batchelor JC, Sanchez-Romaguera V, Yeates SG, Saunders RE. Effect of conductive area trimming on the read range of inkjet printed Epidermal RFID tags. In: 9th European Conference on Antennas and Propagation (EuCAP); 13-17 April 2015, Lisboa, Portugal. 2015

[18] Intermec by Honeywell. Intermec RFID Tags & Media, Meeting the scalable RFID challenge. 611460-B 01/14. Morris Plains: Honeywell International Inc; 2013

[19] Confidex. Confidex UHF RFID products. Confidex Ltd.; 11/2015

[20] CEPT ERC. ERC Recommendation 70-03, Relating to the Use of Short Range Devices (SRD). September 2015.

[21] Lee CW, Lee SJ, Kim M, Kyung Y, Eom K. Capacitive humidity sensor tag smart refrigerator system using the capacitive to voltage converter (CVC). International Journal of Advanced Science and Technology. 2011;**36**:15-25

[22] Abad E, Mazzolai B, Juarros A, Gómez D, Mondini A, Sayhan I, Krenkow A, Becker T. Fabrication process for a flexible tag microlab. Proc. SPIE. 2007;**6589**:65890O

[23] Cartasegna D, Cito A, Conso F, Donida A, Grassi M, Malvasi L, Rescio G, Malcovati P. Smart RFID label for monitoring the preservation conditions of food. Sensors and Microsystems. 2010;**54**:381-385. DOI: 10.1007/978-90-481-3606-3_77

[24] Oprea A, Courbat J, Bârsan N, Briand D, de Rooij NF, Weimar U. Temperature, humidity and gas sensors integrated on plastic foil for low power applications, Sensors and Actuators B: Chemical. 2009;**140**(1):227-232. DOI:10.1016/j.snb.2009.04.019

[25] Yang L, Rida A, Wu T, Basat S, Tentzeris MM. Integration of sensors and inkjet-printed RFID tags on paper-based substrates for UHF cognitive intelligence applications. In: IEEE Antennas and Propagation Society International Symposium; 9-15 June 2007, Honolulu, USA. 2007; p. 1193-1196. DOI:10.1109/APS.2007.4395714

[26] Tani A, Ugaji M, Yamabe Y. A building structural-performance monitoring system using RFID tag with sensors, In: Proceedings of the International Conference on Computing in Civil and Building Engineering; 30 June-2 July 2010; Nottingham, UK. 2010. Paper 221.

[27] Jankowski-Mihułowicz P, Pawłowicz B, Pitera G. The issue of data exchange in the HF band RFID system with autonomous semi-passive transponder. Przegląd Elektrotechniczny. 2015;**91**(9):74-77. DOI: 10.15199/48.2015.09.19

[28] Jankowski-Mihułowicz P. Field conditions of interrogation zone in anticollision radio frequency identification systems with inductive coupling. In: Turcu C, editor. Radio Frequency Identification Fundamentals and Applications Bringing Research to Practice. INTECH; 2010. p. 1-26

[29] GS1 EPCglobal. EPC Radio-Frequency Identity Protocols Generation-2 UHF RFID; Specification for RFID Air Interface Protocol for Communications at 860 MHz – 960 MHz. Ver. 2.0.1, Brussels: GS1; April 2015.

[30] Balanis C. Antenna Theory. 4th ed. Hoboken: Wiley; 2016. 1096 p

[31] Tran N, Lee J-W. Simple high-sensitivity voltage multiplier for UHF-band semi-passive radio frequency identification tags using a standard CMOS process. IET Microwaves, Antennas & Propagation. 2010;**4**(11):1974-1979. DOI: 10.1049/iet-map.2009.0288

[32] W Che, D Meng, X Chang, W Chen, L Wang, Y Yang, C Xu, X Tan, N Yan, H Min. A Semi-Passive UHF RFID Tag with On-Chip Temperature Sensor. In: Custom Integrated Circuits Conference (CICC 2010); 19-22 September 2010; San Jose, CA, USA. IEEE; 2010. DOI:10.1109/CICC.2010.5617397

[33] Griffin JD, Durgin GD. Complete link budgets for backscatter-radio and RFID Systems. IEEE Antennas and Propagation Magazine. 2009;**51**(2):11-25. DOI: 10.1109/MAP.2009.5162013

[34] Jankowski-Mihułowicz P, Węglarski M. Determination of passive and semi-passive chip parameters required for synthesis of interrogation zone in UHF RFID systems. Elektronika ir Elektrotechnika. 2014;**20**(9):65-73. DOI: 10.5755/j01.eee.20.9.5007

[35] Wei P, Che W, Bi Z, Wei C, Na Y, Qiang L, Hao M. High-efficiency differential RF front-end for a Gen2 RFID tag. IEEE Transactions on Circuits and Systems II: Express Briefs. 2011;**58**(4):189-194. DOI: 10.1109/TCSII.2011.2124530

[36] Jankowski-Mihułowicz P, Kalita W. Efficiency of tag antenna unit in anticollision radio frequency identification systems with inductive coupling. Acta Electrotechnica et Informatica. 2009;**9**(2):3-7

[37] Agilent. In-Fixture Measurements Using Vector Network Analyzers. AN 1287-9, 5968-5329E. Santa Clara: Agilent Technologies; 2006

[38] Rumiantsev A, Ridler N. VNA calibration. IEEE Microwave Magazine. 2008;**9**(3):86-99. DOI: 10.1109/MMM.2008.919925

[39] Jankowski-Mihułowicz P, Kawalec D, Węglarski M. Antenna design for semi-passive UHF RFID transponder with energy harvester. Radioengineering. 2015;**24**(3):722-728. DOI: 10.13164/re.2015.0722

[40] Marrocco G. The art of UHF RFID antenna design: Impedance-matching and size-reduction techniques. IEEE Antennas and Propagation Magazine. 2008;**50**(1):66-79. DOI: 10.1109/MAP.2008.4494504

[41] Kim D, Yeo J. Dual-band long-range passive RFID tag antenna using an AMC ground plane. IEEE Transactions on Antennas and Propagation. 2012;**60**(6):2620-2626. DOI: 10.1109/TAP.2012.2194638

[42] Mohammed NA, Demarest K, Deavours DD. Analysis and synthesis of UHF RFID antennas using the embedded T-match, In: IEEE International Conference on RFID; 14-16 April 2010; Orlando, FL, USA. IEEE; 2010. p. 230-236. DOI:10.1109/RFID.2010.5467276

[43] AMS. SL900A EPC Class 3 Sensory Tag Chip—For Automatic Data Logging. Datasheet, V. 1-01. AMS; 2014

[44] Jankowski-Mihułowicz P, Węglarski M, Pitera G, Kawalec D, Lichoń W. Development board of the autonomous semi-passive RFID transponder. Bulletin of The Polish Academy of Sciences Technical Sciences. 2016;**64**(3):647-654. DOI: 10.1515/bpasts-2016-0073

[45] Janeczek K, Jakubowska M, Kozioł G, Jankowski-Mihułowicz P, Passive UHF. RFID-enabled sensor system for detection of product's exposure to elevated temperature. Metrology and Measurement Systems. 2013;**XX**(4):591-600. DOI: 10.2478/mms-2013-0050

[46] Jankowski-Mihułowicz P, Kalita W, Skoczylas M, Węglarski M. Modelling and Design of HF RFID Passive Transponders with Additional Energy Harvester. International Journal of Antennas and Propagation. 2013; Article ID 242840. DOI: 10.1155/2013/242840

[47] Jankowski-Mihułowicz P, Lichoń W, Pitera G, Węglarski M. Determination of the material relative permittivity in the UHF band by using T and modified ring resonators. International Journal of Electronics and Telecommunications. 2016;**62**(2):129-134. DOI: 10.1515/eletel-2016-0017

[48] Jankowski-Mihułowicz P, Tomaszewski G, Węglarski M. Flexible antenna design for HF RFID semi-passive transponder in ink-jet technology. Przegląd Elektrotechniczny. 2015;**91**(4):1-5. DOI: 10.15199/48.2015.04.01

[49] Ohnimus F, Ndip I, Guttowski S, Reichl H. Design and analysis of a bent antenna-coil for a HF RFID transponder. In: 38th European Microwave Conference, 27-31 October 2008; Amsterdam, Holland. IEEE; 2008. p. 75-78. DOI:10.1109/EUMC.2008.4751390

[50] Preis K, Bauernfeind T, Biro O, Koczka G, Ticar I. Investigation of UHF circular loop antennas for RFID. IEEE Transactions on Magnetics. 2010;**46**(8):3309-3312. DOI: 10.1109/TMAG.2010.2044768

[51] ZL Ma, LJ Jiang, J Xi, TT Ye. A compact HF/UHF dual band RFID tag antenna. In: IEEE International Symposium Antennas and Propagation Society (APSURSI); 7-13 July 2013; Orlando, FL, USA. IEEE; 2013. p. 1122-1123. DOI:10.1109/APS.2013.6711221

[52] Shao B, Amin Y, Chen Q, Liu R, Zheng L-R. Directly printed packaging-paper-based chipless RFID tag with coplanar LC resonator. IEEE Antennas and Wireless Propagation Letters. 2013;**12**:325-328. DOI: 10.1109/LAWP.2013.2247556

[53] ST-Microelectronics. M24LR16E-R Product Specification. DOI 018932. December 2011.

[54] Jankowski-Mihułowicz P, Węglarski M. Synthesis of read/write device antenna for HF proximity range RFID systems with inductive coupling. Przegląd Elektrotechniczny. 2012;**88**(3a):70-73

[55] Jankowski-Mihułowicz P, Pitera G, Węglarski M. The impedance measurement problem in antennas for RFID technique. Metrology and Measurement Systems. 2014;**XXI**(3):509-520. DOI: 10.2478/mms-2014-0043

[56] Sharma A, Zuazola IJG, Gupta A, Perallos A, Batchelor JC. Non-uniformly distributed-turns coil antenna for enhanced H-field in HF-RFID. IEEE Transactions on Antennas and Propagation. 2013;**61**(10):4900-4907. DOI: 10.1109/TAP.2013.2275244

[57] Petrariu A-I, Popa V, Gaitan V-G, Finis I. Test results for HF RFID antenna system tuning in metal environment. In: 13th International Conference Carpathian Control (ICCC); 28-31 May 2012; High Tatras, Slovakia. IEEE; 2012. p. 543-546. DOI:10.1109/CarpathianCC.2012.6228704

[58] Ahmad MY, Mohan AS. Multi-loop bridge HF RFID reader antenna for improved positioning. In: Asia-Pacific Microwave Conference (APMC); 5-8 Dec. 2011; Melbourne, VIC, USA. IEEE; 2011. p. 1426-1429.

[59] Qing X, Chen ZN. Characteristics of a metal-backed loop antenna and its application to a high-frequency RFID smart shelf. IEEE Antennas and Propagation Magazine. 2009;**51**(2):26-38. DOI: 10.1109/MAP.2009.5162014

[60] Jankowski-Mihułowicz P, Węglarski M. Determination of 3-dimensional interrogation zone in anticollision RFID systems with inductive coupling by using Monte Carlo method. Acta Physica Polonica A. 2012;**121**(4):936-940

[61] Wobak M, Gebhart M, Muehlmann U. Physical limits of batteryless HF RFID transponders defined by system properties. In: IEEE International Conference on RFID-Technologies and Applications (RFID-TA); 5-7 Nov. 2012; Nice, France. IEEE; 2012. p. 142-147. DOI: 10.1109/RFID-TA.2012.6404500

[62] Ohnimus F, Ndip I, Guttowski S, Reichi H. Design and analysis of a bent antenna-coil for a HF-RFID transponder. In: 38th European Microwave Conference; 27-31 October 2008; Amsterdam, Netherlands. IEEE; 2008. p. 75-78. DOI:10.1109/EUMC.2008.4751390

[63] Hennig A. Feasibility of Deeply Implanted Passive Sensor Transponders in Human Bodies. In: 4th European Workshop on RFID SysTech; 10-11 June 2008; Freiburg, Germany. IEEE; 2008.

[64] Jankowski-Mihułowicz P, Lichoń W, Węglarski M. Numerical model of directional radiation pattern based on primary antenna parameters. International Journal of Electronics and Telecommunications. 2015;**61**(2):191-197. DOI: 10.1515/eletel-2015-0025

[65] Parini C, Gregson S, McCormick J, van Rensburg DJ. Theory and Practice of Modern Antenna Range Measurements. Stevenage: IET; 2014. 799 p. DOI: 10.1049/PBEW055E

[66] Ito T, Tsutsumi Y, Obayashi S, Shoki H, Morooka T. Radiation pattern measurement system for millimeter-wave antenna fed by contact probe. In: European Microwave Conference; 29 Sept. – 1 Oct. 2009; Rome, Italy. IEEE; 2009. p. 1543-1546. DOI: 10.23919/EUMC.2009.5296180

[67] Farzaneh S, Ozturk AK, Sebak AR, Paknys R. Antenna-pattern measurement using spectrum analyzer for systems with frequency translation. IEEE Antennas and Propagation Magazine. 2009;**51**(3):126-131. DOI: 10.1109/MAP.2009.5251209

[68] Ukkonen L, Sydanhelmo L. Threshold power-based radiation pattern measurement of passive UHF RFID tags. In: Progress in Electromagnetic Research Symposium; July 5-8, 2010; Cambridge, USA. 2010. p. 87-90

[69] Abdulhadi AE, Abhari R. Design and experimental evaluation of miniaturized monopole UHF RFID tag antennas. IEEE Antennas Wireless Propagation Letters. 2012;**11**:248-251. DOI: 10.1109/LAWP.2012.2187632

[70] Jankowski-Mihułowicz P, Węglarski M. A Method for Measuring the Radiation Pattern of UHF RFID Transponders. Metrology and Measurement Systems. 2016;**23**(2):163-172. DOI: 10.1515/mms-2016-0018

[71] Icheln C. Methods for Measuring RF Radiation Properties of Small Antennas [dissertation]. Espoo, Finland: Helsinki University of Technology; 2001. 93 p

[72] Jankowski-Mihułowicz P, Kawalec D, Węglarski M. Synthesis of omnidirectional read/write device antenna for UHF RFID system. Elektronika. 2015;**3**:23-24. DOI: 10.15199/13.2015.3.5

[73] Feig. ID ISC.ANTU250/250, Type EU and FCC, UHF Long Range Antenna. Document M40900-3de-ID-B. Weilburg: Feig Electronic; 14 September 2006

[74] Yu H, Wu J, Fan L, Lin Y, Xu K, Tang Z, Cheng C, Tang S, Lin J, Huang M, Lan Z. A novel redox-mediated gel polymer electrolyte for high-performance supercapacitor. Journal of Power Sources. 2012;**198**:402-407. DOI: 10.1016/j.jpowsour.2011.09.110

[75] Wua Z-S, Zhoua G, Yina L-C, Rena W, Lia F, Cheng H-M. Graphene/metal oxide composite electrode materials for energy storage. Nano Energy. 2012;**1**(1):107-131. DOI: 10.1016/j.nanoen.2011.11.001

[76] Jayalakshmi M, Balasubramanian K. Simple capacitors to supercapacitors—An overview. International Journal of Electrochemical Science. 2008;**3**(11):1196-1217

[77] Belleville M, Cantatore E, Fanet H, Fiorini P, Nicole P, Pelgrom M, Piguet C, Hahn R, van Hoof C, Vullers RJM, Tartagni M. Energy Autonomous Systems: Future Trends in Devices. Technology and Systems. CATRENE Working Group on Energy Autonomous Systems; 2009. 84 p.

[78] Vullers RJM., van Schaijk R, Doms I, van Hoof C, Mertens R. Micropower energy harvesting. Solid-State Electronics. 2009;**53**(7):684-693. DOI: 10.1016/j.sse.2008.12.011

[79] Jankowski-Mihułowicz P, Kalita W, Węglarski M. Autonomous sensor with RFID interface. Elektronika. 2015;**3**:18-22. DOI: 10.15199/13.2015.3.4

[80] Jankowska-Mihułowicz M, Chudy-Laskowska K. Constraints in investment decision making in the field of RFID—Opinions of Polish managers. In: 4th International Scientific Conference on Marketing Management, Trade, Financial and Social Aspects of Business; 20-21 October 2016; Košice, Slovakia: University of Economics in Bratislava; 2016. p. 68-73.

[81] Jankowska-Mihułowicz M, Chudy-Laskowska K, Kmiotek K. Behaviour of Polish managers while making investment decisions in the field of RFID. In: 4th International Scientific Conference on Marketing Management, Trade, Financial and Social Aspects of Business; 20-21 October 2016; Košice, Slovakia. University of Economics in Bratislava; 2016. p. 74-82.

[82] Jankowski-Mihułowicz P, Kalita W, Pawłowicz B. Problem of dynamic change of tags location in anticollision RFID systems. Microelectronics Reliability. 2008;**48**(6):911-918. DOI: 10.1016/j.microrel.2008.03.006

[83] Jankowski-Mihułowicz P, Węglarski M. Interrogation zone determination in HF RFID systems with multiplexed antennas. Archives of Electrical Engineering. 2015;**64**(3):459-470. DOI: 10.2478/aee-2015-0035

[84] Jankowski-Mihułowicz P, Kawalec D, Węglarski M. The idea of enhancing directional energy radiation by a phased antenna array in UHF RFID system. International Journal of Electronics and Telecommunications. 2016;**62**(2):115-120. DOI: 10.1515/eletel-2016-0015

[85] Wirth WD. Radar Techniques Using Array Antennas. 2nd ed. IET; 2013. 460 p. DOI: 10.1049/PBRA026E

[86] Ariff MH, Ismarani I, Shamsudin N. Design and development of UHF RFID reader antenna for livestock monitoring. 5th IEEE Control and System Graduate Research Colloquium (ICSGRC); 11-12 August 2014; Shah Alam, Malaysia. IEEE; 2014. p. 125-129. DOI: 10.1109/ICSGRC.2014.6908708

## Chapter 6

Case Study: Installing RFID Systems in Supermarkets

María-Victoria Bueno-Delgado, Francesc Burrull and Pablo Pavón-Mariño

Additional information is available at the end of the chapter

http://dx.doi.org/10.5772/64972

Abstract

Radio frequency identification technology (RFID) is considered as the reference technology for wireless identification and item traceability. Supermarkets are one of those scenarios where the RFID potential can be harnessed. In theory, RFID in supermarkets shows several advantages compared with traditional barcode systems, offering real-time inventory, stock control, cash queues, among others. In practice, its massive and global implementation is still being delayed due to the high quantity of factors that degrade the RFID system performance in these scenarios, causing uncontrolled items and identification losses and, at the end, economical losses. Some works in the scientific literature studied a single or a set of problems related to RFID performance, mostly focused on a specific communication layer: antennas and hardware design, interferences at physical layer, medium access control (MAC) protocols, security issues, or middleware challenges. However, there are no works describing in depth the set of factors affecting RFID performance in a specific scenario and contemplating the entire communication layer stack. The first challenge of this chapter is to provide a complete analysis of those physical and environmental factors, hardware and software limitations, and standard and regulation restrictions that have a direct impact on the RFID system performance in supermarkets. This analysis is addressed by communication layers, paying attention to the point of view of providers, supermarket companies, and final customers. Some of the most feasible and influential research works that address individual problems are also enumerated. Finally, taking the results extracted from this study, this chapter provides a Guide of Good Practices (GGPs), giving a global vision for addressing a successful RFID implementation project, useful for researchers, developers, and installers.

Keywords: RFID, case study, supermarket, performance, GGP

1. Introduction

For over a decade, radio-frequency identification technology (RFID) has been the benchmark of technological innovation in scenarios of mass identification and traceability. RFID technology allows for identifying thousands of items in a few seconds, without direct line-of-sight between the RFID antennas (reader) and the items to identify (RFID tags), reaching up to 10 m of reading distance.

There are thousands of pilot projects and implementations in use of RFID throughout the world [1–5]. One of them is the identification of goods in supermarkets [6–8]. In these scenarios, the products are items to be identified and, instead of incorporating a barcode, they are labeled with RFID tags, usually working at the ultra-high-frequency (UHF) band. Tags are electronic devices composed of a simple circuit, an antenna, and, in some cases, a battery. The simplest tag models do not incorporate batteries (passive tags) and feed their circuits with the energy extracted from the incident electromagnetic wave generated by the reader antennas. This operating mode is usually called *backscattering* [9]. Every tag stores in a small memory the product identification code (electronic product code (EPC)) [10], which, among other data, includes the provider identification code, the type of product, and the unique serial number of the product in which it is attached to. When a tag is in the coverage range of a reader, it automatically sends its EPC code to the reader, and the reader sends it to a middleware subsystem. This subsystem is in charge of querying to a database (working under EPC-IS [11]) about the product data linked to the EPC code, for example, price or expiration date.

The implementation of RFID in supermarkets allows customers to obtain information about the goods they collect when they are doing the shopping, for example, with RFID *checkpoints* installed in strategic places in the shopping zone or built-in in the shopping trolley [12, 13]. Moreover, with RFID, the customer no longer has to remove the groceries from the shopping trolley and place them into the conveyor belt to be traced in order to make the payment. Instead, the customer passes with the shopping trolley through RFID reader antennas (similar to the anti-theft systems), and immediately all products are tracked and identified. The system calculates the final purchase cost and prints the ticket in a few seconds. Incorporating RFID in supermarkets saves time to customers and offers added-value services that, at present, do not exist in most supermarkets. For those companies in this sector, RFID technology permits them to control inventory in real time and enables product traceability, among others. The downside is that there are many factors that significantly degrade the performance of RFID systems in these scenarios, causing to not being able to identify the products at the expected time or even losing information and identified items due to the hardware and software interferences and limitations, which finally translates into potentially significant economic losses.

With the aim of maximizing the performance of RFID systems in these environments, the engineers and technicians perform multiple measurements in their implementations, varying the antennas orientation, testing different brands of tags, changing the position where the tags are attached to the items, varying the number of tags per pallet, and so on. All these tasks are addressed without following specific implementation rules or a specific Guide of Good

Practices (GGPs). Consequently, unexplained variations in the performance occur in many cases, which lead to frustration of the implanter, and distrust of the entrepreneur.

The lack of rules and implementation protocols come from the absence of scientific studies encompassing the set of factors that affect and degrade the RFID performance in specific scenarios, works where the set of problems and solutions proposed by the scientific community are identified and listed. Therefore, this chapter is an attempt in this line, presenting a complete analysis on the main factors that degrade the performance of passive UHF RFID systems working in a supermarket. They have been classified according to the communication layer where they occur, distinguishing among those degrading at the physical layer, medium access control layer, and higher layers. The most relevant solutions found in the scientific literature focusing on minimizing or eliminating the identified problems are also enumerated. The results extracted from the study have permitted us to design a GGP for implementing RFID systems, tackling the hardware/software design and requirements that maximize the performance of RFID systems.

2. Scenario description

The scenario under study is a supermarket where an RFID system will be installed. The system will be composed of more than one reader and antennas, a middleware subsystem with some databases, and all products labelled with RFID tags (see **Figure 1**). The scenario has some desirable checking/reading points:

1. *Entrance to warehouse*. In this place, the check-in of goods arriving to the grocery store is performed. Also, the EPC-IS database is updated, since the new inventoried products are added. Then, the available stock is known in real time.

2. *Crossing gate warehouse—sales zone*. At this point, the check-in/check-out of the products entering and leaving the warehouse is made. The goal is to have the EPC-IS database updated, and to get real-time information about the available stock for sale.

3. *Checkpoints in the corridors or built-in the shopping trolley*. This added-value service allows customers for getting data of interest about any product while they are doing shopping: ingredients, nutritional value, expiration date, or recommended recipes, among others.

4. *Cash register system*. Every cash register is an identification point. The products are identified by the RFID system through the antennas installed on these points. The RFID system connects to the EPC-IS database to get the price of the products. Simultaneously, the EPC-IS updates the stock in order to detect if it is necessary to make new orders to suppliers.

5. *Exit doors*. It works as anti-theft system for those not identified products in the cash register system.

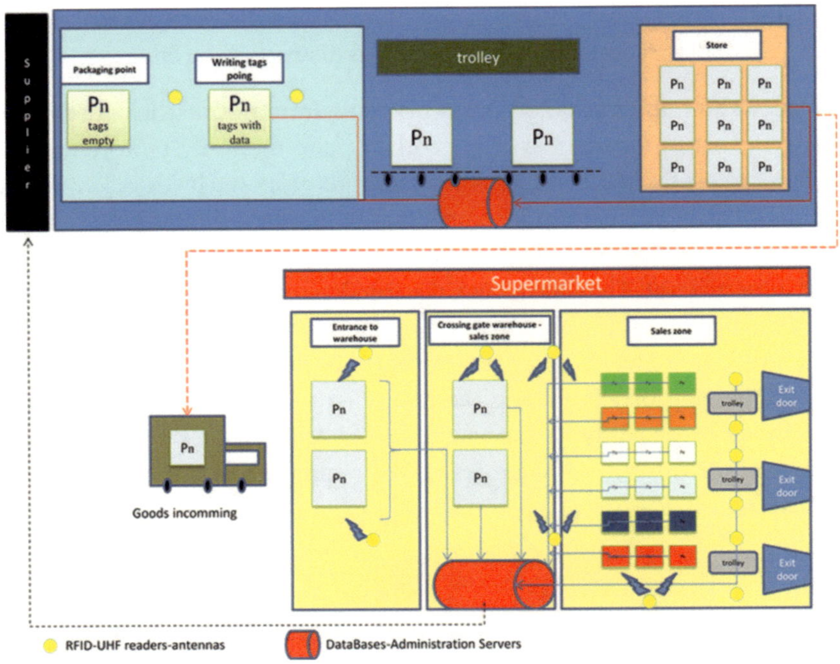

Figure 1. Scenario under study: a supermarket.

In this scenario, some assumptions are taken. First, we require that suppliers label their products with passive RFID tags operating in the UHF band, in the spectrum of the frequencies permitted by the country where the supermarket is located. In addition, tags attached to the goods must store the product's information in EPC code format. Finally, both suppliers and supermarket must connect their databases to an EPCglobal Architecture Framework, called EPCglobal Network [14], which allows product's traceability and localization, in real time, and worldwide.

3. Agents at the RFID physical layer

At the physical layer, the frequencies incompatibility, the electromagnetic noise, and the absorption and reflection phenomena are the agents that have a strong influence in the performance of RFID systems, even triggering the complete loss of information. In the following subsections, each of these issues is addressed, listing the most remarkable and viable solutions found in the current scientific literature.

3.1. Frequencies incompatibility

The International Telecommunication Union (ITU) [15] manages the global radio spectrum by dividing the world into three regions. Each region has a set of frequency allocations. **Figure 2** summarizes the frequency assignments for RFID. For UHF, **Figure 2** shows that tags and

http://dx.doi.org/10.5772/64972

readers work in different frequency ranges according to the operating region. Assuming that in the case study that concerns us, the RFID-UHF system is installed in a supermarket located in Spain, and only those products labelled with RFID tags operating at UHF-Region 1 (862–870 MHz band) can be identified. Therefore, if a bottle of wine is labelled and marketed in Chile with a tag attached to it operating at UHF-Region 2, it cannot be identified in Spain.

Region	LF	HF	UHF	Microwaves
Region 1	125 KHz	13.56 MHz	862-870 MHz (4 W EIRP)	2.446-2.454 GHz
Region 2	125 KHz	13.56 MHz	902-928 MHz (3.2 W EIRP)	2.40-2.4835 GHz
Region 3	125 KHz	13.56 MHz	950-956 MHz (4 W EIRP, China 2 W ERP, Singapur and Taiwan and Philinnines 0.5 W ERP)	2.427-2.470 GHz

Figure 2. ITU regions. Frequencies assignments.

On the other hand, there is a problem of incompatibility among the RFID systems used by the suppliers. Not all good suppliers are working with RFID-UHF systems. For those products with liquid or with a metal container, the suppliers commonly use tags operating at low-frequency (LF) or high-frequency (HF) band, which are less sensitive to the absorption and reflection phenomena (see Section 3.2). Therefore, if, for example, there are bottles of juice labelled with LF tags, they cannot be read by the UHF reader. To solve these problems, new antennas for tags and readers are being designed in order to operate in the whole UHF spectrum (encompassing the three regions) [16–18] and dual HF/UHF antennas to enable interoperability between different systems RFID [19, 20].

3.2. Electromagnetic noise, absorption, and reflection

In a supermarket, there are many things that cause interferences, affecting the performance of the RFID systems: the metals in the shopping trolleys and shelves, the products with liquids, the refrigeration machines, and even the human body. Some of them are impossible to avoid, such as the electromagnetic or environmental noise generated by the electrical equipment in the supermarket, the alarms, the elevators, the automatic doors, or the interferences from the GSM mobile customers [21, 22].

The absorption and reflection phenomena have also a high influence on the performance. Absorption occurs when the passive tags are attached to products with a high quantity of liquid (e.g., a bottle of milk) or when the labelled products are placed near an item with a high percentage of liquid (e.g., the human body). When a reader tries to communicate with a tag in these situations, most of the tag incident signal is absorbed by the liquid. Then, the tag has not enough energy to power its circuit, being unable to send its EPC code to the reader. Reflection happens when tags are near, or attached to metals. The signal emitted by the reader is reflected by the metal, and again the tag is not able to send its EPC code. An interesting example of reflection in which RFID installers do not pay attention is the reflection caused by the typical fluorescent light tubes in supermarkets. In [23], it was shown how these lamps are able to reflect and modulate the incident signal of a reader, causing a reflected signal with much more power than a tag response, especially when the lamps are less than 5 m away from the reader. In the scientific literature, there are some prominent studies dealing with the design of tags nonvulnerable to the above phenomena [24–30].

4. Agents at the RFID medium access control

In the case study of this chapter, thousands of tags attached to products work together with a high number of readers (at least one reader for each checkpoint and cash register).

When a set of tags is in the coverage area of a reader, all are simultaneously fed by the incident signal of the reader and consequently they try to send their EPC code immediately. When two or more tags transmit their EPC code at the same time, a tag-to-tag collision occurs (e.g., when hundreds of products are in the shopping trolley and go through the reader antenna placed in the cash register system). To minimize the impact of these collisions, the readers in the market implement a medium access control (MAC) mechanism based on the worldwide standard EPCglobal Class-1 Gen-2 [31]. It defines an MAC mechanism for RFID readers working at UHF that organize the tags responses by a Frame Slotted Aloha (FSA) protocol [32], controlled by the reader. This is a very simple mechanism with a low rate of identification, which has led the scientific community to propose new alternatives compatible with the standard that significantly increase the rate of identified tags per time unit [33–36].

When two or more readers are operating in the same environment, reader-to-tag and reader-to-reader collisions occur. The former happens when the tags are located in the overlapping coverage area of two or more readers, for example, in **Figure 3**, when a tag is located in the overlapping coverage area of readers R1 and R2, the tag receives the signal from both readers but, since the tag is a very simple device, is not able to select a reader to send its EPC code, even though readers are working at different frequency. The reader-to-reader collisions occur by the interfering signals of those readers transmitting at the same frequency and time instant (see **Figure 4**). Readers are configured with a specific transmit power (Ptx), defined by the standards and regulations. For instance, in Europe the ETSI-EN 302-208 regulation [37] sets

http://dx.doi.org/10.5772/64972

the maximum Ptx to 3.2 W Equivalent Isotropic Radiated Power (EIRP), while in the USA is the FCC-Part 15 [38], which sets to 4 W EIRP.

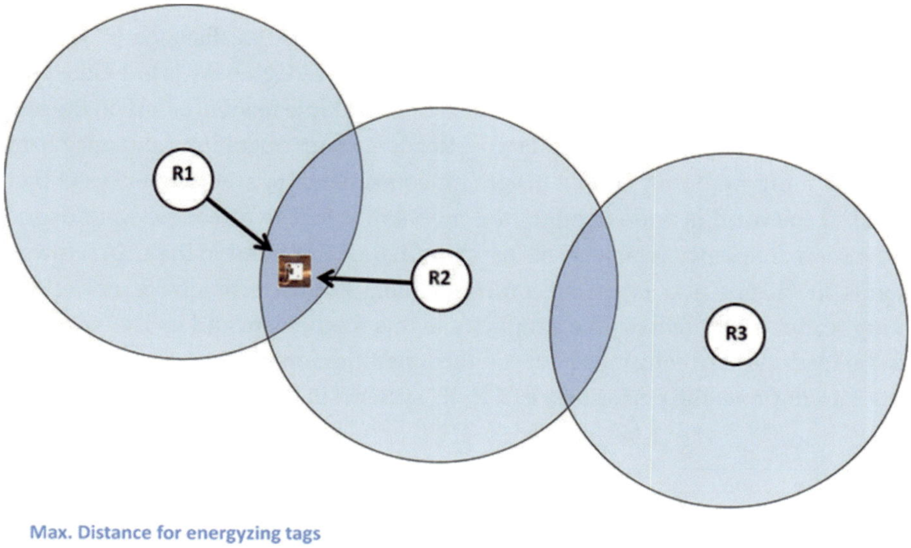

Figure 3. Example of reader-to-tag collision.

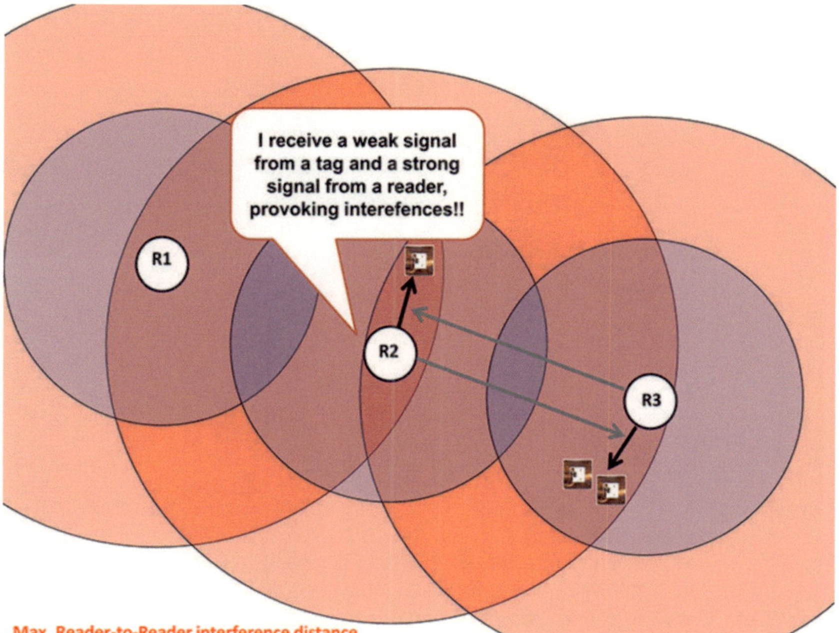

Figure 4. Example of reader-to-reader collision.

The readers' output power limits the maximum reader-to-tag read range, that is, the maximum distance in which readers can feed the tags circuits in order to respond with their EPC codes. But the Ptx also sets the maximum distance in which readers can interfere with each other. In general, in an indoor environment, 3.2 W EIRP allows readers to reach tags placed up to 10-m distance, and interfere with other readers located up to 1000-m distance [39]. In order to minimize the effects of reader-to-reader interferences, the EPCglobal Class-1 Gen-2 standard suggests a communication protocol for scenarios with multiple readers based on the frequency hop spread spectrum (FHSS) mechanism [31]. Readers fix an operating frequency from a set, and they may jump randomly or in a programmed sequence to any frequency set by its ITU region [15]. If the band is wide enough, the probability that two readers were operating at exactly the same frequency is small. This happens in the UHF band in the USA. However, the UHF bands in Europe and Japan are much smaller, so this technique is not effective for preventing reader interferences. The simplicity of this mechanism and its lack of efficiency to address the reader-to-tag collisions have led the scientific community to suggest a number of alternatives to improve the performance of RFID systems in these environments [40–43].

5. RFID middleware

The RFID middleware plays an important role in the global identification and traceability. The EPCglobal Network [14] states the network architecture and the elements in the global RFID traceability network, as well as the communication protocols used among the elements, security issues, and so on.

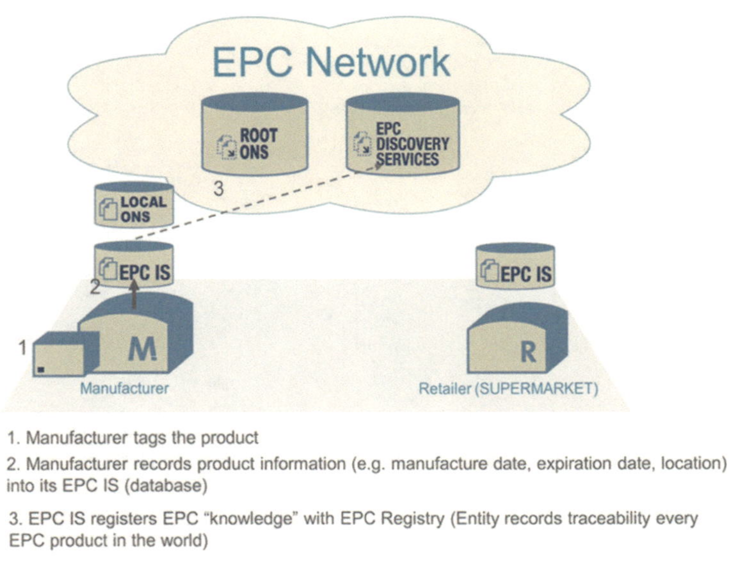

Figure 5. Manufacturer side: recording EPC codes in its EPC-IS and informing to EPC Discovery Services.

When a tag is identified, the reader only gets from it the EPC code [10] of its product (the tag is attached—and customized—to a product). The rest of the data of the identified product is obtained through the middleware, which performs a query to the system database, where all the product data are stored. In the case study that concerns us, this is the database managed by the supermarket. In this case, every EPC code registered is linked to a price. Other data of interest, for example, expiration date, nutritional value, recommended recipes, and so on, are obtained when the supermarket middleware makes a direct query to the manufacturer's EPC-IS (see **Figures 5** and **6**) [11]. For this, the supermarket middleware needs to know the URL or IP that gives access to the EPC-IS. The middleware obtains this sensitive information by querying to a server in the EPCglobal Cloud called root object name server (Root ONS) [44]. This server works like the typical domain name servers (DNS) in the Internet: you ask for a company (sending the company code), and it answers with the IP or URL associated to it (see **Figures 7** and **8**).

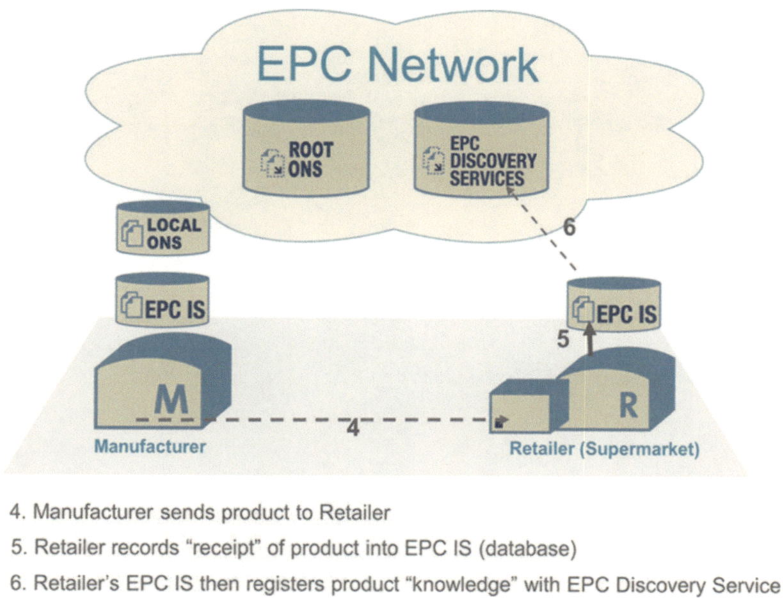

Figure 6. Supermarket side: recording identified tags in its EPC-IS and informing to EPC Discovery Services.

On the other hand, if the data of interest are a record about the product traceability, it is necessary that the middleware makes a query to the EPC Discovery Services [45], a server in the EPCglobal Cloud that stores a traceability record of every product in the world, labelled with RFID tags and storing an EPC code. The EPC Discovery Services stores the locations and other relevant information in the products life, starting at the moment that the product is labelled and recorded at the factory. The products location is updated at the moment that the product is moved, for example, from the factory to the provider, or from the supplier to the supermarket. For instance, when a good enters the supermarket store, it is registered by the middleware in the EPC Discovery Services, indicating its new location.

As a conclusion, if the supermarket is going to operate under the EPCglobal Network, it is necessary to set the agreements between the supermarket and the suppliers, in order to have access to the products information stored in the EPCglobal Network. On the other hand, there are still latent problems in the EPCglobal Network architecture that must be solved to reach a proper functioning: global network synchronization, scalability, security access to the EPC-IS and ONS, and so on. There are some outstanding works in the scientific literature that attempt to minimize and address these problems [46–50].

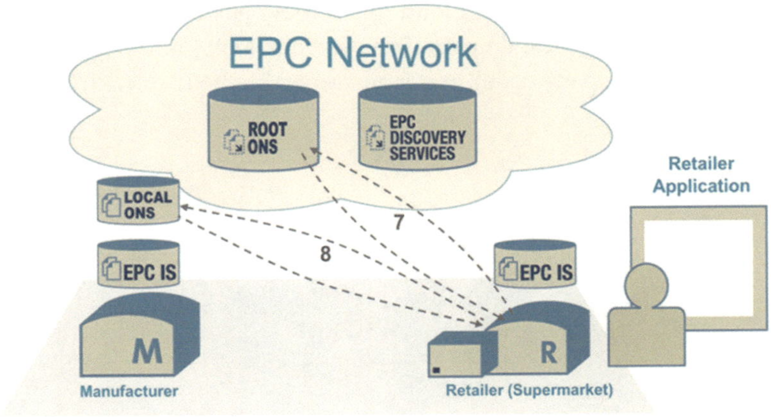

7. Retailer must query to Root ONS. This entity answer a IP address to connect with the Manufacturer's Local ONS

8. Manufacturer's Local ONS is queried for location of EPC-IS

Figure 7. Supermarket queries about the EPC collected to the ONS.

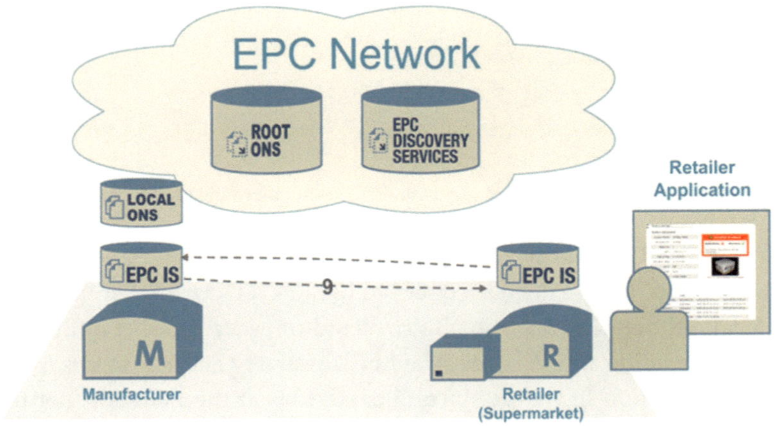

9. Retailer queries Manufacturer EPC IS for desired product information (e.g., manufacture date, expiration date, etc.)

Figure 8. Supermarket gets the added-value information about the EPC collected.

6. Security and privacy issues

In addition to the security issues to solve in the EPCglobal Network, it is necessary to clarify the doubts about data security and privacy of customers, suppliers, and companies in general. Corporations feel vulnerable to the following:

1. Spoofing (industrial espionage). It may happen when there are unauthorized reading products to know their type, composition, quantities, among others.

2. Tampering data that means to destabilize the supply chain or to disturb the operations by rewriting or deleting the EPC codes in tags by a malicious reader, for example, changing the EPC code of a tag by other linked to a product with lower price.

Customers also feel vulnerable to the following:

1. Tracking: customers fear that malicious readers can identify them, for example, with the RFID passport or an identity card, with the aim of being controlled (their habits or movements) by a higher entity (e.g., the government).

2. Hostlisting/profiling: customers fear they can be traced and classified according to the items labelled with RFID that they buy or they have.

The current security and privacy challenges focus on the establishment and management of keys, certificates of authorization, and the use of cryptographic algorithms for encrypting reader-to-tag communications [50–52].

7. Guide of Good Practices for implementing an RFID-UHF system in a supermarket

After reviewing the factors influencing the performance of RFID in supermarkets, this section proposes a Guide of Good Practices (GGP) for the design and implementation of RFID-UHF passive systems in supermarkets. Note that the rules described in this section must be applied once the scenario is defined, as well as the traceability/identification zones/points, for example, like the description addressed in Section 2.

The first step (Task 1 in **Figure 9**) is to decide the operating frequency, since it will determine the entire system. As it was explained in Sections 1 and 3.1, UHF is the most extended and used frequency band in these environments, offering the maximum reading distances between passive RFID tags and readers. Hence, the supermarket and its suppliers should agree about the operation mode, that is, if they will work at the same UHF band under the ITU region (see **Figure 2**). If a provider works with LF or HF, it should use tags with dual antennas, which are able to transmit/receive in HF/UHF or LF/UHF [19, 20]. Moreover, if the supermarket sells products labelled outside the ITU-working region, they must be labelled with tags that work in the whole UHF band [16–18]. On the other hand, the suppliers should address measurements about the absorption and reflection effects in their products labelled with RFID tags

(Task 2 in **Figure 9**). Suppliers must verify the successful identification of their products with liquids or metals. It is necessary something like a certificate of "*quality of identification,*" where suppliers officially state that the tags used to label their products are not susceptible to the absorption and reflection phenomena [23–25].

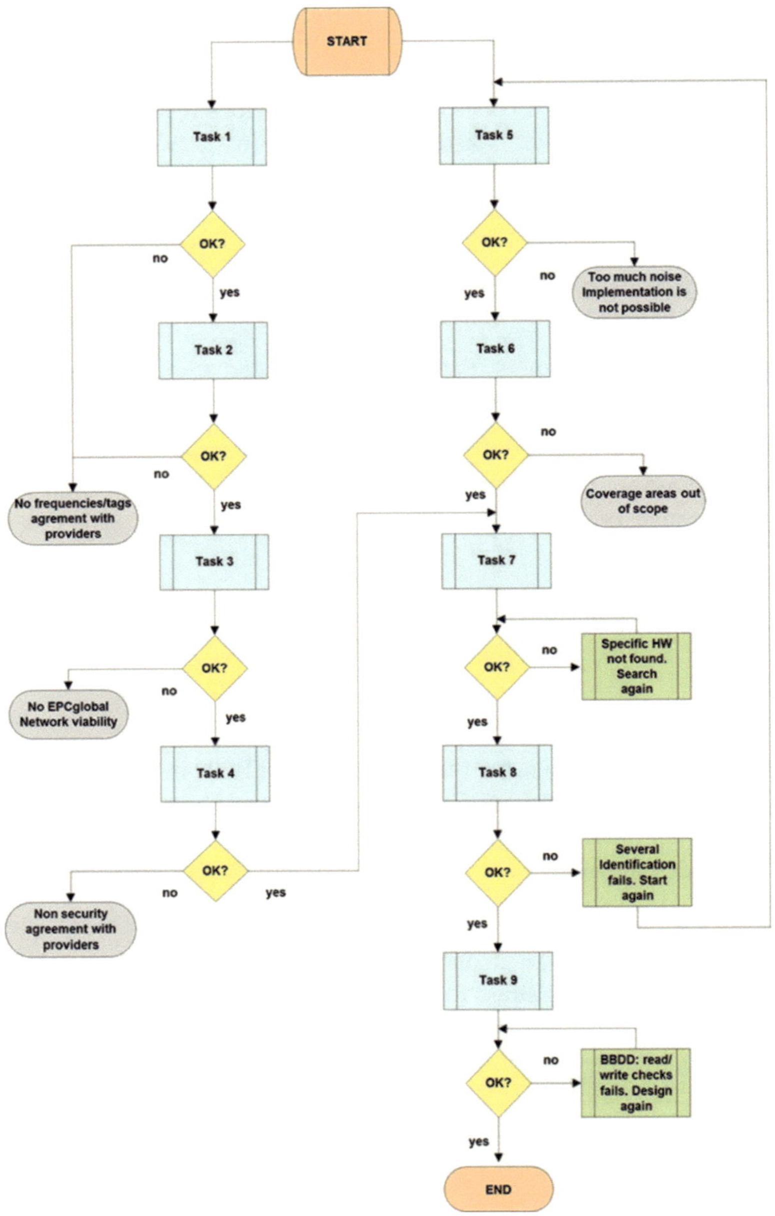

Figure 9. Guide of Good Practices: an RFID-UHF system implementation in a supermarket.

In the globalized world, it seems obvious that both supermarkets and suppliers want to be part of the global network of traceability, the EPCglobal Network. In such case, both must register their EPC-IS [11], designing their databases and middleware compatible for operating with the EPCglobal Network, according to the standard defined in [14] (Task 3 in **Figure 9**). Besides, they must have read/write access in the EPC Discovery Services [45] and they must be registered in order to query to the ONS Root [44]. If a provider does not belong to the network, it cannot ensure global traceability of its products, nor can it provide information about the manufacturer, product type, and so on. However, the products can be identified by the supermarket and a price can be assigned to them through the internal database used in the supermarket.

Regarding secure communications, both the RFID system installed in the supermarket and the suppliers should use security systems to avoid spoofing and/or tampering, but without neglecting the global products visibility (Task 4 in **Figure 9**). This entails that both parties have to manage certificates of authorization for accessing to the EPC-IS, ONS, among others. In addition, for the reader-to-tag communications, a data encryption algorithm must be used and shared by the parties, suppliers, and supermarket [50–52].

If the above points are satisfactorily achieved, it means that both, suppliers and supermarket, can work together under a global identification RFID-UHF system. The following steps (which can be addressed in parallel to the above) are

1. Studying the electromagnetic noise (Task 5 in **Figure 9**). It is necessary to analyze the noise environment where the reader antennas will be installed, detecting all elements of the area which are the source of interferences. This comprises, for instance, the use of a spectrum analyzer connected to a half-wave dipole antenna and to a PC. The analyzer captures the interfering signals and the data are stored on the PC. It is desirable to make measurements at times of the day where there is more work activity, and when more electronic devices are working. In [53], it is described in detail how to perform these measurements.

2. Designing the identification areas (Task 6 in **Figure 9**). Although the starting point is the plan with the ideal deployment described in Section 2 (see **Figure 1**), the results of the previous step determine the final reader antennas location. Those zones where the effects of interferences are the lowest will be the initial identification zones. In each of them, a one-fourth wave dipole antenna, put on the center of a metal plate, will be placed, using a tripod. A signal generator and a PC will be used to capture the measurement data. The aim is to create a coverage map to decide how to properly orient the antennas and how to align them to offer the best performance. In [53], it is described how to perform these measurements in detail. If the measurement results are optimistic, it is time to choose the hardware, installation, startup, and identification tests.

3. Selecting RFID hardware (Task 7 in **Figure 9**). This task encompasses having an extensive knowledge about how the RFID readers and tags work (physical and logical operation). It is recommended to use bistatic antennas, with circular polarization, and a distance between the reader and the reader antennas (cable) less than 5 m. The reader will have at least 4 I/O ports, and it will work to the maximum output power according to the ITU

region where it is operating. The reader-to-tag communication protocol must be EPCglobal Class-1 Gen-2 [31] or an improved version, compatible with the standard, that permits to modify the frame-length parameter (Q) [32–34]. Readers must implement a reader-to-reader anti-collision protocol based on FHHS or a similar technique, being compatible with the current standard [31]. Finally, readers should be able to run the *EPCKill* command, defined by the EPCglobal standard. This command enables that those readers placed at the exit doors of the supermarket can automatically disable tags leaving the supermarket. Then, those tags cannot be read anymore, preventing customers from *Tracking* and *Hostlisting*.

4. Installation and identification tests (Task 8 in **Figure 9**). It is recommended to make the installation antenna by antenna. For every new reading point installed, the coverage range must be tested, and an intensive reading identification test is required. The performance is usually measured by the number of identified tags per time unit. The testing procedure will be conducted by varying the following parameters: frame-length (Q), number of tags per pallet/shopping trolley, speed pallet/trolley, tag-antenna distance, tag position according to the antenna, and so on.

5. Write/Read database/EPC-IS (Task 9 in **Figure 9**). If, after performing the previous steps the identification results are acceptable, it is time to implement the databases, the middleware, and the EPC-IS, to enable the supermarket operations through the EPCglobal Network. Note that the supermarket can use a unique database with all products data, distinguishing those data that will not be shared by the EPCglobal Network, for example, price of product, in/out-of-stock, for sale, sold, and so on. The databases must be tested (read/write operations), as well as the readings in the EPC-IS of the suppliers, Root ONS, and EPC Discovery Services.

If all the above steps are addressed and the testing results are satisfactory, the system is ready to operate. **Figure 9** shows a specification and description language (SDL) diagram with the GGP explained here.

8. Conclusions

This chapter has addressed a complete analysis of those hardware, software, and environmental factors that degrade the performance of passive RFID systems, focusing the study on a scenario of great potential for RFID technology and of interest to the society: a supermarket. In general, in the scientific literature these factors are studied individually or only a set of them and most of the works are usually focused on a communication layer. By contrast, this chapter provides a study in-depth about the set of factors affecting RFID performance in a specific scenario but contemplating the entire communication layer stack, and taking into account the requirements and needs of suppliers, supermarket companies, and final customers.

Throughout this chapter, the most remarkable works in the scientific literature that address how to eliminate or minimize the impact of the problems at physical, communication, or middleware layer have been reviewed: frequencies incompatibility, electromagnetic noise, reader-to-reader and reader-to-tag collisions, data security, scalability, global synchronization, and so on. As a result of this study, a protocol for implementing RFID systems in supermarkets is proposed as a Guide of Good Practices composed of nine defined tasks. It gives a complete vision for addressing, step by step, a successful RFID system implementation project, being useful for researchers, developers, and installers.

Author details

María-Victoria Bueno-Delgado*, Francesc Burrull and Pablo Pavón-Mariño

*Address all correspondence to: mvictoria.bueno@upct.es

Telecommunications Networks Engineering Group (GIRTEL), Technical University of Cartagena, Cartagena, Spain

References

[1] Q. Cao, D.R. Jones, H. Sheng. Contained nomadic information environments: Technology, organization, and environment influences on adoption of hospital RFID patient tracking. Information & Management Journal. 2014;51(2):225–239. DOI: 10.1016/j.im.2013.11.007

[2] M. Bertolini, G. Ferretti, G. Vignali, A. Volpi. Reducing out of stock, shrinkage and overstock through RFID in the fresh food supply chain: Evidence from an Italian retail pilot. International Journal of RF Technologies. 2013;4(2):107–125. DOI: 10.3233/RFT-120040

[3] A. Parreño-Marchante, A. Álvarez-Melcón, M. Trebar, A. Grah, P. Filippin. Improvement of Traceability Processes in the Farmed Fish Supply Chain. In: Z. Zhang, R. Zhang, J. Zhang, editors. LISS 2012. Springer Berlin Heidelberg; 2013. p. 1065–1070. DOI: 10.1007/978-3-642-32054-5_150

[4] Y. -M. Hwang, J. Moon, S. Yoo. Developing a RFID-based food traceability system in Korea Ginseng Industry: Focused on the business process reengineering. International Journal of Control and Automation. 2015;8(4):397–406. DOI: http://dx.doi.org/10.14257/ijca.2015.8.4.36

[5] E. C. Jones, C. A. Chung. RFID and Auto-ID in Planning and Logistics: A Practical Guide for Military UID Applications. CRC Press, Taylor & Francis Group; 2011. 430 p

[6] E. Bottani, R. Montanari, A. Volpi. The impact of RFID and EPC network on the bullwhip effect in the Italian FMCG supply chain. International Journal of Production Economics. 2010;124(2):426–432. DOI: doi:10.1016/j.ijpe.2009.12.005

[7] S. Piramuthu, W. Zhou. RFID and Sensor Network Automation in the Food Industry: Ensuring Quality and Safety through Supply Chain Visibility. Wiley-Blackwell UK; 2016. 320 p

[8] O. Boyinbode, O. Akinyede. A RFID based inventory control system for Nigerian supermarkets. International Journal of Computer Applications. 2015;116(7):7–12. DOI: 10.5120/20346-2531

[9] P. V. Nikitin. Theory and measurement of backscattering from RFID tags. IEEE Antennas and Propagation. 2006;48(6):212–218. DOI: 10.1109/MAP.2006.323323

[10] GS1. EPCglobal standard, EPC code [Internet]. Available from: http://www.gs1.org/epc-rfid [Accessed: July 11, 2016]

[11] GS1. EPC Information Services (EPCIS) [Internet]. Available from: http://www.gs1.org/sites/default/files/docs/epc/epcis_1_1-standard-20140520.pdf [Accessed: July 11, 2016]

[12] K. Ambekar, V. Dhole, S. Sharma, T. Wadekar. Smart shopping trolley using RFID. International Journal of Advanced Research in Computer Engineering & Technology. 2015;4(10):3875–3877

[13] P. Chandrasekar. Smart shopping cart with automatic billing system through RFID and ZigBee. In: International Conference on Information Communication and Embedded Systems; February 27–28, 2014; Chennai. IEEE; 2014. p. 1–4. DOI: 10.1109/ICICES.2014.7033996

[14] GS1. EPCglobal Architecture Framework (EPCglobal Network) [Internet]. Available from: http://www.gs1.org/sites/default/files/docs/architecture/architecture_1_2-framework-20070910.pdf [Accessed: July 11, 2016]

[15] ITU – International Telecommunications Union. Available from: http://www.itu.int [Accessed: July 11, 2016]

[16] K. ElMahgoub. Slotted triangular monopole antenna for UHF RFID readers. Applied Computational Electromagnetics Society Journal. 2016;1(1):24–27

[17] Q. Xianming, C. K. Goh, Z. N. Chen. A broadband UHF near-field RFID antenna. IEEE Transactions on Antennas and Propagation. 2011;58(12):3829–3838. DOI: 10.1109/TAP.2010.2078432

[18] Z. N. Chen, Q. Xianming, H. L. Chung. A universal UHF RFID reader antenna. IEEE Transactions on Microwave Theory and Techniques. 2009;57(5):1275–1282. DOI: 10.1109/TMTT.2009.2017290

[19] L. Zöscher, R. Spreitzer, H. Gross, J. Grosinger, U. Mühlmann, D. Amschl, H. Watzinger, W. Bösch. HF/UHF dual band RFID transponders for an information-driven public

transportation system. E & I Elektrotechnik und Informationstechnik. 2016;133(3):163–175. DOI: 10.1007/s00502-016-0405-y

[20] Z. L. Ma, L. J. Jiang, J. Xi, T. T. Ye. A single-layer compact HF-UHF dual-band RFID tag antenna. IEEE Antennas and Wireless Propagation Letters. 2012;11:1257–1260. DOI: 10.1109/LAWP.2012.2225821

[21] M. Russoa, P. Šolić, M. Stella. Probabilistic modeling of harvested GSM energy and its application in extending UHF RFID tags reading range. Journal of Electromagnetic Waves and Applications. 2013;27(4):473–484

[22] R. Ferrero, F. Gandino, B. Montrucchio, M. Rebaudengo. Experimental Investigation on the Interference between UHF RFID and GSM. In: 2015 International EURASIP Workshop on RFID Technology (EURFID); October 22–23, 2015; Rosenheim. IEEE; 2015. p. 140–143. DOI: 10.1109/EURFID.2015.7332399

[23] G. Ibrahim, A. Plytage. UHF RFID systems; Their susceptibility to backscattered signals induced by electronic ballast driven fluorescent lamps. IEEE Transactions on Antennas and Propagation. 2010;58(7):2473–2478. DOI: 10.1109/TAP.2010.2048841

[24] S.-K. Kuo, J.-Y. Hsu, Y.-H. Hung. Analysis and design of an UHF RFID metal tag using magnetic composite material as substrate. Progress in Electromagnetics Research B. 2010;24:49–62. DOI: 10.2528/PIERB10070107

[25] Y. Kim. Design of near omnidirectional UHF RFID tag with one-off seal function for liquid bottles. Microwave and Optical Technology Letters. 2013;55(2):375–379. DOI: 10.1002/mop.27285

[26] H.-W. Son, H.-G. Jeon, J.-H. Cho. Flexible wideband UHF RFID tag antenna for curved metal surfaces. Electronics Letters. 2012;48(13):749–750. DOI: 10.1049/el.2012.1030

[27] T. Björninen, L. Sydänheimo, L. Ukkonen, Y. Rahmat-Samii. Advances in antenna designs for UHF RFID tags mountable on conductive items. IEEE Antennas and Propagation Magazine. 2014;56(1):79–103. DOI: 10.1109/MAP.2014.6821761

[28] L. Catarinucci, R. Colella, M. D. Blasi, L. Patrono, Luigi, L. Tarricone. Experimental performance evaluation of passive UHF RFID tags in electromagnetically critical supply chains. Journal of Communications Software & Systems. 2011;7(2):59–70

[29] M. Laniel, J.-P. Émond. Mapping of RFID tag readability in relation to the food content in a refrigerated sea container at 915 MHz. Innovative Food Science & Emerging Technologies. 2010;11(4):703–706. DOI: 10.1016/j.ifset.2010.06.005

[30] M. D. Blasi, V. Mighali, L. Patrono, M. L. Stefanizzi. Performance evaluation of UHF RFID tags in the pharmaceutical supply chain. In: D. Giusto, A. Lera, G. Morabito, L. Atzori, editors. The Internet of Things. Springer, New York, NY; 2010. p. 283–292. DOI: 10.1007/978-1-4419-1674-7_27

[31] GS1. EPCglobal Class1-Gen2 standard [Internet]. Available from: http://www.gs1.org/epcrfid/epc-rfid-uhf-air-interface-protocol/2-0-1 [Accessed: July 12, 2016]

[32] S. Kang, Z. Prodanoff. RFID model for simulating framed slotted ALOHA based anti-collision protocol for multi-tag identification. In: C. Turcu, editor. Current Trends and Challenges in RFID. InTech; DOI: 10.5772/16601

[33] J. Vales-Alonso, M. V. Bueno-Delgado, E. Egea-Lopez, J. J. Alcaraz-Espin, F. J. Gonzalez-Castaño. Multi-frame maximum-likelihood tag estimation for RFID anti-collision protocols. IEEE Transactions on Industrial Informatics. 2011;7(3):487–495. DOI: 0.1109/TII.2011.2158831

[34] N. Bagheri, P. Alenaby, M. Safkhani. A new anti-collision protocol based on information of collided tags in RFID systems. International Journal of Communication Systems. 2015. DOI: 10.1002/dac.2975

[35] D. Klair, K. -W. Chin, R. Raad. A survey and tutorial of RFID anti-collision protocols. IEEE Communications Surveys & Tutorials. 2010;12(3):400–421. DOI: 10.1109/SURV.2010.031810.00037

[36] T. F. La-Porta, G. Maselli, C. Petrioli. Anti-collision protocols for single-reader RFID systems: Temporal analysis and optimization. IEEE Transactions on Mobile Computing. 2011;10(2):267–279. DOI: 10.1109/TMC.2010.58

[37] ETSI. ETSI EN 302 208-2 V2.1.1 [Internet]. Available from: http://www.etsi.org/deliver/etsi_en/302200_302299/30220802/02.01.01_60/en_30220802v020101p.pdf [Accessed: July 12, 2016]

[38] FCC. part-15 [Internet]. Available from: https://www.fcc.gov/general/rules-regulations-title-47 [Accessed: July 12, 2016]

[39] D.-Y. Kim, J.-G. Yook, H.-G. Yoon, B.-J. Jang. Interference analysis of UHF RFID systems. Progress in Electromagnetics Research B. 2008;4:115–126. DOI: 10.2528/PIERB08010607

[40] M. V. Bueno-Delgado, P. Pavon-Marino. A maximum likelihood based distributed protocol for passive RFID dense reader environments. Journal of Supercomputing, Special Issue on Advances in Communication Networks for Pervasive and Ubiquitous Applications. 2013;64(2):456–476. DOI: 10.1007/s11227-012-0779-5

[41] M. V. Bueno-Delgado, P. Pavon-Marino. A centralized and aligned scheduler for passive RFID dense reader environments working under EPCglobal standard. Simulation Modelling Practice and Theory, Special Issue on Internet of Things. 2013;34:172–185. DOI: 10.1016/j.simpat.2012.07.006

[42] M. V. Bueno-Delgado, R. Ferrero, F. Gandino, P. Pavon-Marino, M. Rebaudengo. A geometric distribution reader anti-collision protocol for RFID dense reader environments. IEEE Transactions on Automation Science and Engineering. 2013;10(2):296–306. DOI: 10.1109/TASE.2012.2218101

[43] K. R. Kashwan, T. Thirumalai. TDMA Based Collision Avoidance in Dense and Mobile RFID Reader Environment: DDFSA with RRE. In: Microelectronics, Electromagnetics and Telecommunications. Springer India; 2015. p. 497–505. DOI: 10.1007/978-81-322-2728-1_46

[44] GS1. Object Name Server (ONS) [Internet]. Available from: http://www.gs1.org/epcis/epcis-ons/latest [Accessed: July 12, 2016]

[45] M. Lorenz, J. Müller, M. -P. Schapranow, A. Zeier, H. Plattner. Discovery Services in the EPC Network. In: C. Turcu, editor. Designing and Deploying RFID Applications. InTech; 2011. p. 109–130. DOI: 10.5772/16658

[46] S. M. Kywe, J. Shi, Y. Li, R. Kailash. Evaluation of different electronic product code discovery service models. Advances in Internet of Things. 2012;2(2):37–46 . DOI: 10.4236/ait.2012.22005

[47] P. Manzanares-Lopez, J. P. Muñoz Gea, J. Malgosa-Sanahuja, J. C. Sanchez-Aarnoutse. An efficient distributed discovery service for EPCglobal network in nested package scenarios. Journal of Network and Computer Application. 2011;34(3):925–937. DOI: 10.1016/j.jnca.2010.04.018

[48] A. Dahbi, H. T. Mouftah. A Hierarchical Architecture for Distributed EPCglobal Discovery Services. In: IEEE Global Communications Conference (GLOBECOM); December 6–10, 2015; San Diego, CA. IEEE; 2015. p. 1–7. DOI: 10.1109/GLOCOM.2015.7417836

[49] S. H. Choi, B. Yang, H. H. Cheung, Y. X. Yang. RFID tag data processing in manufacturing for track-and-trace anti-counterfeiting. Computers in Industry. 2015;68:148–161. DOI: 10.1016/j.compind.2015.01.004

[50] J. Garcia-Alfaro, J. Herrera-Joancomarti, J. Melia-Segui. Security and Privacy Concerns About the RFID Layer of EPC Gen2 Networks. In: G. Navarro-Arribas, V. Torras, editors. Advanced Research in Data Privacy. Springer International Publishing Switzerland; 2015. p. 303–324. DOI: 10.1007/978-3-319-09885-2_17

[51] B. R. Ray, J. Abawajy, M. Chowdhury. Scalable RFID security framework and protocol supporting Internet of things. Computer Networks. 2014;67:89–103. DOI: 10.1016/j.comnet.2014.03.023

[52] S. Chang, L. Lu, X. Liu, H. Song, Q. Yao. Vulnerability aware graphs for RFID protocol security benchmarking. Journal of Computer and System Sciences. 2015;81(6):1027–1041. DOI: 10.1016/j.jcss.2014.12.015

[53] ComptTIA RFID+ certification. Available from: http://certification.comptia.org [Accessed: July 12, 2016]